WOMEN & EVANGELISM

AN EVANGELISTIC LIFESTYLE FROM A WOMAN'S PERSPECTIVE

▶ A Self-study Course for the Woman with a Heart for Evangelism

DEVELOPED BY THE INSTITUTE OF EVANGELISM BILLY GRAHAM CENTER

SHARON BEOUGHER
AND
MARY DORSETT

Women and Evangelism:
An Evangelistic Lifestyle from a Woman's Perspective
Copyright © 1994 by the Billy Graham Center, Institute of Evangelism,
Wheaton, IL.

This course manual accompanies cassette tapes which contain instruction and examples of evangelism. The views expressed on the
tapes do not necessarily reflect the official positions of the Billy
Graham Center, Institute of Evangelism.

Unless otherwise noted, Scripture quotations are taken from the Holy
Bible, New International Version © 1973, 1978, 1984 International
Bible Society. Used by permission of Zondervan Bible Publishers.

ISBN 1-879089-15-7
Printed in the United States of America

$\mathcal{J}$able of $\mathcal{C}$ontents

$\mathcal{U}$nit One: Foundations

$\mathcal{U}$nit Two: Inner Circle Evangelism

$\mathcal{U}$nit Three: Community Evangelism

$\mathcal{U}$nit Four: Evangelism and Vision

$\mathcal{A}$ppendices

About the Authors

Sharon Merritt Beougher grew up in Texas and North Carolina. She attended the University of North Carolina where she received her Bachelor of Music Education with an emphasis in piano. She later attended Southwestern Baptist Theological Seminary in Forth Worth, Texas, where she received a Master of Arts in Religious Education. Before her marriage, she served on staff in four different churches, one being in Plymouth, England, with responsibilities in the areas of children, youth and singles. Sharon is a certified trainer in Evangelism Explosion, Master Life Discipleship Program, and the Christian Discipleship Seminar. She has been involved in discipling relationships throughout the years since her involvement in InterVarsity Christian Fellowship in college.

Sharon is married to Dr. Tim Beougher, Assistant Professor of Evangelism at Wheaton College, and has the privilege of being the mother to four children: Kristi, age 9; Jonathan, age 7; Kari, age 5; and Karisa, age 2. Her recent energies have been devoted to her family as well as teaching piano in the home.

᠔   ᠔   ᠔   ᠔   ᠔   ᠔   ᠔   ᠔   ᠔   ᠔   ᠔   ᠔

As a young woman, **Mary Dorsett** received the B.A. in English Literature from the University of Missouri, St. Louis in 1970. Two years later, as a young wife and mother, she understood that salvation through Jesus was a free gift that He was offering to her. From that time, she has sought to grow in her understanding and obedience to the Savior. In 1991, she received the first M.A. in Evangelism awarded by Wheaton College.

Mary has been a part of the Wheaton College community since 1983. She is privileged to spend time in prayer/discipleship groups with coeds and also in extending hospitality – especially through cookies – to a wide range of students. Mary and her husband, Lyle, who teaches in the Christian Education/Educational Ministries Department of Wheaton, are the co-founders of *Christ for Children International*. CFCI (whose primary focus is on evangelism and discipleship) works among the poor children of Mexico and Mary serves as Vice President and general coordinator for the mission.

Along with many more mundane duties, Mary gratefully and delightedly serves as mother to son Michael and daughter through marriage, Connie. Mike and Connie are both Wheaton graduates who now teach in the inner city of Chicago. Another daughter, Erika, has been with Jesus since she suddenly died at the age of ten in 1983. Even so, the Dorsett home remains full as the Lord brings many adopted sons and daughters form the campus community. Some are part of their lives for just a brief time, but a special group has become a permanent part of the Dorsett family and daily bring joy and blessing.

ACKNOWLEDGMENTS

This educational project grew out of an effort in the Spring of 1991 by the Institute of Evangelism to provide inspiration, insight, and instruction to women who have a heart for evangelism. During that Spring semester, *Women in Evangelism* was offered as a course for credit for Wheaton College students. So much interest was generated by the course that it was opened to the community, and the resulting enrollment quickly swelled to more than 1,600! The venue was moved off campus to the Wheaton Bible Church, where the sanctuary accommodated a standing-room-only attendance for each of the eight Tuesday evening sessions.

Dr. Robert Coleman, Director of the School of World Mission and Evangelism at Trinity Evangelical Divinity School and Director of the Billy Graham Center's Institute of Evangelism, conceived the original course outline and content, and supervised its progress and the ensuing development of this manual. Dr. Timothy Beougher, Assistant Professor of Evangelism at Wheaton Graduate School and Associate Director of Educational Programs for the Institute of Evangelism, and Dr. Lyle Dorsett, Professor of Evangelism at Wheaton College and Associate Director for Urban Ministries for the Institute of Evangelism, oversaw the course presentation. Dr. Edith Blumhofer, Project Director for the Institute for the Study of American Evangelicals, moderated each evening session. Dr. James Kraakevik, Director of the Billy Graham Center, provided administrative support throughout the project, as did LTC(Ret) David Olmsted, Associate Director of Administration in the Institute of Evangelism. Mr. Mark Cedar, Field Coordinator for the Institute of Evangelism, prepared many technical aspects—particularly the audio component—and researched other appropriate messages by noted women evangelicals to supplement the messages of the eight principal speakers. Mr. Dale Haas, Broadcast Services Coordinator for Wheaton College, provided the technical mixing and editing for the master tapes of the audio component. Mrs. Diane Garvin, secretary for the Institute of Evangelism, gave countless hours of her time to this project, helping in innumerable ways.

After several drafts, selected representatives from various segments of society and the church fieldtested the material. We acknowledge with thanks those who graciously devoted their time evaluating the material and providing valuable feedback.

We are also deeply appreciative of the speakers who graciously allowed us to use their messages in this course. The accompanying audio tapes include not only their presentations, but also additional excerpts from a variety of messages given over the last few decades, all of which are used by permission.

Session One	**The Message of Evangelism**
*Elisabeth Elliot	*"Evangelism and Missions"*
Anne Ortlund	*Putting your confidence in the Gospel of Christ*
Gwynne Johnson	*"Filling Up to Overflow"*

Session Two	**A Verbal Witness in Evangelism**
Mary Whelchell	*Evangelism in the Marketplace*
Debbie Laws	*Transitioning into the Gospel with people*
Gigi Tchividjian	*Her personal testimony*
Mini Jane Johnston	*Witnessing through tracts*
Winnie Christensen	*"Building a Relationship with God"*

Session Three	**Evangelism and Prayer**
*Evelyn Christenson	*"Prayer and Evangelism"*
Millie Dienert	*Prayer Seminar #2, 10/10/85, Wheaton College*
Carolyn Peterson	*'The Great Commission Through Prayer"*

Session Four	**Evangelism with Children**
Henrietta Mears	*'The Lordship of Jesus Christ*
Martha Wright	*"Inspirational Thoughts About Child Evangelism*
Ann Hibbard	*"Evangelism in Family Situations"*
Karen Mains	*"Teach Your Children About God"*
*Jill Briscoe & Judy Golz	*"Evangelism and Family (Part A)"*

Session Five	**Evangelism with Spouses ...**
*Jill Briscoe & Judy Golz	*"Evangelism and Family (Part B)"*
Moody Radio Broadcast	*Being unequally yoked*
Marta Alvarado	*"Ministry Starts in the Home"*

Session Six	**Relationship Evangelism**
*Ann Kiemel Anderson	*"Evangelism and Relationships"*
Roberta Hestenes	*Living in right relationship to others*
Joanne Shetler	*"Women as Evangelists"*
Judy Streeter	*Growing relationships through your home life*

Session Seven	**Evangelism and Bible Study**
*Anne Graham Lotz	*"Evangelism and the Bible"*
Martha Reapsome	*"Reaching My World: Personal Evangelism"*

Session Eight	***Evangelism and the Creative Arts***
*Jeanette Clift George	*"Evangelism and the Use of Drama"*
Gloria Gaither	*Story of the talents*
Karen Patitucci	*Use of drama through the church*

Session Nine	***Evangelism Through Social Ministry***
*Mother Consuella York	*"Evangelism and Social Action"*
Connie Fairchild	*On social action*
Joni Eareckson Tada	*"Social Concern and Evangelism"*

Session Ten	***Cross-Cultural Evangelism***
*Melody Green	*"Evangelism and a World Christian View*
Marilyn Laszlo	*"Pioneering for Jesus Christ"*
Colleen Townsend Evans	*Breaking through barriers of prejudice*

Session Eleven	***Evangelism and Disciplemaking***
Kay Arthur	*"A Study on Discipleship"*
Nita Outhous	*On disciplemaking*
Vonette Bright	*"Beautiful Life: A Celebration for Women"*
	Wheaton College, 1985
June Moss	*"Managing Your Time"*

Session Twelve	***Women Need Women***
*Edith Blumhofer	*"The History of Women in Evangelism"*
Lucy Swindoll	*"Supply of God"*
Corrie Ten Boom	*"Representative of Heaven"*

* *Women in Evangelism* series speaker

What you have in your hands now results from the combined labor of all those persons—homemakers, evangelists, missionaries, lay persons, and educators. We believe the course constructively confronts the key evangelism issues facing women. By God's grace, we offer it to help you be more effective in your high calling to "go and make disciples."

INTRODUCTION TO THE COURSE

I. STUDY IN GOOD WAYS

The course has four Units of three Sessions each. If you try to study too many lessons at once, you might become confused with too much material. If you wait too long between sessions, you might forget some important points or lose the flow of the process. Work through the material at a pace that fits your schedule.

> Your hopes should be high as you begin this course—purpose to be used of God to affect your world for His glory. Now is the time to begin enjoying personal and professional fulfillment as you study, grow, and reproduce what you have learned.

◆ *Make time for study*

It will be best for you to study one lesson per week over the next three months. Try to set aside two or more hours for a session each week on a regular schedule—as if you were going to a class. That should give you time to read carefully, listen to the tapes, do all the exercises, and work on the assignments.

◆ *Write lesson exercises*

Whether you are studying this course by yourself or in a class with other people, you need to pause often to review what you have read. If possible, complete each "Stop and Apply" exercise from memory, writing your responses in the Manual. Of course, you may check the text or the answer sheet in Appendix E to make sure your answers are correct. You will not receive a "grade" for this work, so you need to be your own monitor to make sure you are learning the necessary points.

These periodic exercises are built-in units of review as you proceed through each lesson. They are good indicators of the key principles found in each session.

◆ *Listen to tapes*

Audio cassette tapes which supplement the Manual come with the course. The tape excerpts elaborate on lesson principles. You will need to have a tape player available for each study period, along with a note pad and pencil. Let these messages inspire you as well as instruct you!

◆ *Use the Scriptures*

Always have your Bible beside you as you study this Manual. Most scriptural references here are from the New International Version (NIV). You might want to use more than one translation to compare other readings. The conscientious Christian always should check what she is learning with the teaching of the Holy Scriptures, following the example of the "noble Bereans":

> *"Now these [the people in Berea] were more noble-minded than those in Thessalonica, for they received the word with great eagerness, examining the Scriptures daily, to see whether these things were so" [Acts 17:11].*

II. SELF-STUDY VERSUS GROUP STUDY

A. *Using a Mentor*

It is not easy to study by yourself. When you are in a class, the teacher guides you through the subject you are studying. Your fellow students share their opinions and make you think. Tests are given to encourage you to make progress. And you do not have the kind of interruptions or distractions that are part of your usual day.

If you are taking this course as a self-study effort, you may feel that nobody notices what you are doing, or that nobody cares what you are doing. This can discourage you. You might feel like quitting after just a few sessions.

You need a person to take an interest in your efforts, to check your progress, and to give you a reaction to your finished work. Such a person is a *Mentor*, someone who knows your study goals and understands your ministry.

Who should that be? Ideally, it would be someone who is a maturing Christian. Your mentor could be a church leader, a close friend, your spouse, or a relative. If the person you select will look through the Manual right now, as you are beginning the course, there will be a general understanding of the subject. Then later, the Mentor can give useful advice just by listening to what you have to say.

Complete the Student and Mentor Agreement form included with this Manual and mail it *immediately* to the Institute of Evangelism, Billy Graham Center, Wheaton, Illinois, 60187, USA. Be sure to do this *before* you begin your study. This will officially register you for this course to receive future certification for your work.

Here is what your Mentor will be expected to do.

◆ *Counsel*

Before you start your first session, you and your Mentor should talk together. What experience have you had thus far? What opportunities lie ahead of you? What needs for personal growth do you have in mind? How do you think this course will help you? You will be more focused if you get the Mentor's reflections on such questions.

◆ *Review*

At the end of each Unit (approximately every three weeks if you do one session each week), the Mentor will meet with you again for about an hour. At that time, the two of you will discuss what you have been reading in the lessons and hearing on the tapes. You will share any questions that have come to mind about the material, and any ideas that your study has generated.

Most of the time, though, will be for the Mentor to review your progress on the exercises given for each session. This conversation should give you someone else's honest opinion about how well you are applying the principles you are studying.

Your Mentor's counsel for these three review sessions will encourage you to keep moving ahead on schedule, and to do your best possible work.

◆ *Report*

When the course is completed, the Mentor will fill out (with appropriate comments) a Review Form provided with this Manual.

You can see that the Mentor you select will have to invest time and thought in helping you. Make sure, therefore, that the person is a growing Christian sister who shares your desire to see lost persons won to Christ and to be discipled.

B. Group Study

If you are taking this course as part of a group, the responsibility of Mentor (as far as filling out the forms) should be fulfilled by the group leader.

The accountability dynamic of counseling and reviewing can be accomplished in any number of ways through procedures or relationships set up within the group.

III. EARN YOUR CREDIT

When you have completed all the work in this course, we estimate that you will have invested at least thirty-six hours of your time. That stewardship of yours deserves to be officially recorded. There are two ways the Billy Graham Center will do that.

◆ Continuing Education Units (CEU)

For thirty-six hours of work in this course, you will receive four (4) Continuing Education Units. This is NOT academic credit to apply toward studies in a college or seminary. This is professional credit which shows that you are improving your knowledge and skills for serving the Lord.

◆ Certificate of Achievement

So that you may have your own record of those credits, and to verify your work for church leaders and ministry colleagues who might be interested, you will receive a properly inscribed certificate bearing your name, with the course title, *Women in Evangelism*, notation of the CEU number (4), and the validating signatures of Institute of Evangelism administrators. This will be sent to you when the Center receives the Mentor Final Review Form.

Your diligence in fulfilling all the requirements of this course is a matter of your personal honor as a Christian, and of the integrity of your Mentor who will endorse your claim for credit.

$\mathcal{U}$NIT ONE:

Foundations

SESSION ONE
The Message of Evangelism

GOALS FOR THE CHAPTER:

It is the purpose of this opening chapter to discuss the concept of biblical evangelism. After reading this chapter, you should be able to:

1. Define evangelism.

2. Understand the commitment to evangelism that was practiced by the early church.

3. Outline the main points in the message of the Gospel.

4. Understand the command to evangelize.

I. INTRODUCTION

Here are two separate, yet related stories:

It was obvious that Gus was lonely; he seized every possible opportunity to talk. Each day as Frances and her husband, Tony, arrived at the hospital to visit Tony's Dad, Gus would watch them with eager eyes and soon they knew his life's story. Having beaten cancer once, a recurrence of the deadly disease looked likely. Frances and Tony tried to encourage him. She brought him flowers one day and each night Gus was included in their parting prayers.

On the fourth day, Frances arrived to find Dad asleep in his bed, so she turned her attention to Gus who began relating his fears about death. She asked him if he knew what would happen after he died. He said he hoped there was a heaven and that he would be allowed to go there.

Following his thought, Frances asked "if you do die, why do you think God should let you into heaven?"

"Well, I've tried to live a good life," he responded.

*"That's good," she assured him, "but no one has ever made it to heaven on his own merits." Gus looked confused. Frances could almost hear his surprised mind wondering, "well then, how **do** you get to heaven?"*

Frances asked him if he had ever heard the Bible verse that says "for God so loved the world that he gave His one and only Son, that whoever believes in him shall not perish but have eternal life" [John 3:16]. Gus wasn't sure. He had been to church occasionally, but he never formed a very clear picture of what God was trying to say to him.

Frances went on to explain that God wanted to have a close, loving relationship with each of us but that we separate ourselves from God when we sin. "Because God is perfectly holy—imagine a totally pure, spotless Being—He cannot tolerate the presence of sin. Anything unholy or sinful must be forever separated from our completely holy God because He is unable to pollute His purity with our sinfulness. Not only that, to be true to His sense of justice, God cannot leave sin unpunished. That means that the only ones who can be assured of going to heaven are those who have never sinned. Yet the Bible tells us (and we instinctively know) 'that all have sinned and fall short of the glory of God' [Rom. 3: 23]. No amount of good works will ever be enough to make up for the penalty of our sin."

Frances and Gus both acknowledged that they were left in a hopeless situation, but then she hurried on to tell Gus the good news. "God doesn't stop there. He loves us so much that He found a way to save us from our rightly deserved punishment. God became a man in Jesus and He willingly paid the penalty for our sins when He died on the cross. And then, because He really is God, He rose again to life because He is more powerful than death. Our pardon is now waiting for each of us. To claim it we only need to believe and totally depend upon Jesus as our Lord and Savior. Our pardon is God's free, no-strings-attached offer to each of us. It is there for everyone but God respects us enough that He will never force anyone to believe Him. The decision is ours."

Now Frances could tell Gus the right answer to why God lets us into His perfect heaven—"We get to heaven because of believing what Christ has done for us on the cross—a work we know is finished by His resurrection from the dead." She asked Gus if he would like to have that assurance and he tearfully nodded. Together they prayed that God would take away his sin and begin to live in and through Gus' life. Her friend's eyes were shining as he asked: "Why didn't someone tell me about this a long time ago?"

Tears welled up in Lisa's eyes and then overflowed as her words tumbled out. For years she had struggled with insecurity and now her college friends, whom she trusted, had disappointed her.

"I've tried so hard to be good. I've been teaching Sunday School, and I pray every day. Why did God do this to me? All I ever wanted Him to do for me was to give me good friends and security. Do you think it's wrong to want good friends?" she queried.

No, of course Nell didn't think it was wrong to want good friends, security and a sense of belonging. But as Nell continued to probe, she discovered the true root of the problem. Lisa was doing "good things" in an attempt to buy blessings from God. A church attender all her life, she knew many facts about God. She knew that Jesus, God's only Son, had died on the cross for the sins of the whole world. She could even quote many portions of the Bible, yet she remained outside the walls of the kingdom because she had never met the King in person.

As they talked, Nell asked her "who controls your life? Do you know and love Jesus as a Savior, or is He merely an interesting concept to be discussed and debated? Is your highest priority the goals you set for your life, or do you daily say to God, 'More than anything I want Your will for my life? I'll try to do everything Your way today because I believe that You know what is best for me.' "

"But what if He doesn't want what I want? What if I don't like His way?" Lisa asked.

Nell had anticipated the question and had some ready answers. "If the God who controls the universe cared enough to become human and die on the cross for your sins, can you honestly think it's realistic to worry that He might not have your best interests at heart?"

After a bit more discussion, Lisa and Nell turned their attention to God in prayer. Lisa admitted that she wasn't doing so well at controlling her own life and she asked Him to take over. More tears flowed, but now they were tears of relief.

About a week later Nell got a letter from Lisa which read in part:

Over and over again I read and heard that we must recognize our sins and accept Christ's sacrifice and love. I knew I sinned but it all seemed very intangible. My wrongdoings didn't convict me enough and I just couldn't grasp the crucifixion and resurrection.

I'm sure you knew that I initially did not want to admit that I was in the wrong. It was hard for me to accept the fact that I was on my own path and that while I thought I was following God's path, in actuality the two paths were parallel, but not the same. I would have continued along my own merry way if God didn't bump me over to His path. I wanted to be accepted by people; He wanted me to seek Him... I wanted second best, not first. After looking at how God moved in the Bible... I realized how much I had insulted Him. In my mind He wasn't good enough to be my friend. Now I more completely understand all that He has done for me. Your question, "Do you love Jesus?" really made me think about this.

Even though I still do not love Him with all my heart, mind, and soul, it is my desire to do so. Jesus has been a great friend to me and I am willing to have my loneliness overflooded by His compassion.

II. EVANGELISM DEFINED

You might think these are two markedly different stories, but both are examples of evangelism in action. Confusion over the topic often arises because evangelism is seldom explained in terms that everyone can comprehend. Yet we must have a clear understanding of evangelism if we are to understand and study the topic.

A working definition of evangelism should look something like this:

> The **compassionate sharing** of the good news of Jesus Christ with **lost people**, in the **power of the Holy Spirit**, for the purpose of **bringing them to Christ** as Lord and Savior, that they in turn might **share Him with others**.

Several key words in this definition give us insight into the nature of the task. First, it is to be "compassionate." He felt compassion for the multitudes, for they were like lost sheep [Matt. 9:36]. When He approached Jerusalem for the last time, he wept [Luke 19:41]. As messengers of God, we need to learn to cultivate this virtue of compassion that lovingly reaches out to share the good news of Jesus Christ with lost people.

The purpose of our endeavors is to introduce "the lost" or the unbelievers in the world to Jesus Christ that they might know Him as Lord and Savior. This is our main goal. We are not introducing them to a philosophy, a concept, a religion, a

Let me introduce you to My Lord and Savior, Jesus Christ!

denomination, or even a church. We want them to know Jesus as a person. From the media we gain many insights into the character of the President of the United States. We learn about his wife and children, his favorite hobbies and sports, even his most cherished dreams, but all of our information is secondhand. Only those who have spent any time with him can say that they know him personally. Many people go through life talking of Jesus—they may even quote Him—but they have never come to know Him firsthand. This is the ultimate goal of evangelism: to help someone else know Jesus personally as the Lord and Savior of her life.

Anyone who comes to know Jesus in this intimate way will find that her life will be transformed by His power. He becomes as real as our mother, father, husband, or child. The more we pursue knowing Him, the deeper our love for Him grows and the greater our ability to be filled with His Spirit. For Christians our relationship with Jesus produces an ever-deepening love for God that shows itself in our obedience to His plan for our lives.

STOP AND APPLY

1. Write your definition of evangelism:

2. The ultimate goal of evangelism is to help another to know _____ personally as the _____ and _____ of her life.

III. THE FIRST EVANGELISTS

Jesus spent most of His last three years teaching and working with His disciples that they might understand the need for His death and the life-giving message of His resurrection. After Jesus went back to heaven, these same followers, filled with the power of the Holy Spirit, then went into all of the world taking the wonderful truth about Jesus with them. They lived and eventually died for one purpose: to share this life-changing news about Jesus.

Evangelism was not a duty or occupation for them. They were so excited and so confident of the message—salvation through Jesus—and of the power of the Holy Spirit which guided them, that they would have burst if they had tried to remain silent. Can you imagine not telling anyone if you had just inherited five million dollars or discovered the cure for cancer? Neither could the disciples imagine not sharing with the world the cure for our sin and spiritual poverty.

The Book of Acts tells us that these first believers attracted others because of their joy, their love for others, and their deep conviction about Jesus. Totally committed to their task of telling others about God's plan for salvation through faith in Jesus, their lives and actions were guided by

Acts 1: 8 "...you will be my witnesses..."

the Holy Spirit. They attracted others because they were totally surrendered to God's power and their message was evident in the way they lived their lives.

Evangelism is not a duty or a heavy burden but rather an awesome privilege God shares with us so that we, in turn, can share with others. Evangelism should never be viewed as a "difficult duty" or "combat assignment." We are not commanded to "hit people over the head and drag them against their will into the kingdom." Rather, we are instructed to share the *GOOD NEWS* about Jesus in such a way that others will clearly see Him for themselves, recognize their own sinfulness and need, and acknowledge Him as their Lord and Savior.

One of the last things Jesus did before returning to heaven was to give His disciples instructions about their new responsibilities. Jesus understood human nature and He knew that His followers (and we today) would not accomplish very much if they were not clear about what He expected of them.

He told them to wait in Jerusalem until they received the power of the Holy Spirit. "You will receive power when the Holy Spirit comes on you; and you will be my witnesses in Jerusalem, and in all Judea and Samaria, and to the ends of the earth" [Acts 1: 8]. Without the Spirit's supernatural power, all of their efforts would have been fruitless. No one reading this would consider mixing up a cake or preparing a batch of bread if she knew she had no oven in which to bake it. The power of the oven transforms the raw materials into a useful—even highly desirable—finished product. So it is with Christians. The power of the Holy Spirit takes our human efforts and transforms them with His spiritual power so that new believers can be added to the kingdom of God.

Jesus knew that His poor, mostly uneducated, provincial disciples were going to journey to much of the civilized world within their lifetime. They would face the rigors and dangers of travel, the need to communicate in foreign languages, opposition and persecution, and, for many, death at the hands of their enemies. When gauged by human standards, it appeared to be a hopeless task. Yet between the time of Jesus' return to heaven and the end of the Book of Acts (around forty years), the church grew from an original band of about 500 to approximately 200,000 believers. That's 400 times larger than when it started![1]

IV. THE POWER BEHIND EVANGELISM

How could such a small group accomplish so much? They lived to carry out the Great Commission which their Lord and Savior, Jesus, had entrusted to them. Jesus knew they would need help if they were to succeed, and thus He began and ended His instructions with an assurance:

> *"All authority in heaven and on earth has been given to me. Therefore go and make disciples of all nations, baptizing them in the name of the Father and of the Son and of the Holy Spirit, and teaching them to obey everything I have commanded you. And surely I will be with you always, to the very end of the age" [Matt. 28:18b–20, emphasis added].*

Imagine how these words encouraged that small, scared group of followers. Yet because of the power of God's Holy Spirit working through them, they were able to accomplish all that they had been commanded to do. Nothing God assigned them proved too difficult to these Spirit-filled believers. The Holy Spirit helped them overcome the perils of the task.

However, the Holy Spirit plays an even more important role in evangelism. Scripture teaches us that it is His job to change hearts. We are commanded to go, preach, teach, and make disciples, but only the Holy Spirit can convict and change hearts.

Right from the start this takes a great deal of pressure off of us. Our job is to present the message—the good news about Jesus—in the most appealing way that we can, but the conviction of sin and the changing of hearts is the work of God. Only God's Holy Spirit can transform lives. Jesus spoke of the work of the Holy Spirit when He said, "When he comes, he will convict the world of guilt in regard to sin and righteousness and judgment" [John 16:8]. In the First Epistle to the Corinthians, Paul echoes a similar theme when he accuses his readers of following men instead of God. "I planted the seed, Apollos watered it, *but God made it grow*. So neither he who plants nor he who waters is anything, but only God, who makes things grow" [1 Cor. 3: 6–7, italics added].

V. THE MESSAGE TO BRING

Perhaps you have never tried to tell anyone about Jesus because you did not know how to explain it properly. It all seems so confusing; there is so much to say and you do not have any idea where to begin. If this describes you, be encouraged by the fact that you are not alone. Many Christians do not know how to communicate the truth about Jesus to someone else. Therefore, before we talk about doing evangelism, we need to look at the main points of the Gospel message.

A. God's Original Plan

The Book of Genesis tells us that God is the Creator of the universe. Adam and Eve represented the climax or high point in the creation process because they were created in the very image of God [Gen. 1: 27]. Before the fall, God spent time in the Garden of Eden with both Adam and Eve. They knew Him personally as a close friend. Because of this intimate relationship, they understood who He was and what was expected of them. God had created Adam and Eve in the very image of Himself, and He delighted in their companionship. All of creation lived in harmony; it was an ideal existence. This was God's original and loving plan for all of us.

B. The Human Predicament

Unlike our complex world, the rules in the Garden of Eden were fairly simple. Adam and Eve could eat whatever they liked as long as it was not from one tree in the center of the garden. Yet they chose to disobey, and sin entered the universe.

Because of their sin, each infant born since the time of Adam and Eve begins life with the same disposition to love self more than to obey God's law. Only one human, Jesus Christ, has ever lived a selfless, sinless life. The rest of us, like spoiled children, have demanded our rights to make our own choices and live our own way. Romans 3: 23 says, "For **ALL** have sinned and fall short of the glory of God."

But many of us rationalize, "Well, I know I'm not perfect but compared to many of the folks I know, I'm a pretty good person and God is so nice and loving that I know He'll let me into heaven." Just being a "nice person" does not guarantee admission into heaven, because even nice people are still sinners. Furthermore, the Bible tells us "that the wages of sin is death" [Rom. 6:23]. "Well," we wonder, "just a little bit of sin can't be all that harmful, can it?"

C. God's Holiness

Because God is perfect, holy, without sin or blemish, and totally pure, He cannot tolerate any sin in His presence. He is completely holy and pure, and is not able to violate His nature. No one would expect a lion to fly like a bird or a parrot to act like "the king of the beasts." They are by nature very different, and no amount of wishful thinking will alter their natures. Likewise, God cannot violate His nature. To stand in the presence of God requires one to be holy as He is holy. His law makes perfectly clear what is expected of us, but we have chosen to disregard these commands.

D. Sin

Sin is choosing our way over God's. It is our willful defiance of His plan for our lives. It is anything which separates us from Him. Just as Adam and Eve were separated physically from God when they were forced to leave the Garden of Eden, no descendant has subsequently experienced the intimate fellowship with our Creator that Adam and Eve originally enjoyed.

But sin has a far worse consequence—it also separates us spiritually from God now and throughout eternity. We need to remember that the penalty for sin is always death. That leaves every human condemned—not just in the present, but for the eternity which we all face.

If someone walked into a crowded shopping mall and began murdering people and then publicly declared that he intended to continue murdering folks, no sane person would think it intolerant of the police to jail such a man. We would demand justice and we would insist on recompense for the victims and punishment for the criminal. Yet, we lightly excuse our own sin and expect God to forget about justice. Most of us want two standards: one that is "just" for those we consider evil, and one that "forgives and forgets" for ourselves and our loved ones. But God cannot do that and still remain true to Himself.

That leaves us standing before God, the righteous Judge, awaiting our justly-deserved sentence of death. We have no one to blame but ourselves. We chose a life of sin because it looked easy or attractive to us. In our self-centeredness, we said to God, "not your way, but MINE for MY life." And we are counting on God to forget about judgment or punishment because He is a "loving God."

E. The Solution: Jesus

So now we have been caught in sin, properly tried and convicted. What hope is there? None without Jesus. Jesus said:

> *"For God did not send His Son into the world to condemn the world, but to save the world through Him. Whoever believes in Him is not condemned, but whoever does not believe stands condemned already because he has not believed in the name of God's one and only Son" [John 3:17–18].*

Later in the same Gospel, Jesus says of Himself, "I am the way, the truth and the life. No one comes to the Father except through Me" [John 14:6].

To understand what Jesus is saying, we need to look at His life. No intelligent and educated person denies that He actually lived on planet Earth approximately 2,000 years ago. His historical presence is accepted even by those who do not agree with His teaching. His death on the cross is duly recorded in secular as well as Christian records of the time. No one argues this dimension of His life.

But Jesus also claimed to be God. It is at this point that the debate begins. All agree that Jesus was human, but is it possible that He is also God? The Bible answers the question with a resounding "Yes!" Jesus plainly states His divinity in John 10: 30 when He says, "I and the Father are one."

Throughout His life, He had sought to reveal His dual nature to His disciples and those with spiritual understanding, but one of His strongest statements came when he stood before the High Priest and the council of Jewish elders who sought to kill Him. Still, He spoke the words of truth about His nature. When they asked Him, " 'Are you then the Son of God?' He replied, 'You are right in saying I am' " [Luke 22:70]. God's solution to the problem of human sinfulness was to send His sinless Son to take the rightful punishment due each person who has ever lived.

F. Calvary and the Cross

"But God demonstrated His love for us in this: While we were still sinners, Christ died for us" [Rom. 5:8]. This extraordinary verse announces wonderful news. God in heaven saw our wretched and hopeless plight. We humans, created in His own image, were to be forever separated from Him because of our sin—unless He intervened and saved us.

We previously ruled out the possibility of God just "winking" at our sin. He cannot pretend that sin does not exist, but He could send someone to take our punishment for us. This someone would have to be perfect so that He did not stand under judgment with us. Of Jesus it is said, "God made Him who had no sin to be sin for us, so that in Him we might become the righteousness of God" [2 Cor. 5:21]. Or again, "He committed no sin, and no deceit was found in his mouth" [1 Peter 2:22].

Jesus, who never sinned in His life, willingly chose to take the punishment for our sins. He would trade His life for ours so that we could once again be united with His Father in heaven. Justice has been done; the full penalty for sin was paid at the crucifixion. What, then, is required of us? Only that we turn from our sins and believe that Jesus, the Son of God, died for us on the cross.

Crucifixion has been described as the most horrible way of death ever devised by humans to torture one another, and no one would willingly seek such agony for the sake of a lie. Yet it is Christ's death on the cross that provides the stumbling block for many. We humans have a strong need to do things for ourselves; we are suspicious of "free" gifts. We do not like being in debt to anyone. So we "water down" the message of "salvation through faith alone" and add requirements like keeping the Ten Commandments, receiving the sacraments, or being baptized so that we can feel that we did at least a tiny part in saving ourselves. But once we add anything to God's plan we nullify it. Ephesians 2:8–9 makes it clear,

> *"For it is by grace you have been saved, through faith—and this not from yourselves, it is the gift of God—**not of works**, so that no one can boast." [emphasis added]*

Thus the idea that Christ's atonement is a free gift causes many to stumble.

Others fall away when confronted with the need to turn from their sins. Incredibly, there are humans who really do not believe they are sinners. But the majority of us falter because we do not like the idea of allowing God to have the place of authority in our lives. Like rebellious teenagers, we refuse to surrender our rights to whatever we want, or we reason that "His plan for me won't be as much *fun* as mine." Yet living for our own selfish pursuits never brings lasting happiness but only a growing restlessness that asks "is this all there is?" No one who has ever really surrendered control of her life into the hands of our living God has regretted her decision. But many have regretted they waited so long to do so!

Life as a Christian is not always easy, but it offers deep satisfaction and inner peace. There is an unshakable security in knowing that the very God who created the universe willingly indwells our frail humanity. For that is what happens when one chooses to trust and believe that Jesus is her Lord and Savior. "Therefore, if anyone is in Christ, he is a new creation; the old has gone, the new has come!" [2 Cor. 5:17].

G. Our Choice

The late C.S. Lewis is frequently quoted as saying that humans have three choices when confronted with the divinity of Jesus. He is either a liar, a lunatic, or Lord. There is absolutely no gain for Him (or anyone else) if He is a liar who claimed to be God, but really wasn't. A liar would ultimately be working for some sort of material prosperity, power, or prestige. But Jesus neither sought nor received any of these. Others believe that He was well-meaning, but ultimately deceived about Himself—in other words: insane. Read the Gospels for yourself and you will not find the words of a crazy man. The final conclusion is the only logical one. Jesus is who He says He is—the incarnate Son of God. Since this is true, one naturally wonders why so many in the world choose to ignore or refute His claims. Ironically, the answer lies in the cross, the instrument of salvation.[2]

Faith in Jesus requires us to acknowledge our sinfulness and to recognize our own inability to atone for these sins. Hanging on the cross, Jesus paid the penalty each of us owes, but to receive our pardon *we must* acknowledge our sin for what it is, recognize our need for forgiveness, and turn from our sinful ways.

Most people will never become serial murderers or hardened criminals, but all of us are sinners just the same. As difficult as it might be to believe, God says that lying to avoid unpleasant consequences, cheating "a little" now and then, losing our tempers, and demanding our own way are equally terrible in His sight. Sin is sin, and it is all equally offensive.

Acts 3:19–20 entreats us to "Repent, then, and turn to God, so that your sins may be wiped out, that times of refreshing may come from the Lord and that he may send the Christ who has been appointed for you—even Jesus." This is God's desire for us, but He will never force His will on us.

The choice now is ours. Just as God's holiness convicts ALL of sin, His mercy and love offer redemption to ALL. Each of us must decide for ourselves whether we will accept His gracious offer or continue to try "and do it for ourselves."

STOP AND APPLY

Fill in the blanks:

1. We are commanded to go, preach, teach and make disciples, but only the _____ _____ can convict and change hearts.

2. God's original plan was for us to delight in His _____ and for all of creation to live in _____.

3. The human predicament is that _____ have sinned and fall short of the glory of God and that the wages of sin is _____.

4. Because God is perfect, He cannot tolerate _____ and is not able to violate His _____. To stand in the presence of God requires one to be _____.

5. Sin is choosing our way over _____. The penalty for sin is always _____.

6. The solution to avoid our deserved judgment is found in _____. Jesus was completely human but also completely _____.

7. But God demonstrated His _____ for us in that while we were yet sinners _____ died for us. Jesus willingly took the _____ for our sins.

8. We have the choice to accept His gracious offer. To do so we must _____ our sin for what it is, _____ our need for forgiveness and _____ from our sinful ways.

9. Just as God's holiness convicts _____ of sin, His mercy and love offers redemption to _____.

VI. WHY WE EVANGELIZE

A. Glorify God

The primary reason for evangelism is that it gives God the glory that is His due and is therefore pleasing to Him. Jesus, Himself, agreed that the first and greatest commandment was to "Love the Lord your God with all your heart and with all your soul and with all your strength and with all your mind" [Luke 10:27]. We were originally created in God's image and for His glory, but sin has warped that relationship. Consequently, when another soul is brought back into fellowship with God, this brings Him more of the glory that is His due. It also means one more person added to the throng that will spend eternity praising Him.

B. Obedience

The Great Commission commands all believers to be actively involved in the task of evangelism. Jesus left His disciples [and us] with this charge ringing in their ears:

> "All authority in heaven and on earth has been
> given to me. Therefore go and make disciples of all
> nations, baptizing them in the name of the Father
> and of the Son and of the Holy Spirit, and teaching
> them to obey everything I have commanded you.
> And surely, I will be with you always, to the very
> end of the age" [Matt. 28:18–21].

C. Excitement

Evangelism is an exciting privilege. If you found a starving baby on your doorstep and lovingly nursed it back to health, you would be excited. You would want all your friends to know how you had saved a precious life from certain death. Now, because of your care, the baby could look forward to a healthy, productive, satisfying life. Evangelism does the same thing. It finds dying people and leads them to Jesus, the Bread of Life, so that they can find nourishment for their souls both now and throughout eternity. Evangelism has been described as one beggar telling another beggar where to find bread. It should never include "forcing" another to believe, nor should the evangelist attempt to compel unwilling people to listen. The evangelist should always respect the feelings of the one with whom she is talking. No one should be forced to listen, but all should have the opportunity to hear, if they desire it.

D. Compassion

A man or woman burdened by sin cannot experience lasting peace or eternal life. Most people in this condition know that they have a need, but often they cannot put it into words or explain it to others. A good evangelist will listen to what they are saying and be able to relate the surface or "felt need" to the root of the problem. Perhaps, like the story of Lisa at the beginning of the chapter, they feel betrayed by their friends. But their real need is to sort out who is number one in their lives. Lasting peace comes only when God occupies the throne of our lives. Lisa needed to put God first. Once she did that, the rest of the problems began to be resolved.

Gus' "felt need" concerned what would happen to him in the hospital—what would be the result of his tests. But his real need was to know what happened after death. At one time or another all humans ponder the question of "life after death." It has become the subject of much interest in recent years.

One school of thought holds that all paths lead to God; consequently all of humanity will ultimately go to heaven when they die. Persons adhering to this view do not really care if you believe anything in particular because "God is love" and would not send anyone to hell. Yet to hold to this philosophy makes Jesus a liar and God the Father a fool who sacrificed His own Son for no reason.

Over and over in the Gospel, Jesus warns us of the torments of hell. Each time judgment is depicted, the world is divided into two categories—those bound for heaven and those bound for hell. Moreover, if everyone is destined for heaven, then the death of Jesus on the cross was unnecessary and God foolishly suffered when there was no need.

When Jesus speaks of hell in Matthew 13:42, He says, "They [the angels] will throw them [the wicked] into the fiery furnace, where there will be weeping and gnashing of teeth." A few chapters later He speaks of the day when He will stand in judgment of all who have ever lived. "Then He [Jesus] will say to those on His left, 'Depart from Me, you who are cursed, into the eternal fire prepared for the devil and his angels.... Then they will go away to eternal punishment, but the righteous to eternal life" [Matt. 25:41, 46]. Over and over Jesus speaks of the torment of hell's fires. Since we have already established that Jesus is not a liar but truly the Son of God, we must believe Him when He speaks of this awful punishment awaiting those who die in sin.

Our goal is never to "scare anyone into heaven" by scorching her with the fires of hell, but the reality of those flames should kindle in every Christian a roaring desire to share the way of escape with all who will listen. Hell gives evangelism an urgency. For some, today is the last chance to hear of the way to salvation. Tomorrow they will be eternally beyond our words. That is why the task is so critical. We need to take the warning in Hebrews 9:27–28 seriously:

> *"Just as man is destined to die once, and after that to face judgment, so Christ was sacrificed once to take away the sins of many people; and He will appear a second time, not to bear sin, but to bring salvation to those who are waiting for Him."*

VII. WHY SOME IGNORE EVANGELISM

If the gospel is so compelling and so urgently needed by a sick and dying world, why are not all Christians actively seeking to bring this message of hope to the dying world all around us? The answer to this sad question is multifaceted, but some of the reasons include embarrassment, ignorance, fear of rejection, and being overwhelmed by the task.

A sampling of attendees at a Billy Graham Crusade were asked the question, "What is your greatest hindrance in witnessing?" The most common response was fear of how the other person would react. More than 25% felt they did not know enough to share the Gospel adequately. Other responses included: apathy, too busy, and an inconsistent personal lifestyle.[3]

No one likes to be put down or ridiculed by someone else—especially in a public or group setting. Our modern society has allowed the theme of "live and let live" to so corrupt our way of thinking that many Christians fear rejection if they mention Jesus to someone who does not believe in Him. The claims of the Bible are derided as "narrow" and Christians are "unloving" when they speak of Jesus as the only path to the Father. In these situations we need to remain polite but firm.

VIII. CONCLUSION

Paul reminds the younger Christian, Timothy, "All Scripture is God-breathed and is useful for teaching, rebuking, correcting and training in righteousness, so that the man [or woman] of God may be thoroughly equipped for every good work" [2 Tim. 3:16–17]. Paul's words serve as an encouragement and warn us also. We need to know Scripture and doctrine so that we can clearly and logically explain its message to those who are not believers. If we combine a solid knowledge of the Bible with a sense of urgency and a genuine concern for those who have not heard the message, we will be the kind of Christians that the Holy Spirit can readily use for spreading the Gospel.

Jesus tells us that "the harvest is ready" and that we should "Ask the Lord of the harvest, therefore, to send out workers into his harvest field" [Matt. 9:37]. *We are the harvesters*. We need to pray that we will not only be properly trained and ready, but that we will recognize a ripe harvest field when we see it. Training and experience will make us more proficient, but prayer for discerning eyes is the key to our success.

If, after reading this, you feel inadequate for the task, do not despair. The next session is designed to give you some helpful, practical advice for proceeding with this wonderful assignment.

STOP AND APPLY

1. What are the four reasons given for why we should evangelize?

   _____

   _____

   _____

   _____

2. Identify three people that do not know Jesus as the Lord and Savior. Begin to pray for them daily. Ask God to open their hearts to hear and accept His plan of salvation.

   (1) _____

   (2) _____

   (3) _____

Now if you haven't already done so, listen to cassette tape #1A in the series featuring *Evangelism and Missions* by Elisabeth Elliot. Also on the tape are excerpts from Anne Ortlund and Gwynne Johnson.

ENDNOTES

[1] Robert Coleman, *Master Plan of Discipleship* (New Jersey: Revell, 1987), p. 39.

[2] C.S. Lewis, *Mere Christianity* (New York: Macmillan, 1943), p. 56.

[3] Tim Beougher, *Overcoming Walls to Witnessing* (Minneapolis: Billy Graham Evangelistic Assn, 1993), p. 7.

SESSION TWO
A Verbal Witness in Evangelism

GOALS FOR THE CHAPTER:

After reading this chapter, you should be able to:

1. Know what constitutes an effective verbal witness.

2. Understand how to approach the one to whom you hope to witness.

3. Familiarize yourself with three methods of evangelism.

4. Understand how to call for a decision.

5. Learn the principles for handling objections.

6. Demonstrate confidence to share the gospel verbally with at least one person.

I. INTRODUCTION

Now it came to pass that a group existed who called themselves fishermen and organized themselves into a club. And lo, there were many fish in the water all around. And the fish were hungry.

Month after month and year after year these fishermen met in their club to talk about their call to fish, the abundance of fish, and methodology on fishing.

Continually they did research for new and better ways to fish. They sponsored costly nationwide and worldwide conferences to discuss fishing, to promote fishing, and to brainstorm on fishing.

Large training centers were set up, and courses were offered on the needs of fish, the culture of fish, and where to find fish. Those who taught had doctorates on fishiology, but had little experience in actual fishing. They just taught others how to fish.

And those who were sent out to fish did exactly as those who sent them. They organized more clubs. They analyzed the fish and discussed what was necessary in order to catch fish. But one thing they did not do. They did not fish.

Imagine their hurt when one day a person suggested that those who don't catch fish are not really fishermen, no matter how much they claimed to be. Yet it did sound correct. By definition a fisherman is one who catches fish. Is a person a fisherman if year after year he never catches a fish? Is one following if he isn't fishing?[1]

As you read this chapter, keep the words of Jesus in mind: "The harvest is plentiful, but the workers are few. Ask the Lord of the harvest, therefore, to send out workers into His harvest field." [Luke 10:2] There are people ready and waiting to respond to the claims of Christ, but they need a "harvester" to come. This requires a *verbal witness*. Of course "lifestyle evangelism"—witnessing through your attitudes and actions—is important, and certainly your life should reflect what you are sharing, but a verbal witness is as necessary to the process of evangelism as the right wing of a plane is to the left wing. If we "witness" with *just* our life, it is not complete. There are pieces to the puzzle that are missing. A verbal witness is necessary to finish the puzzle.

A. The Urgency for a Verbal Witness

There is an urgency to our sharing with others. One day this week, sit down and read the obituary page in the newspaper. Time is running out. "As long as it is day, we must do the work of him who sent me. Night is coming, when no one can work" [John 9:4]. We do not have forever; night is coming.

The story is told of an apprentice demon, soon to be sent to earth on his first mission, who is preparing for a last-minute strategy session with his master. The young demon is a fast learner. He has realized that the unbelieving world is already in his master's power and that it would be a poor use of his time and resources to focus his schemes on the lost. Rather, his strategy is to focus on neutralizing the Christians in their evangelistic work. "They could do the most harm," he reasons, "so I must keep them from the destructive work, modeled so well by Paul 2,000 years ago." He shudders at the thought of Paul's success.

The demon then shares his strategy with his master. "I'll try to convince Christians that there is no such thing as sin," he says. "Then they will stop sharing the good news. The answer will soon become irrelevant if I eliminate the question."

"This is only a part of my plan," says Satan, "but it cannot be the focus, for most of our enemies realize the reality of sin. Even those in our power sometimes, in rare moments of clear thinking,

realize sin's destructiveness. You'll confuse some of the enemy, but not all of them on this."

"Well then, I'll convince the church that there is no hell, that even if there is sin, there are no eternal consequences."

"Good thinking," replies Satan. "You will confuse some with this, but still, the prospect of judgment is so ingrained in men, even those in our power, that this will not neutralize the enemy. Most will see through the deception."

The young demon thinks for a moment, and then a look of triumph floods his face. "I've got it! I'll convince them that there is no hurry. They can have their doctrines of sin, heaven and hell. I'll just help them rationalize away their lack of conviction on these matters by whispering in their ears, 'There is no hurry; don't inconvenience yourself. Save it for later.' They are all so prone to be concerned with their own cares and problems anyway, that they will buy right into it."

"You have done well," says Satan. "You will see great success in neutralizing the enemy with this strategy."[2]

Christ will soon return. When He gets here, the harvest will be finished. "Therefore keep watch, because you do not know the day or the hour" [Matt. 25:13].

B. What Constitutes a Verbal Witness?
A verbal witness contains four parts: the approach, the method of sharing, calling for a response, and handling any objections. Each of these will be discussed in the rest of this chapter.

II. THE EVANGELISTIC APPROACH

An evangelistic approach means moving from general conversation to talking specifically about Christ. This is important because it helps set the person who is approached at ease and helps stimulate interest. Your goal is to help the other person feel comfortable and also to stimulate interest in spiritual things.

A. Secular Life
What constitutes a good approach? Begin by talking about the person's *secular life.* Ask about the person's family. Where appropriate, give the person a sincere compliment and begin things on a positive note. Ask about her hobbies and interests. Ask where she grew up or where she has lived. Ask about work or sports she

enjoys. Let the person talk about herself. Then at an appropriate time, you can relate these to her "deeper needs." Learn to really listen to the person with your eyes as well as your ears. Keep your attention focused on her. Don't interrupt her or keep thinking about what you are going to say next. By listening to the person, you will earn the right to be heard.

Nearly every conversation can point to an "open nerve" or point of felt need in a person's life. An "open nerve" is an area of need in a person's life that can be used as a bridge to the Gospel. For example, consider the following list of rather common concerns found in our society.

☑ Lack of purpose and meaning in life

Identify "Open Nerves" by Listening

☑ No joy or happiness

☑ Loneliness and emptiness

☑ Lack of peace and contentment

☑ Fear of death

☑ Dissatisfaction with life

☑ Boredom

☑ Bitterness and resentment toward God or others

☑ Sinful habits

☑ Worry and fears

☑ Problems with drug abuse or alcohol

☑ Marriage problems

☑ Guilty conscience

☑ Failure complex and low self-image

☑ Problems in raising children

☑ Inability to live up to one's own moral standards

A dramatic illustration of this principle tells of a woman reading a newspaper:

She read about a car crashing into a house and killing a baby inside. She grieved over the loss to the mother and then wondered about the welfare of the errant driver, also a woman. After resisting the impulse for several days, she wrote a sympathetic letter to the guilty driver and told her that God cared about her need. She included her phone number and waited.

The desolate woman called back, and after a long conversation the two strangers agreed to meet. Because of that visit and the Christian's witness to God's love, the sorrowing woman trusted Christ as her Saviour. She came to a Bible study group and to church and the love she encountered helped bring her family members to Christ also. She had to go to jail for her involuntary crime, but her faith kept her strong and made an impact on other prisoners. The chain of blessing went on adding links because a Christian woman spoke simply and lovingly toward a needy individual.[3]

A more commonplace example of touching an "open nerve" involved two neighbors in an ordinary conversation:

Elizabeth was a Christian. One day her neighbor confided in her about her worry and fears that something would happen to her children or husband. Every time she heard something on the news about a plane crash or auto accident or earthquake she would have terrible thoughts that she might lose one of them. Elizabeth picked up on this nerve of excessive worry and shared with her how she had once been worried about a lot of things, but that something very important had happened to her. It changed her life and freed her from the bondage of worry. Then she proceeded to share the gospel with her neighbor and led her to Christ.

In summary then, learn to ask questions! Listen! Be observant! Be sensitive! Be friendly!

B. Church Background

After you have established a friendly rapport, seek to discover if the person has any religious or church background. Constantly be on the lookout for clues that come up in conversation. You might ask if she attended a church in the area or if she attended church as a child. For example, a young mother found a clue and used it to deepen her conversation with a friend:

Friend: *We looked all around for a good preschool for Jonathan that had a positive atmosphere and teachers who really cared about the children. After calling all around and* *asking neighbors, we discovered that the best one was at First Baptist Church.*

Believer: *That is good to know. Do you also go to that church?*

Friend: *No, we don't attend anywhere regularly. But on Christmas and Easter we usually go to the church at the corner.*

C. Transition Questions

Ask *questions* that will lead to a spiritual discussion. Continuing with the previous conversation:

Believer: *I used to attend only on holidays, until I visited a church where the people really seemed excited about being able to know God as a person. I found out how I could know that if I died tonight I would go to heaven, as well as be able to live each day with peace in the midst of unbelievable stress and worry. Could I ask you a question: If you were to die tonight, do you think you would go to heaven?*

While this illustration works well in one circumstance, some other questions might be more appropriate at other times. By being familiar with the following list, you will have several options available to meet nearly any need.

1. If you were to die tonight, do you think you would go to heaven?

    or If you were to die tonight and stand before God and He were to say to you, "Why should I let you into heaven?" what would you say to Him?

2. Through the years have you come to know Christ personally, or are you still on the way?

3. Do you think about spiritual things often? Are you interested in spiritual things?

4. In your personal opinion, what is a Christian?

5. Do you know what the Bible says about eternal life?

6. What do you think of Jesus Christ?

7. Do you think heaven is a perfect place?

    or How close have you come to a perfect life?

or If God lets you go to heaven as you are, what will happen to heaven's perfect record?

or Do you see any hope in the Bible verse 2 Cor. 5:17?

8. I notice you have a Bible on your shelf. What do you think is the central message of the Bible?

9. "You know, I heard the best message in church yesterday!" Share about the message briefly, then say, "By the way, are you interested in spiritual things?"

STOP AND APPLY

Check the correct statement:

1. The four components of a verbal witness include:
   - ❏ the approach, the tone of your voice, getting the person to ask questions, and calling for a decision.
   - ❏ the approach, the method of sharing, calling for a response, and handling any objections.
   - ❏ the approach, having a memorized presentation of the Gospel, calling for a response, and being able to argue your case.

2. The three subjects most often used to move conversation from general things to a personal relationship with Christ include:
   - ❏ denominational preference, childhood, and hobbies
   - ❏ secular life, denominational preference, and favorite kinds of books
   - ❏ secular life, church background, and asking questions

3. In your own words, define an open nerve and give two examples:

4. Identify a person in your life who is hurting, and write down what you feel are her open nerves.

_____

_____

_____

_____

5. Pick three of the transition questions that you would feel most comfortable using in a conversation. List them below.

_____?

_____?

_____?

III. METHODS OF EVANGELISM

Once you have brought up the subject of spiritual things and the gospel, it is important to share the facts of the gospel with anyone who is open. While there are **many** excellent ways and plans to share the gospel, we have chosen to examine three diverse methods: personal testimony, the Bridge Illustration, and the use of a Gospel booklet.

D.L. Moody was confronted one day by a person who disapproved of his method of witnessing. Moody replied that he was not overly fond of it himself and asked, "What methods do you use?" "Oh, I don't have a method," the critic replied. "Well," Moody retorted, "I think I like the way I do it better that the way you don't!"[4]

The important thing is not which method you use, but that you have one that you know how to use.

A. Personal Testimony

A personal testimony is simply telling the story of what Jesus has done in your life. The Gospel accounts are filled with such stories. For instance, as soon as Andrew realized Jesus was the Messiah, "The first thing Andrew did was to find his brother Simon and tell him, 'We have found the Messiah' "[John 1:41]. Later in that same chapter, Philip shares his testimony with Nathanael. "We have found the one Moses wrote about in the Law, and about whom the prophets also wrote—Jesus of Nazareth, the son of Joseph" [John 1:45]. Soon Nathanael believed too.

In John 4:29, the sinful Samaritan woman (who had been married five times and was presently living with a man who was not her husband) believed in Jesus for herself and shared her testimony with the village saying, "Come, see a man who told me everything I ever did! Could this be the Christ?"

A personal testimony has a great deal of value because people are interested in personal stories. Nobody can refute your testimony—it is something that happened to you. Being honest about needs in our lives helps others to relate and be willing to discuss their lives with you.

> *Margaret was in England for a year working in a church with youth and college students. She was supposed to speak at a Christian Union meeting at an Arts College in Plymouth but when she arrived, she found only three students. Being told that one of the three was not a Christian, she immediately changed her topic and shared her personal testimony of how she had come to know Christ. Kathy, the unbeliever, called her later that week; they met for coffee where Kathy opened up and shared some of her life with Margaret; before they left the restaurant, Kathy asked Christ to be her Lord and Savior.*

In preparing your testimony, it is helpful to write out what you want to say. Not that you will read it, but the actual writing of it helps you to focus on important milestones in your relationship with Christ. Your basic outline should include:

1. My life before I became a Christian.

2. How I became a Christian.

3. Specific ways Christ has changed my life since I became a Christian.

Testimonies will differ. You may have become a Christian as an adult or as a young person. Some testimonies are dramatic; others appear to be more ordinary. The main point is to realize that you DO have a testimony.

For those of you who became a Christian at an early age, you might talk about your home life, people who influenced you, your early understanding of what following Christ meant, and how you came to relate personally to Jesus as Lord and Savior. Try to identify some specific areas where Christ has made a difference in your life.

You might want to include examples of how your relationship with Christ has helped you to avoid specific sins or temptations.

Before you actually use the worksheet to develop your personal testimony, consider the following "do's" and "don'ts":

DO:

1. Begin your testimony with an attention-getting sentence:
   "I used to think I knew what was going on in life. Boy, was I wrong."
   "I used to be afraid of dying but not anymore."
   "I grew up in a church but did not understand its purpose until recently."
   "I was not always this interested in Christian things."

2. End your testimony with a decision sentence:
   "And that is how I became a Christian. Does what I said make sense?"
   "Do you feel you have come to know Christ, or are you still on the way?"

3. Modify your testimony so others can identify with you. Identify with weaknesses and needs as honestly as you can. Find the open nerve.

4. Give enough details to arouse interest.

5. Use Scripture (Heb. 4:12; 2 Tim. 3:16–17)

6. Focus on Christ, not yourself.

7. Stress the personal relationship you have with Christ.

8. Make sure you clearly communicate the Gospel in your testimony.

DON'T:

1. Use "church" and "Christian" talk.

2. Ramble on and on (3–4 minutes is adequate)

3. Avoid the point—Christ is the new life.

4. Overemphasize how bad you used to be—don't stretch the story!

5. Use words that are general (fantastic, super, great). Be specific!

6. Mention denominations, groups, or people in a derogatory manner.

7. Give the impression that the Christian life is a bed of roses and that you are perfect. Paint an accurate picture. Christ said we could have an abundant life, but He never said it would be easy.

8. Speak in a judgmental or a critical way. Convey love and acceptance.

9. Preach—share about Christ instead.

Writing your testimony takes some effort, but remember: you are introducing the King of Kings and Lord of Lords. Let's suppose that tomorrow you were responsible for introducing the king of a foreign country at a government meeting. You would write out your introduction to him as accurately and carefully as possible and then rewrite, polish, memorize and practice it until it was perfect. How can we do less for Jesus!

Perhaps it would be helpful for you to read an example of a testimony before you write yours:

Before I received the gift of eternal life, I used to be terrified of death and dying. The thought of death terrified me because I did not know what was beyond death's doors. I remember that one time I was coming home from work and suddenly all I could see was some headlights coming toward me swerving from the other lane. I can still hear the screeching sounds of both cars and the sirens blaring from the ambulances and police. But, miraculously, I was not hurt despite the seriousness of the accident. I was paralyzed with fear at the prospect of death being at my door.

Soon after that a friend of mine shared with me a tract showing me that God loved me and had a wonderful plan for my life, that Jesus had died on the cross to pay the penalty for my sins and that He was offering eternal life to me. I decided to take Him at His Word. I believed He really could offer me the gift of salvation.

Since then, my fear of death and dying is gone. About a year ago I was flying to Texas to see my family. All of a sudden there was some engine trouble on the plane and we all had to prepare for an emergency landing. My whole life flew before me but in the midst of a possible tragedy, God had given me complete peace in my heart because I knew for certain that if I were to die, I would go to heaven. What a joy and difference that made as I faced that danger! Do you know for certain that if you were to die tonight, you would go to heaven?

STOP AND APPLY

1. Write your own personal testimony. Take a piece of paper, write down your thoughts on each point, and then put it together.
   a. My life before becoming a Christian:
   b. How I became a Christian:
   c. Specific ways Christ has changed my life since I became a Christian:

2. Practice your personal testimony with your Mentor and with one other person. Write that person's name here:

   _____

B. Bridge Illustration

Another popular method of sharing the gospel is the Bridge Illustration. You can share this illustration with an individual or a group in about fifteen minutes. You might begin by asking: "Have you ever thought much about what it really means to be a Christian?" Then offer to show them a diagram that would clarify what it means to be a real Christian and how each one of us can know for certain if we have eternal life.

When you present the Bridge, it is better to draw the illustration as they watch. That way they can see everything in its sequence, participate in the verses and respond to your questions. Also, after you are finished, the other person can keep the drawing to refer to at a later time.

To learn how to share the Bridge Illustration, you will need to memorize the drawing itself as well as the Scripture passages with their references. Turn to Appendix A and go through the Bridge Illustration step by step.

C. Use of Gospel Booklets

A Gospel booklet is an excellent way to share the gospel. You may wonder how something so small could be used so powerfully. However, many people have come to know Christ because of a tract. But in order for a booklet to be of any benefit, you need to always have one with you! You cannot give away a booklet you do not have!

Melissa once shared a tract with a shoe saleswoman in Texas. She just talked generally with the woman as she tried on shoes, showing her interest in the saleslady as a person. As she left, she asked the woman if she could share a small pamphlet with her explaining that it contained information about the most important decision she could ever make. The shoe saleslady took it and Melissa went on her way. Four years later, after moving to another state, someone wrote to Melissa sharing that a woman had joined their church and given her testimony. She told how a customer named Melissa had given her a little booklet which she read when she got home, resulting in her accepting the truth about Christ. "The word of God is sharper than a two-edged sword!"

Most Christian bookstores carry a wide variety of booklets which explain the basic message of the Gospel. One popular tract is *Steps to Peace with God* by Billy Graham which uses Scripture, pictures, and text to help the reader understand the basic concepts required for salvation. It includes a "sinner's prayer" to help guide the seeker or aid the evangelist who is a bit nervous or new at sharing her faith.

1. Benefits of a Tract

There are many benefits to using an evangelistic booklet:

a. It presents the Gospel very *clearly*.

b. It helps give you *confidence* when you may be nervous.

c. It gives you a *guide* to keep you on the subject.

d. It presents the *claims of Christ* clearly without getting sidetracked.

e. It has the Bible verses *printed out* in case you forget.

f. It gives *visual* help as well as verbal.

g. It offers suggestions for *Christian growth*.

h. It can easily be *taught* to other Christians.

i. The person to whom you are talking will then have something to *take with her* and read again later.

2. "What Do I Say When I Give Out the Booklet?"

You might consider one of the following suggestions:

"Several years ago I discovered the real purpose in life and ever since my life has been different. This little booklet shows how I made that discovery and how you could know it too. Could I share this with you?" (Then hand her the tract.)

"This little booklet contains some of the most important information you could ever know in your entire life. I would like to challenge you to read it before you go to bed tonight and then tell me your impressions of it."

STOP AND APPLY

Put a **T** for True and an **F** for False regarding the benefits of using a tract:

_____   1. It presents the Gospel clearly.

_____   2. It guarantees Christian growth.

_____   3. It can easily be taught to others.

_____   4. It gives confidence when you may be nervous.

_____   5. It usually insures that the person will accept Christ.

_____   6. The person to whom you are talking can take it with her.

_____   7. It gives visual help as well as verbal.

_____   8. It does not use Bible verses to avoid offending those who do not read the Bible.

Before you finish this course, share a gospel booklet with at least one person (Christian or non-Christian) who could benefit from it. Write down her name:

_____

IV. CALLING FOR A DECISION

As was said in the first chapter, the harvest is ripe! Make no mistake about it—people are ready.

Jean was in a small ladies' Bible study group that met weekly to discuss a guide on Christian homemaking. A co-worker of one of the members of the group started coming to this study. She was originally from Yugoslavia and had question after question about the study. Her comments led the members of the group to believe she was not a Christian. The leader asked her two questions which confirmed her suspicions and proceeded to share the Bridge Illustration with her. After hearing it, Jean immediately prayed to receive Christ and with tears in her eyes said that she had been searching and searching for the "Right Way." She shared that some Mormons had come to her door several weeks earlier and they had gotten her thinking about spiritual things. She did not feel comfortable with what they shared, but she did not know where to turn. The Holy Spirit had already prepared her heart and that group of ladies was privileged and excited to reap the harvest. What a glorious opportunity! The fields are white!

A. Definition

So what exactly is a "decision for Christ"? It is nothing magical or mysterious; it is simply the human means of exercising saving faith. Think of it as that moment in which a person who understands the facts of Christianity embraces them in his or her heart (by an act of the will) by choosing to depend on Christ alone as Lord and Savior.

Tying the evangelistic knot can be an unsettling experience. Besides the fact that sinful humans rebel and fight against giving control of their lives to anyone, including Christ, Satan will fight hardest at the point of their surrender to Jesus.

When we decide to accept Jesus as Lord and Savior, we enter into a covenant agreement with Him. We give Him permission to take over our lives. Repentance and faith are both involved in this decision. Together they form the process known as conversion. The symbolism of bride and groom can help our understanding:

It is significant that marriage is one of the illustrations the New Testament uses for being and becoming a Christian. It is obvious that merely believing in a fellow or a girl, however intense that belief might be, does not make one married. If, in addition, we are emotionally involved and have that "all gone feeling" about the other person we still will not be married! One finally has to come to a commitment of the will and say, "I do," receiving the other person into his life and committing himself to the other person thereby establishing a relationship. It involves total commitment of intellect, emotions and will. One must believe in Jesus Christ; and personally receive Him into one's life; and thus become a child of God. The pattern is the same in marriage; a fellow first believes in a girl, then must receive her into his life and thus becomes married. Mere intellectual assent to facts does not make a person a Christian any more than mere intellectual assent to facts makes a person married.[5]

B. Before a Person Makes a Decision

Before a person is ready to make a decision, there must be an adequate understanding of God's love, man's sin, and Christ's work. After you have shared the gospel, there are two key questions to ask:

> *"Does this make sense to you?"*
> and/or
> *"Is there anything preventing you from putting your trust in Jesus Christ right now? Would you like to receive the gift of eternal life which Christ is offering to you?"*

C. If the Answer is "Yes"

If the answer is "YES," then you need to clarify what she is about to do. You can do this by covering three key points and asking three key questions:

Point 1. *Recognize God's solution*—After you discuss the problem with your friend, be sure she understands God's solution.

Question: Do you recognize that Jesus Christ died on the cross to pay for your sins?

Point 2. *Repent of sins*—Be sure she understands that to repent of her sins means to turn away from her sins and go the opposite direction.

Question: Do you understand that you have a sin problem you cannot solve by yourself? Do you really want Christ to deliver you from your sin? Are you willing to repent of your sins and follow Him?

Point 3. *Respond by choosing to place trust in Christ*—Saving faith is the choice we make to rely upon Christ.

Question: Do you place your trust in Jesus Christ as your Lord and Savior?

After you have asked these questions, you can use the chair illustration to further explain *saving* faith:

You see this chair here?
Do you believe that chair exists?
Do you believe that it would hold you up?

But you see, it is not holding you up for the obvious reason you are not sitting on it. That is the way I was with Christ. I believed Jesus existed. I believed He was divine. I could trust Him for finances, health or protection, but saving faith is trusting in Christ *alone* for salvation. As far as my eternal welfare is concerned, I was trusting in my own efforts.

> *Saving faith is putting our trust in Jesus Christ alone for eternal life. Several years ago I repented of my sins and transferred my trust from myself to Jesus Christ; from what I had been doing for God to what He has done for me on the cross. By a simple act of faith I transferred my trust from what I had done to what Christ had done for me. Just as I am now transferring my trust from this chair that I have been resting on (representing my good works) to this one representing Christ. (Get up and actually sit in the other chair.) Now I'm resting on only one thing: that is, Jesus Christ. No longer am I trusting what I have done; rather, I trust what He has done for me.*[6]

After the person is sure about her decision, tell her that you can lead her in prayer and she can tell God what she just told you. You can either give her ideas of what to say and let her pray, or she can repeat verbatim the prayer after you. Assure her that the Lord is looking at her *heart* more than He is listening to her lips.

Feel free to use your own words or consider the following version of the sinner's prayer:

> *Dear Jesus, I know that I am a sinner and need Your forgiveness. I believe that You died for my sins. I want to turn from my sins and ask You to take over the control of my life. I commit myself to You as Lord.*

Keep in mind that people react to their decisions in a variety of ways. Do not always expect bells to ring! Remember that the goal of the decision is not the pursuit of an emotional high but a reasonable response to truth. Some new believers feel an "emotional high," while others "feel" as though nothing has changed. Therefore do not ask someone "How do you feel?" This can easily mislead a new Christian. God want us to live by *faith*, not by feeling.

D. If the Answer is "No"

If the person answers "NO" to your commitment question, you can respond by saying: "Have I explained everything clearly enough so that you know what you need to do when you are ready?" If she is still uninterested, do not close the door of opportunity. Be courteous and express appreciation for allowing you to share.

E. Principles to Keep in Mind at the Point of Decision

1. **Understand that salvation involves a personal decision to transfer trust from self to Christ.** Intellectual belief is not enough! Hearing is not enough. We need to convey to people that we do not earn eternal life by changing our lifestyles, but rather by giving Christ the right to lead us and then our lives will change. It is important to realize that you are putting your trust in Jesus Christ as your Lord as well as your Savior. A mom can tell her children five times to pick up the toys in their room. They can hear her and understand what she is saying, but often they don't do anything about it. A decision has to be made to obey and please her.

2. **Understand the necessity of calling for a decision.** The nature of the gospel demands a response. But human nature often causes us to harden our hearts to the ways of God, or to procrastinate about the decision. Remember the illustration about Satan's strategy to get us to procrastinate and put off what we know we should do.

3. **Underscore that saving faith involves more than knowledge of facts.** Saving faith demands that knowledge become personalized through choice. It is not just an intellectual acknowledgment.

4. **Stress the fact that the issue in salvation is not "*Will God accept me?*" but "*Will I accept His gracious offer?*"**

5. **Focus your appeal to the individual.** With those who seem to be complacent, emphasize the urgency of the decision. With those who seem only to be concerned on an intellectual level, examine the uniqueness of Christ's claims. With those who are sincerely seeking, show them that the invitation is open to them.

Be careful not to manipulate people, and do not press for a decision until you are sure that the person understands the gospel. Then do not allow a seeker to believe that she is saved through merely saying the words of a prayer, but rather through a sincere heart.

STOP AND APPLY

1. What are two key questions to ask before a person is ready to make a decision?
   a. Does this make _____ to you?
   b. Would you like to _____ the gift of eternal life?

2. You have shared the gospel with a person and she has chosen *not* to accept Christ as Lord and Savior. Of the following suggestions, mark the two which give the appropriate response for this particular situation:
   ___ Ask if you have explained everything clearly enough.
   ___ Ask if she is willing to place her trust in Christ as Lord and Savior.
   ___ Ask if she is willing to repent of her sins and follow Him.
   ___ Be courteous and express appreciation for letting you share.
   ___ Be sure she understands God's solution.

3. Write down one example of a sinner's prayer:

V. HANDLING OBSTACLES

It is natural for people to make excuses. Resistance or disinterest can arise from many different causes: it is a natural defense mechanism; it can be a stalling technique; there could be an unwillingness to forsake sin; or, perhaps there is an honest expression of doubt and confusion.

A. Principles in Dealing with Excuses

There are several principles in dealing with excuses:

1. Remember that an excuse frequently hides the real reason.

2. Avoid an argument. Leading people to faith in Christ is much more than merely giving an answer to excuses. You can win the debate but lose them for Christ.

3. The same excuse does not mean the same thing to every person.

4. Meet excuses in the right spirit—with humility.

5. Use sincere compliments when appropriate (e.g. "That was an excellent question.")

6. Present the entire Gospel if at all possible.

B. Methods of Handling Objections

The first method to handle objections is to **preclude** them. A smooth, well thought-out presentation can prevent many objections and sidetracking. Billy Graham precludes some objections by saying, "Now some of you are saying." James Kennedy's *Evangelism Explosion* uses the introduction to preclude some objections by emphasizing the need to start with a person's secular life in order to earn the right to ask personal questions. Then they cannot say, "That is too personal."

The second way to handle objections is to **postpone**. For example, "That is a good question. But I believe what I am about to say may be helpful. If you don't mind, could I continue and come back to that if you are still unsure?"

The third method is to **answer quickly and move on.**

The fourth way to handle objections is to **research and return**. There is nothing wrong with admitting that you do not know the answer to a particular question. Do not let it discourage you or throw you off if you are asked a question you cannot answer. Tell them you will be glad to find the appropriate answer and come back to them to explain it. Howard Hendricks, author of *Say It With Love,* tells how one of his professors responded to a question he could not answer:

"That is one of the most perceptive questions I have ever been asked. Frankly, I cannot answer it now. My answer would be too superficial, but I'll think about it."[7]

STOP AND APPLY

Fill in the blanks:
The four ways to handle objections are to: _____ them; _____ them; _____ quickly and move on, and _____ and return.

VI. CONCLUSION

A verbal witness is necessary to bring people to Christ. It will involve an ***approach*** that takes a person from secular conversation to a discussion of the person's church background and then on to some kind of transition question.

The verbal witness will also involve a ***method***. Three methods have been presented: personal testimony, the Bridge Illustration, and sharing a Gospel booklet. However, there are many other good methods available. Use the one with which you are most comfortable, but be sure to have a method!

Finally, a verbal witness will involve ***calling a person to a decision***, clarifying what she is doing, and often handling objections.

Keep Colossians 4:5 in mind: "Make the most of your chances to tell others the Good News. Be wise in all your contacts with them. Let your conversation be gracious as well as sensible, for then you will have the right answer for everyone" (Living Bible).

In conclusion, remember that it is important not to assume responsibility God never intended you to assume. It is not your responsibility to cause someone to become a Christian. You cannot do that. 1 Cor. 3:6 says, "I planted the seed, Apollos watered it, but ***God*** made it grow." Our job is not to produce the end result but to be faithful in the process. When we stand before our Lord, the main question will not be, "How many people have you led to the Lord?" but rather, "Have you been faithful to do what I have asked you to do?" Rev. 2:10 promises: "Be faithful, even to the point of death, and I will give you the crown of life."

Now if you haven't already done so, listen to cassette tape #1B in the series which begins with *Evangelism in the Market Place* by Mary Whelchell. Also on the tape are excerpts from Debbie Laws, Gigi Tchividjian, Mini Jane Johnston, and Winnie Christensen.

ENDNOTES

[1] John M. Drescher, "A Parable of Fishless Fishermen," *Discipleship* 18 (1983): 42.

[2] *Tell It Often—Tell It Well* (San Bernardino, CA: Here's Life Publishers, 1985), pp. 134-35.

[3] Howard Hendricks, *Say It With Love* (Wheaton: Victor Books, 1978), p. 33.

[4] Leighton Ford, *The Christian Persuader* (New York: Harper and Row Publishers, 1966), p. 68.

[5] Paul Little, *How To Give Away Your Faith* (InterVarsity Press, 1978), p. 59.

[6] James Kennedy, *Evangelism Explosion* (Wheaton, Illinois: Tyndale House Publishers, 1983), p. 39.

[7] Hendricks, p. 41.

SESSION THREE
Evangelism and Prayer

GOALS FOR THE CHAPTER:

After reading this chapter you should be able to:

1. Understand the Scriptural command for evangelistic prayer.

2. Grasp the connection between prayer and evangelism.

3. Recognize some of the main principles involved in prayer and evangelism.

4. Examine some of the methods associated with evangelism and prayer.

5. Be aware of the importance and effects of evangelistic prayers.

I. INTRODUCTION—WHY PRAY FOR EVANGELISM?

After reading the last two chapters, it is assumed that you now understand the message and some methods for evangelism. These are important topics, but if you work without prayer you will surely meet with failure. Perhaps the simplest definition of prayer is "conversing with God." Prayer can and does take many forms, but evangelistic prayer seeks to win the lost to relationship in Christ through the power of the Holy Spirit. Motive and methods give you the rationale and structure for doing the task of evangelism, but only the Holy Spirit can give the power and the success. Someone has compared it to owning a wonderful, shiny, new car. There are two ways to get it down the highway: you can push it, or you can tap into the power and let the gasoline fuel it for you. Most of us do not foolishly push our cars to work or the grocery store. Why, then, do we suppose that we can fuel our spiritual lives without tapping into the power source? You get gasoline at the filling station, but you get *spiritual power* from the Holy Spirit when you pray and ask for it.

A. Prayer is Commanded

1. Jesus makes it clear that prayer facilitates the harvest process.

Jesus went through all the towns and villages, teaching in their synagogues, preaching the good news of the kingdom and healing every disease and sickness. When He saw the crowds, He had compassion on them, because they were harassed and helpless, like sheep without a shepherd. Then He said to His disciples, "The harvest is plentiful but the workers are few. Ask the Lord of the harvest, therefore, to send out workers into his harvest field" [Matt. 9:35–38].

His Harvest Field

The command to pray for evangelism—the harvest field—does not originate with the church but with Jesus Himself. He is the One who tells us that the vital link between unsaved humanity and the Kingdom of Heaven is prayer—not random or sporadic prayer, but a specific plea for more harvesters to be found who will go into the fields and perform this vital task.

Agricultural harvesters are those who go into ripe fields and systematically dig up, pick, or cut the crop from the field and then transport it back to the owner's barn. Spiritual harvesters have similar responsibilities: they gather souls that are ready to leave the fields of the world and guide them to the Kingdom of God. Although the work requires discipline and can often be difficult, it brings unbelievable joy when a new believer enters into God's family. The cost will never outweigh the utter delight of leading another from the fields of darkness to the Kingdom of Heaven. The harvester does not transform an unbeliever into one of God's children; that is the work of the Holy Spirit. However, the harvester often becomes the vehicle used by the Holy Spirit to accomplish His task. Why God allows humans to be part of His glorious task of harvesting is a mystery. Yet the role we are to play is clearly delineated, and one of those tasks is to pray for more harvesters. Jesus tells us that there are not enough workers to bring in all the ripe fruit that is waiting in the fields.

In other words, souls all around you are waiting to be harvested but there is no one to take the message. Consider the following challenge issued in the August 1991 edition of *The Church Around the World:*

"Ripe Mission Field at Our Door"

According to a nationwide survey by Barna Research, one out of four unchurched people would willingly attend a church service if a friend invited them. This represents 15 to 20 million adults in our communities who are ready to reply favorably if you ask them to go to church with you.

---

2. Jesus gives us a promise of help.

Knowing the human tendency toward timidness, Jesus gave us a promise of assistance:

> *And I will do whatever you ask in My name, so that the Son may bring glory to the Father. You may ask Me for anything in My name, and I will do it. If you love Me, you will obey what I command. And I will ask the Father, and He will give you another Counselor to be with you forever—the Spirit of truth. The world cannot accept Him, because it neither sees Him nor knows Him. But you know Him, for He lives with you and will be in you. I will not leave you as orphans; I will come to you [John 14:13–18].*

The secret to our success lies in asking what Jesus has commanded. From the previously cited passage in Matthew, we see that Christ commands us to pray for more workers for the harvest; and from this passage in John, we find the assurance that Christ will always answer and empower us when we seek to obey *His* commands. There is no doubt about the outcome. If we pray for harvesters, we will be heard.

B. Prayer promotes intimacy with God

How did Jesus know the mind of God so clearly? He spent long periods in solitary prayer learning the plan of the Father for His life. If Christ needed time in prayer each day to discern the will of God for His life, why do we think it unnecessary for ours? Or worse yet, do we make a mockery of the process by beginning or ending a strictly human endeavor with a glib prayer asking God to sprinkle His divine blessings on our self-centered effort?

Christ never insisted on His own way! Over and over He sought to know and obey the will of the Father, even when it led to the cross. Christ reconciled us to His Father because He was willing to pray—even in the face of death—"Not my will but Yours be done" [Luke 22:42]. Through prayer He was able to discern the will of God for His life and then He chose to obey.

Unfortunately, many Christians view God as a distant and rather impersonal force. However, these same folks often expound the wisdom of spending quality and quantity time with their families and friends building loving, trusting, and enduring relationships. They would never dream of going a day or a week without speaking to their husbands, children, parents, or other housemates. They set a high priority on interpersonal relationships but exclude God from this category—not so with Jesus. God the Father was more real to Jesus than a beloved husband is to a loving wife. Furthermore, Jesus delighted in the time He spent alone with the Father.

C. Prayer enables us to conform our lives to God's plan for us and for evangelism

Prayer involves two-way conversation between a person and God. It should never be a monologue on the part of the petitioner. Our society increasingly stresses the importance of good communication. Spouses, parents and children, co-workers, and friends are constantly encouraged to be open and honest with each other. Our newspapers, magazines, and bookstores are filled with "how to" advice concerning this important topic. Yet it is ironic that society recognizes the vital role of communication in our interpersonal lives, but often fails to apply the same truth to our relationship with God.

When a wife answers the phone and her husband speaks, she has no need to ask who is calling. His unique voice is immediately recognizable to her. Regular communication through prayer tunes our "spiritual ear" so that we easily learn to identify God's voice, and it helps us to grow in spiritual knowledge and wisdom. With practice the listener can increasingly hear, understand, and then obey the will of God as He reveals it through prayer and Scripture. The process of listening, not just talking, to God enables the Christian to perceive evangelism from God's perspective and follow His plan for soul winning.

D. Prayer brings power

Before His Ascension, Jesus predicted the effects of the Holy Spirit living in the lives of His followers. "But you will receive power when the Holy Spirit comes on you; and you will be my witnesses in Jerusalem, and in all Judea and Samaria, and to the ends of the earth" [Acts 1:8].

At the time of His Ascension, Jesus gave His disciples the command and the authority to go into the world and preach the Gospel to all nations, but they still lacked the ability to carry out Christ's directive. The needed power would come at Pentecost. But during the ten-day interval after the Ascension, the disciples spent their time alone in the upper room seeking God in prayer. They knew that their mission would fail if they attempted it on their own. The same is true today.

Evelyn Christenson in her book, *Battling the Prince of Darkness*, recounts the story of a frail, elderly lady who served on the board of her organization:

> I can still see my almost ninety-year-old (now deceased) board member Edith sitting in board meetings with a little pile of pictures in her lap. She couldn't stand it until she had shown us that month's pictures. Of what? Children, grandchildren, birthday parties, vacations? Oh, no. Missionary friends from her "special mission field" regularly sent her the names and pictures of those they were trying to win to Jesus. Edith would then pray, by name, for them until they accepted Jesus. In her sleepless, pain filled nights, Edith often prayed all night. The pictures were that month's harvest of her new converts! Her pain-ridden wrestling for those souls was the power that produced their release from Satan's evil kingdom.[1]

The unsaved became Christians because someone cared enough to pray. Edith had found the secret of praying for souls one at a time until they were safely part of the Lord's kingdom.

E. Evangelism battles Satan

Many non-Christians erroneously believe that there is a safe, neutral middle ground between the Kingdom of God and the Kingdom of Satan. Reading 1 John 5:19 makes it clear that everyone belongs to Satan until each person chooses to become a child of the Lord. "We know that we are children of God, and that the whole world is under the control of the evil one." Those who are not part of God's heaven are automatically slated to spend eternity in hell with Satan. That is why Satan so opposes evangelism. Every soul saved is one "stolen" from him. No wonder he works so hard to discredit the lifesaving words of the Gospel. Jesus won the battle when He died on the cross—the doors of heaven are now open to all who will accept Christ's redemptive power. Knowing this defeat, Satan works all the harder to see that as few as possible find the true path to salvation. Satan will always oppose evangelism.

1. Pray Defensively

Defensive prayer protects the Christian who evangelizes lost souls. Satan seeks to destroy those who bear the good news of Jesus to the darkened souls of the lost, but the power of God to protect His own supersedes that of Satan. The wise evangelist not only prays for protection for herself, but also enlists prayer partners who ask God to protect her and enable her to carry out her task.

At the end of the sixth chapter of Ephesians, the Apostle Paul lists the spiritual armor that is available to all Christians who go forth in battle for the Lord. Today we might see these as bulletproof vests, crash helmets, special plexiglass cages or other protective devices. The purpose of this spiritual protection is to enable us to successfully fight Satan and the Kingdom of Darkness—to fight *and win!*

Pray a "Shield of Protection" for the Christian

We put on this special covering through prayer. Those involved in evangelism need to pray daily for this protection [defensive] and then pray to take the battle to the gates of hell [offensive] and prevail. Wise evangelists daily arm themselves with the protection and power of the Holy Spirit.

2. Pray Offensively

While defensive prayer protects Christians, offensive prayer for evangelism asks God to soften the hearts and prepare the ears of the hearers that they might be receptive to the message of the Gospel. Offensive prayer asks that Satan will be blocked in the lives of unbelievers and that they will be open to hear the voice of the Holy Spirit. Acts 26:18 puts it this way: "to open their eyes and turn them from darkness to light, and from the power of Satan to God, so that they may receive forgiveness of sins and a place among those who are sanctified by faith in me."

A few years ago, Floyd McClung wrote a book titled *Living on the Devil's Doorstep* that tells of his battle with Satan in the city of Amsterdam. With its permissive society—legal drugs and prostitution—its red-light district has gained a notorious reputation. In the years that the McClungs and YWAM [Youth With A Mission] have ministered there, they have battled the power of evil and the occult. They have watched as it sucks young people to an early grave and an eternity in hell. The YWAMers and others involved in the fight against Satan know that prayer is the front line of their defense *and* their offense against the enemy. Spiritual warfare is not a game. Satan and his demons are real and they seek to devour anyone who attempts to "steal" souls locked in their dark world.

Pray for a "Softened Heart" in the lost

Like Christ, Christians who aggressively battle evil do not hide inside their houses and hope that Satan will be defeated. They take their battle to the streets, the bars, the houses of prostitution, and any place that they find hurting people. But before, during, and after their encounters with these folks, they pray that they will be the conquerors in this spiritual battle and that new souls will be added to the Kingdom of God as a result of their efforts.

We should only pray to God, but we can and should address Satan, if the situation arises. When Jesus was confronted by the devil in the desert, Christ quoted Scripture and gave commands that reinforced His position of authority over the Evil One. We should follow this example. When battling the devil for the soul of an unbeliever, quote Scripture and use the name and power of Christ's blood to claim the soul for God's kingdom.

Robert Savage authored a volume entitled *Pocket Prayers* in which he encourages Christians to use the words of Scripture when praying for friends or loved ones. The following list of Scriptures all relate to the great need for faith in the life of the unbeliever. By simply restructuring the sentence, it is easy to turn any of the passages into a prayer. For instance, Psalm 105:4 could be prayed

"Dear Lord, may _____ look to you and your strength and seek your face always." Certainly not all-inclusive, this list is intended to help you to use Scripture in this special way.

Prayer	Ref.
"Dear Lord, please help _____ to want to seek you with all her heart because You have said that if a person seeks You with heart and soul, You will be found."	Deut. 4:29
"God in heaven, You have said You love those who love You, and will be found by those who seek You. Please help _____ to fulfill this requirement that she may know the joy of being in full fellowship with You."	Prov. 8:17
"Father in heaven, there will come a day when _____ will no longer have breath to seek for You. Help her call on You today and find salvation in Your Son, Jesus Christ. Help _____ realize that time is limited. Impress upon _____ the need for urgency."	Isa. 55:6
"Loving Father, _____ knows nothing of Your righteousness and unfailing love. I humbly ask Your Holy Spirit to break up the unplowed hardness of heart that keeps _____ from hearing Your voice. Unstop her ears and help _____ to seek You until she is fully surrendered to You and can experience the showers of righteousness that Hosea speaks of."	Hosea 10:12
"Jesus, You have said that if we ask, seek, and knock, the door will be opened. Give to _____ an unrelenting desire to ask, seek, and knock to know the truth about You. May _____ fervently seek You with all her heart and may Your Holy Spirit illumine her mind with the truth."	Luke 11:9
"Jesus, You have promised that those who hear Your Word and believe that You came to bring eternal life will not be condemned. Lord, Your promise is always true and so I ask that You would help _____ to realize that she currently stands condemned by Your Word. Help her to recognize her eternal peril and humbly return to You."	John 5:24
"Holy Spirit, _____ foolishly doesn't recognize her need for repentance and new life in Jesus. Convict _____ of the utter folly of not surrendering her life to Jesus."	Acts 2:38
"Dear Lord, I see _____ struggling with many problems in life. But she is ignoring the basic problem in her life—the need for You to be on the throne. By the power of Your Holy Spirit, I ask that _____ is convicted of this error and established in true faith so that she might know the times of refreshing that can only come from Your hand."	Acts 3:19

"Father, Your plan has been established from the foundation of the earth. Please help _____ recognize that You are not a distant or remote God, but one who wants to have a vital, alive relationship with every person."	Acts 17:26–27
"Lord Jesus, the warnings are clear. Salvation is only found in You. Help _____ to recognize that the days are growing shorter when she will be called to judgment for all of eternity."	Heb. 2:3
"Only foolish people harden their hearts to You, Lord. Help _____ see that rebellion is the act of a willful child, but faith in Jesus is the only path to deep inner peace, both now and throughout eternity."	Heb. 3:15

STOP AND APPLY

Circle the answer that best describes why we should pray for evangelism:

1. Prayer is:
   (a) talking to God
   (b) listening to God.
   (c) both "a" and "b."

2. Prayer is:
   (a) suggested.
   (b) commanded.
   (c) helpful.

3. Prayer promotes:
   (a) intimacy with God.
   (b) a personal relationship with God.
   (c) both "a" and "b."

4. Prayer enables us to conform our lives to:
   (a) God's plan for us.
   (b) the needs of people.
   (c) the world.

5. Prayer brings:
   (a) success.
   (b) God's judgment.
   (c) power.

6. Evangelism battles:
   (a) people.
   (b) Satan.
   (c) the world.

---

7. Both offensive and defensive prayers should be used in evangelism. Put an "*O*" or a "*D*" before each of the following statements.

___Prayers for protection for the Christian who is evangelizing.

___Prayers to soften hearts and prepare hearers.

___Prayers to block Satan in the lives of unbelievers.

___Prayers to clothe Christians with spiritual armor.

___Prayers to send forth workers into the field.

II. PRAYING FOR EVANGELISM

A. Direction of Prayer

Just as human relationships are based on good communication, so, too, is ours with God. Ask yourself if you are working in God-given or human strength and direction. If your communication with God is poor, perhaps you need to concentrate more on Him and less on yourself. Talk with Him as you would to a beloved and respected parent or spouse. Speak of your love for Him, as well as mentioning problems or concerns.

What if a wife met her husband at the door each day with a list of what is wrong or things that she wanted him to do:

> *Good evening, Husband:*
> 1. *The dog got sprayed by a skunk—where were you when I needed you?*
> 2. *The back screen door is torn and needs fixing,*
> 3. *I think the roof is leaking and it's going to cost so much to fix,*
> 4. *I'm so tired from doing all the chores—how come you don't help more? and,*
> 5. *[apologetically] Yes, I know you do a lot of good things and I appreciate it but [whine] I NEED MORE.*

Now how's that for a lover's litany? Yet, that is what we often do with the Lord. We only communicate when we want something, and we seldom ever stop to say "thank you" or "I love and worship you." Begin your time with the great Lover of your soul by offering Him praise and worship. Tell Him you love Him; He never tires of hearing it. After you have spoken of your love, then proceed to other types of prayer.

Many Christians find it helpful to follow the "ACTS" plan. Begin with *adoration*, follow with a time of *confession* where you humbly and openly confess all known sins and submit yourself in obedience to God. *Thank* Him for all the ways that you see Him working in your life and those around you. *Supplication* completes this four-layered plan of prayer. It is now that you will want to lay your petitions before Him.

1. Pray for conviction of sins.

The Lord cannot use us if we knowingly live a life of sin. If you are serious about evangelism, ask Him to convict you of any sin in your life that will hinder you from completing the task that He is assigning you. This is a difficult prayer for some because it presupposes that you really want to weed out any sin that comes to your attention. That means turning your back on it and firmly resolving not to commit it again!

2. Pray for the church to have power.

"I will give you the keys of the kingdom of heaven; whatever you bind on earth will be bound in heaven, and whatever you loose on earth will be loosed in heaven" [Matt. 16:19]. Christ has chosen to delegate much of His authority to the church, but, unfortunately, the church seldom uses it properly. Christ gave it to us that we might take the good news about Him to all the unsaved in the world. Instead, it is often used to further human ambitions or build monuments here on earth. Christ wants us to use this power to enlarge the kingdom of heaven, and He wants us to pray that others will come to know Him as their Lord and Savior.

a. There is power in the name of Jesus.

Jesus clearly told His disciples that His name held power: "Until now you have not asked for anything in my name. Ask and you will receive, and your joy will be complete" [John 16:24]. Jesus was telling His disciples that His name stood for (or represented) Himself. When we pray in the name of Jesus, we are not invoking magic or a trite formula. We are coming before God in the name of the one whom He [God] has exalted above all other names [Phil. 2:9].

Imagine the doors that open every time the voice says, "This is the President of the United States." His name is not just his personal possession but a reflection of his power. Yet no earthly leader will ever compare in power to that of Christ, and Christ has said to evangelize the world *"in My Name."*

b. There is power in the blood of Jesus.

Why does Satan fear and hate the blood of Jesus? Because it atoned for the sins of the world. Our society is so sanitized that blood makes most of us squeamish, but it was different in Israel. There the people saw the daily animal sacrifices; they watched the blood flow and smelled the burning meat. They relied on these offerings to appease God. Without that blood they were in deep trouble; without the animal sacrifice they were responsible for the consequences of their own sins.

It is much the same today. We can choose to accept the punishment of hell caused by sins we have each committed, or we can receive our pardon by acknowledging that the blood of Jesus already paid the debt for each of us.

Occasionally we read an inspiring story where one person out of love for another offers to die in the place of a friend. It is not often that such self-sacrifice occurs; when it does, it is usually front-page news. Now imagine the power behind the blood of the person whose death was able to save *everyone* who has ever been born. Even the power of a million nuclear bombs pales in comparison, and Jesus places the knowledge of this life-changing power at our disposal when we carry out His task of world evangelization.

Countless evangelistic stories attest to the power and necessity of such prayer. For instance, the story is told of a missionary working in a small town on the border between Brazil and Uruguay:

> *One morning he went and began passing out tracts on the Uruguayan side of town and was rebuffed by all he met. Discouraged he crossed over to the Brazilian side and met with the opposite reaction. The people were not only polite, they were friendly and interested.*
>
> *Much to his surprise, he spotted a woman who had also crossed the street and was shopping on the Brazilian side. When he offered her a tract, she graciously accepted even though she rudely refused him earlier that morning. Then he began to notice a pattern. Everyone on the Brazilian side of the town accepted his material openly and graciously regardless of the side on which they lived.*
>
> *Puzzled, he began to pray about this reaction and felt the Lord bring the Scripture from Mark 3:27 to mind: "In fact, no one can enter a strong man's house and carry off his possessions unless he first ties up the strong man. Then he can rob his house." Further investigation revealed that a group of Brazilian Christians had been praying for the strong man [the devil] to be bound in their town.[3]*

3. Pray for Revival

Although some Christians use the terms "*evangelism*" and "*revival*" interchangeably, *evangelism* refers to the conversion of unsaved souls to faith in Jesus Christ, while *revival* refers to the process whereby Christians are renewed and empowered to do the tasks assigned them by God—especially evangelism.

a. God has promised revival under certain conditions.

The text most often associated with revival is found in 2 Chronicles 7:14: "If my people, who are called by my name, will humble themselves and pray and seek my face and turn from their wicked ways, then will I hear from heaven and will forgive their sin and will heal their land."

Notice that God includes an important "if" in this powerful promise. Revival always presupposes that God's people are willing to reform totally their sinful ways, become humble, and pray for God to restore them to their former spiritual health. Although God can and often does restore individual souls who take this promise and its requirements seriously, it is primarily intended for the people of God as a whole.

When the history of Christianity is charted, it looks rather like a long line of mountain peaks separated by deep, dark valleys of negligence and sin. As early as the Book of Revelation [end of the first century], Christ was calling Christians to repent of their evil ways and return to Him with wholehearted commitment. Aside from the obvious need to turn from sin, the church needs times of revival because they inspire people to a fresh and vigorous commitment to spread the Gospel at home and abroad.

Great revivals are never self-contained events. The joy of being in right relationship with the Lord wells up and spills over, first to the surrounding community and then into the world as these spiritually refreshed and invigorated disciples go out and tell others about the power of God to change lives.

b. Revival is the work of the Holy Spirit

Just as there is power in prayer because the Holy Spirit works in and through prayers, so He is responsible for revival. Over the years, many countries and places have experienced revival. For instance, Wheaton College has experienced several of these dramatic outpourings of the power of the Holy Spirit. Preceding each occasion, one finds that the student body spent significant time in prayer. In 1936, a Wheaton student asked the famous evangelist J.

Edwin Orr, when he felt that Wheaton might experience revival. Orr answered, "When Christians get right with God about their sins." Less than a month later, revival came to Wheaton and for more than twelve hours students took turns confessing their sins and seeking God's forgiveness. Many of the students involved felt the call of God on their lives and have spent over fifty-five years laboring in the harvest fields.[4]

In 1943, a similar outpouring occurred and this time faculty joined with the students in seeking God's forgiveness for sin in their lives. Results of that February meeting eventually reached the far corners of the world as over thirty percent of the graduating class of 1943—including Billy and Ruth Graham—ultimately became involved in some form of full-time ministry.

Seven years later, in 1950, the campus again witnessed a dramatic answer to their prayers for forgiveness and spiritual cleansing. As before, these renewed lives scattered to the far corners of the world and took the Gospel to all who would hear. One of the more prominent results of this revival can be found in the establishment of radio station ELWA in Liberia. From 1954 until its takeover during the coup of 1990, it broadcast in 42 languages to Africa, Europe, the Middle East, and Russia. The Holy Spirit used these surrendered men and women to be His hands, feet, and voice to the unbelieving world.

B. Pray Simply

Many people who are willing to pray for evangelism falter because they do not know how to begin. Evangelistic prayer need not be complex. In his book, *A Force in the Earth*, David Shibley suggests that Christians who wish to pray for evangelism keep the following points in mind:[5]

☑ Pray that the nations of the world and their leaders will be such that the atmosphere is peaceful and conducive to evangelism.

☑ Pray that Satan and his demons will be bound so that harvesters can do their job.

☑ Ask the Father to send the Holy Spirit to prepare the hearts of those who do not know Him that they might become ripe fruit.

☑ Quote Jesus and ask the Lord of Harvest to send forth workers into the fields that He has prepared.

☑   Beseech God to send His angels to do battle with the evil forces that would keep people from Christ. Some may wonder if angels are part of God's plan for the harvest, but Hebrews 1:14 teaches: "Are not all angels ministering spirits sent to serve those who will inherit salvation?"

C. Pray Regularly

Most people never notice that Jesus spent great quantities of time alone with His Father in prayer. Before beginning His three-year public ministry, He spent forty days praying in the desert. Furthermore, the Gospels chronicle many other occasions:

- *"Jesus got up, left the house and went off to a solitary place, where he prayed"* [Mark 1:35].
- *"leaving them, he went to the hills to pray"* [Mark 6:46].
- *"Jesus often withdrew to lonely places to pray"* [Luke 5:16].
- *"One of those days Jesus went out into the hills to pray, and spent the night praying to God"* [Luke 6:12].

These are only a few examples of His prayer life. If Christ found a time of regular conversation with the Father to be vital to His ministry, it's foolish to assume that we can ever be successful without following in His footsteps.

If you do not have a regular time alone with the Savior, resolve to make this a part of your daily life. It is best to begin with a modest commitment and make sure that you keep it—perhaps five or ten minutes at the start. Then as prayer becomes a natural part of your daily schedule, the Holy Spirit will guide you.

> ### STOP AND APPLY
>
> Plan how you are going to accomplish this regular time with the Savior, and be prepared to share your plan with your Mentor.

D. Pray Fervently and Persistently

Americans live in an "instant society." We want what we want when we want it. We hate lines, waiting, and any inconveniences. An attitude of instant self-gratification is diametrically opposed to that taught by Christ. Nowhere does He teach that the life of the disciple will be anything but difficult. However, He also reminds us that persistence pays off—just as the woman in the parable in Luke 18 eventually receives justice.

Praying for the conversion of a loved one, a friend, or even the unsaved of another country does not always bring immediate response. But the prayer is never forgotten by God, who hears all our utterances. History is replete with the stories of men and women who have faithfully prayed for the salvation of spouses, children, or loved ones. These prayer warriors often persevere for years before they see any fruit for their efforts.

In his small volume, *The Work of Faith Through George Mueller*, the editor, Abbie Morrow, recounts an interview between Mueller and the Reverend Charles R. Parsons. Morrow quotes the venerable saint from Bristol, England as saying:

> "Thousands of souls have been saved in answer to the prayers of George Mueller. He will meet thousands, yes, tens of thousands in heaven!... The great point is to never give up until the answer comes. I have been praying for fifty-two years, every day, for two men, sons of a friend of my youth. They are not converted yet, but will be! How can it be otherwise? There is the unchanging promise of Jehovah, and on that I rest. The great fault of the children of God is, they do not continue in prayer; they do not go on praying; they do not persevere. If they desire anything for God's glory, they should pray until they get it. O how good, kind, gracious and condescending is the One with whom we have to do! He has given me, unworthy as I am, immeasurably above all I had asked or thought! I am only a poor, frail, sinful man; but He has heard my prayers ten thousands of times, and used me as the means of bringing tens of thousands into the way of truth. I say tens of thousands, in this and other lands. These unworthy lips have proclaimed salvation to great multitudes, and very many have believed unto eternal life."[6]

According to David Shibley, in *A Force in the Earth*, God heard and answered the persistent prayer of George Mueller for the salvation of his friend. Shibley writes:

The day came when Mueller's friend came to Christ. It did not come until Mueller's casket was lowered in the ground. There, near the open grave, this friend surrendered his heart to the Lord. Persistence had paid off![7]

E. Pray Boldly

All greatly-used saints of God [whether they are famous or not] know that they must approach the heavenly throne as boldly as Christ did. Christ prayed with confidence and certainty that the Father would hear and answer any prayer that would bring glory to Himself and advance the Kingdom of God on earth. That was why Christ could know that the Father would raise Lazarus from the dead, cure ten lepers, restore sight and hearing, or preserve and strengthen the timid disciples so that they could form the strong backbone of the Christian church.

This power in evangelism is not only granted to the prominent but also to the simple members of the Kingdom. As a youngster, Evelyn Christenson watched her mother

> ...as she prayed for every single member of her extended family. Not one of whom knew Jesus Christ when she found Jesus. And my mom had the privilege of leading every single one of them to Jesus Christ before they died. And she prayed for twenty-five years for my dad, and she prayed thirty years for my only brother to find Jesus. That was my mom. When she died at the age of ninety-one, they all said that my mother had won more people to Jesus Christ in her town than all of the pastors put together. Because she was some great, wild evangelist? [Oh no] My mom was a simple little lady who knew how to pray. And she prayed for them, she loved them, she involved herself in their lives—lived a sacrificial life for them. And had the privilege of leading—I don't know how many—it's hundreds of people to Jesus. My little mom. So you see I was brought up in that kind of atmosphere, and I was rather surprised when I got a little older and realized that plans and programs and projects somehow replace the power.[8]

STOP AND APPLY

1. If you want to pray regularly, it helps to set _____ _____ of prayer.

2. Prayer can fall into the ACTS plan. This stands for:
   A _____
   C _____
   T _____
   S _____

3. In evangelism it is important to pray specifically for the church to have _____ and to pray for _____ of sins.

4. Check the following that may keep you from spending time with God on a regular basis:
   ❐ watching too much TV   ❐ not interested
   ❐ staying up too late   ❐ lack of discipline
   ❐ don't know how   ❐ unconfessed sin
   ❐ involved in too many   ❐ distracted by
     activities   housework
   ❐ don't have a plan   ❐ haven't made it a
   ❐ other (list them here)   priority

5. Has someone been a faithful prayer warrior for you? If so, share about this person with your Mentor.

III. THE IMPORTANCE OF PRAYER TO EVANGELISTIC OUTREACH

A. Prayer Supports and Undergirds Evangelism

Ask sincere evangelists and they will tell you that without prayer, their efforts are doomed to failure. Even Billy Graham, who has preached to more people than any person who has ever lived, finds that his success is entirely dependent upon prayer. Time and again, his crusades have relied on prayer support to overcome the powers of evil which seek to destroy the outreach. Some of this prayer support is visible. Members of the Billy Graham Evangelistic Association work with churches from each crusade city and organize teams of local believers who commit themselves to pray for the success of the crusade. In addition, they each intercede for several unbelieving men and women whom they hope will attend the meetings. For up to a year before the crusade, these praying people meet on a regular basis to pray specifically for friends and loved ones. Once the crusade begins, they invite these prayed-for friends to accompany them to one of the meetings. Most of the people who go down to the platform at a crusade are ones who have been brought in such a fashion. Their hearts have already been softened by the Holy Spirit to accept the message they hear.

When Pearl Goode died in 1972, Ruth Graham spoke at her funeral. She pointed to the casket told the congregation, "Here lie the mortal remains of one of the secrets of Bill's [Billy Graham's] success." From 1954 until her death, Pearl Goode was at every one of the Billy Graham crusades. She came not to join in the inspiring and festive atmosphere that often accompanies the meetings. Instead, she quietly remained in her hotel room praying—sometimes all night—for the spiritual success of the outreach. Without fanfare or publicity, she poured out her heart to God on behalf of the efforts of thousands of men and women each of whom had a part to play. Only God can say how many souls are now part of His kingdom because of the prayers of Pearl Goode.[9]

B. Prayer Must Always Precede Evangelism

Prayer for a specific evangelistic outreach strikes most of us as logical and necessary, but there is another type of evangelistic prayer that is not always so obviously required. Pre-evangelistic prayer should be a daily part of the prayer life of all believers. Although some Christians appear to receive a special gift of evangelism from the Holy Spirit, *all Christians* are commanded to share their faith whenever possible with all who will listen. Jesus makes it quite clear that we are all to be involved. His words in Matthew 10:32–33 contain both a promise and a warning: "Whoever acknowledges me before men, I will also acknowledge him before my Father in heaven. But whoever disowns me before men, I will disown him before my Father in heaven."

If you have never prayed in this way, begin by asking the Holy Spirit to help you. Then keep your eyes open for places or people where you can share the good news about Jesus. The Holy Spirit loves to be creative, so you might find yourself praying for some unlikely candidates. The following are merely a few ideas to get you started on this great adventure.

1. Take Joshua walks

Much of America seems bitten by the desire to exercise and stay healthy. More and more of us are attempting to "stay fit" in a variety of ways. Concern for physical health is not bad, but our bodies will one day die. While out jogging or walking around your neighborhood, why not use the time to pray for souls? Pray for the houses that you pass. If you know something about the residents, pray specifically for God to soften their hearts and lead you to find ways to reach out and build a bridge to them. Pray that God will give you an open door, and boldness to clearly and succinctly explain the gospel to them. Then pray that the spiritual blinders will fall off their eyes and that they will accept this life-changing truth as reality in their lives.

When the Holy Spirit gives the "go ahead" signal, consider inviting these people to a church service, an evangelistic Bible study, or possibly a neighborhood discussion about the claims of Christ. Look for ways that you can creatively present authentic biblical truth about Jesus in such a manner that your friends will find it irresistible.

2. Form or use existing prayer chains

Most churches have prayer chains that usually work overtime when someone is ill or in unusual distress, but often they go days, weeks, or months without praying for unsaved souls. Mobilize this untapped resource in your church and turn it into a powerful evangelistic weapon for advancing the kingdom. Have these hidden prayer warriors beseech God to protect and embolden the ones who that day will be involved in the process of evangelism. Ask God to protect and defend those who battle the kingdom of Satan, but also plead with God to help His people break down the strongholds of the evil one that inhabit every community.

3. Pray for church services

Evelyn Christenson tells of a pastor who walks around his church on Saturday night and prays for the folks who will be sitting in each pew the next morning. Even if you cannot go to your church on Saturday night, why not covenant to pray for the unbelievers—whether new or regular attenders—who will worship with you on Sunday morning?

4. Take advantage of pictorial directories

If "a picture is worth a thousand words," then consider the link between pictorial directories and evangelism. High school and college yearbooks or other pictorial directories provide a rich field for prayer and harvesting. Young people are especially open to new ideas and are just beginning to form opinions on a variety of subjects. If you are committed to helping these young people find the path to Jesus, agree to take one or more pictures, post them in some prominent place in the house and then pray daily for the salvation of the young faces that greet you.

5. Establish Prayer Triplets

One effective method of evangelistic prayer involves the formation of a Prayer Triplet. In a little pamphlet published by Evelyn Christenson Ministries, Prayer Triplets are introduced as "a simple convenient way to win people to Christ. You just link up with two Christians and pray together regularly for the salvation of nine friends or relatives who do not know Jesus personally."

The format for a Prayer Triplet group is wonderfully simple. As the pamphlet explains:

Format for a Prayer Triplet

1. Choose two Christian friends or relatives to make your triplet.

2. Each of you choose the names of three people who do not know Jesus as personal Lord and Savior.

3. Agree on a time to meet once a week to pray together for your nine. Just 10 or 15 minutes in your home, at work or school, before or after a meeting, etc. is all it takes.

4. Pray together for the nine people by name to accept Christ as their personal Lord and Savior. Include their personal needs and families.

5. As much as possible, as God leads, involve yourself with your three in a friendly, helpful way. Pray for each other as you seek to do this.

6. When your friends become Christians, continue to pray for them even if your triplet takes on other names to pray for.

7. If possible, incorporate them into your church, Bible study and/or fellowship after they accept Jesus.

> ### STOP AND APPLY
>
> Seriously consider the challenge to form a Prayer Triplet, and be prepared to discuss this with your Mentor. Pamphlets on Prayer Triplets can be procured from:
>
> *Evelyn Christenson Ministries*
> *4265 Brigadoon Drive*
> *St. Paul, MN 55126*

IV. THE EFFECTS OF EVANGELISTIC PRAYERS

A. It fulfills the biblical mandate

When we ask God to raise up workers, we are fulfilling the vital command of Jesus [Matt. 9:36–38]. In doing so, we become united with believers around the globe who are likewise involved in a similar pursuit, and we are actively advancing the kingdom of God on earth.

B. It strengthens individuals and churches

When churches are united in their purpose and obedience to Christ, they become attractive to the secular world that surrounds them. Christ, Himself, tells us in John 12:32: "But I, when I am lifted up from the earth, will draw all men to myself." Not surprisingly, then, the healthiest churches in every country of the world are those that seek to follow the words and example of Jesus most clearly.

C. It opens our eyes to "hidden" or new harvest fields

Sometimes Christians overlook other obvious connections to the secular world. Have you considered the spiritual state of the friends of your children, the woman who does your hair, the people at your health club, the lonely, talkative widow who lives on your street, or the single Mom who needs a friend and someone to help carry her burden?

D. It enlarges the Kingdom of Heaven and brings glory to God

When a soul is reborn into His eternal kingdom, glory is restored to God. Only God is worthy of the praise and adoration of all of creation. Evangelism, then, gives to God the glory that He deserves because it restores a rightful relationship between Creator and creature. Every soul that is added to God's heaven represents a precious life saved from eternity in hell. The church today is involved in a spiritual battle of cosmic proportions. Each morning brings us one day closer to the return of Christ and an end to our opportunity for evangelism. Let us greet each day on our knees.

Now if you haven't already done so, listen to cassette tape #2A featuring *Prayer and Evangelism* by Evelyn Christenson. Also on the tape are excerpts of messages by Millie Dienert and Carolyn Peterson.

ENDNOTES

[1] Evelyn Christenson, *Battling the Prince of Darkness* (Victor Books, 1990), pp. 107–108.

[2] Robert C. Savage, *Pocket Prayers* (Tyndale House, 1982).

[3] David Shibley, *A Force in the Earth* (Florida: Creation House, 1989), pp. 73–74.

[4] Mary Dorsett, "Revival" (*Wheaton Alumni Magazine*, Apr/May '89).

[5] Shibley, pp. 74–77.

[6] Abbie C. Morrow, *The Work of Faith Through George Muller* (Cincinnati: M.W. Knapp, 1899), p.149.

[7] *Ibid.*, p. 84.

[8] Evelyn Christenson, Talk given at Wheaton College, Wheaton, Illinois on April 9, 1991, pp. 3–4 of transcript.

[9] John Pollock, *Billy Graham: Evangelist to the World* (Minneapolis: World Wide Publications, 1979), p. 113.

$\mathcal{U}$NIT TWO:

Inner Circle
Evangelism

SESSION FOUR
Evangelism With Children

GOALS FOR THE CHAPTER:

After reading this chapter, you should be able to:

1. Consider various methods of evangelism for reaching children.

2. Understand God's ideal plan for the family as parents seek to lead their children into relationship with Him.

I. INTRODUCTION: GOD'S PURPOSE FOR THE FAMILY

The picture of baby Obed bouncing on "Grandmother Naomi's" knee at the end of the Book of Ruth vividly illustrates family evangelism as God intended for it to be. This child of God-fearing parents would grow up to father a new generation of God-fearing children that would include Jesse, the father of King David, who was called "a man after God's own heart."

From earliest times, God intended for families to be founded on a mutual love and devotion to Him. Parents would naturally incorporate His word and plan for their lives into every aspect of child-rearing. Children would find in their parents models of godly behavior and seek to imitate them. Families who wholeheartedly sought His will would be blessed with His presence and His peace no matter what the outward circumstances.

Unfortunately sin entered the picture, and since that time humans have struggled to conquer their selfish and self-centered desires. Today most families in America are self-centered—not God-centered. The result is damaged family relationships or "dysfunctional families" as they are currently labeled.

II. CHILD EVANGELISM

A. The Changing Realities for America's Children

Those raised in the 1950s or even the "turbulent '60s" like to think of the American family as bearing at least a passing resemblance to the ones portrayed on *Father Knows Best, Ozzie and*

Harriet, Leave It to Beaver, or even *The Brady Bunch*. Yet these television sitcoms of those decades (where parents always find time for the needs of their children and "all ends well") are sadly unrealistic to most modern American children. A 1989 article in *Christianity Today* disclosed that:

☑ 1 in 2 American children has a mother at work.
☑ By the year 2000, 7 out of 10 preschoolers will have a working mother.
☑ In 1980, 20% of American children lived in a one-parent family; ten years later that number rose to 25%.
☑ 1 in 4 American children fails to finish high school.
☑ 1.5 million run away or are thrown out of their homes.
☑ *12.4 million live below the poverty line.*[1]

The Chicago Tribune also found that of the twelve most industrialized nations in the world, the United States leads in the number of teen pregnancies.[2]

Time is running out for many American children. Yet churches have traditionally placed a low priority on time and monies spent on this needy, hurting, and potentially fruitful home mission field. Only recently have more and more church leaders awakened to the fact that relevant children's outreach programs are the main—and in some cases, *the only*—hope for tomorrow's generation of leaders.

B. The Age of Accountability

For years, studies have been done by numerous denominations and church groups to determine the age at which people are most likely to become believers. Various reports on the topic have been written, and although minor statistics may differ, the overwhelming evidence concludes that children and youth are the group most open to accepting the Gospel. The older one gets, the less likely that person will become a Christian. Many factors conspire against older persons, who more often think of themselves as self-sufficient, saved by their own merits, not interested in spiritual matters, or "turned off to God."

Children, like adults, have deep needs. Unlike many adults, however, their minds are often much more open to the claims of Christ. They have not systematically hardened themselves to the main tenets of faith (as have so many older people), nor have their minds become so preoccupied with things of the world that they impatiently dismiss all talk of religion. Most people become Christians during their childhood or youth.

Much has been written about the age at which a child is able to exhibit saving faith. Some argue that it is impossible before the age of ten or twelve, while others hold that even toddlers can understand and believe. Many great Christian leaders became Christians as children. Isaac Watts made his decision at age nine. Jonathan Edwards recognized Jesus as the Lord of his life at age seven. Corrie Ten Boom and Ruth Graham both surrendered control of their lives to Jesus when they were little five-year-old girls. In *The Effective Invitation* by R. Alan Street, the story of Leighton Ford, an internationally known evangelist, vividly underscores the reality of a child's conversion:

> The children filed into a house at Canadian Keswick for Frances Thomas' daily "Happy Hour." Five-year-old Leighton, a bit taller and thinner than most, took his place on the front row.
>
> Amid her flannelgraph, chalkboard, and colorful teaching accouterments the former missionary to China held the youngsters spellbound with the story of Nicodemus, that distinguished Jewish teacher who once asked Jesus, "How can a man be born when he is old?" And then, as she did after each meeting at Keswick, Miss Thomas asked the children to raise their hands if they wanted to respond to God's invitation for salvation. Leighton's hand shot up.
>
> "No, Leighton," Miss Thomas whispered, "You're too young. Please be still."
>
> Again she gave the invitation and again Leighton raised his hand. She tried once more to dissuade him.
>
> The third time Leighton's hand was raised Miss Thomas perceived that the boy of five had understood and was prepared to make a commitment to the Savior.[3]

There is also biblical evidence for child conversion. Paul speaks of Timothy who learned of faith in Christ from his grandmother, Lois, and his mother, Eunice. Timothy, who would become Paul's trusted assistant and beloved spiritual son, grew up in a household where his mother was a believer but his father was not. Still, Paul says of Timothy that "from infancy you have known the holy Scriptures, which are able to make you wise for salvation through faith in Christ Jesus" [2 Tim. 3:15].

The Gospel of Matthew presents a beautiful picture of Jesus interacting with children and warning His disciples that all believers must "become like little children" [Matt. 18:3]. Matthew 19:14

says, "Let the little children come to me and do not hinder them, for the kingdom of heaven belongs to such as these." The Kingdom of Heaven is clearly open to anyone with the faith to believe.

What about infants? Some parents may worry that infants who die before reaching an age when they can possibly be expected to make a decision will not be part of the kingdom. But such fears are not substantiated by any biblical evidence. Not only is God just, but He is also merciful and loving. There is no reason to believe that He will punish souls who are incapable of making an informed decision. The story in Matthew 2 of King Herod's murder of all baby boys under the age of two in Bethlehem is usually referred to in biblical texts and commentaries as "the slaughter of the innocents." The implication is that these young souls were considered innocent before God and would be received by Him in all love and fairness. It is also comforting to remember the story of King David when the first son born to him and Bathsheba died. Although deeply grieved, David tells his servants, "While the child was still alive, I fasted and wept. I thought, 'Who knows? The Lord may be gracious to me and let the child live.' But now that he is dead, why should I fast? Can I bring him back again? *I will go to him*, but he will not return to me" [2 Sam. 12: 22–23]. David firmly expected to see the child in heaven.

C. Churches and Children

Realistically, the church cannot sit back and expect parents to play their God-given role in the lives of America's children and youth. Too many modern families are in chaos. These young and precious lives are therefore easily influenced. Gangs, cults, drug dealers, and a variety of other anti-Christian forces have long recognized this fertile field. Unless large numbers of Christians shake off the apathy and lethargy that has rendered most of us impotent in the face of crises, we can expect to lose a great portion of the next generation.

The successful church should consider the following points when planning an outreach to children and youth:

1. *Offer training seminars for bewildered parents to help them fulfill their God-given role*. They need principles as well as specific methods so they will not relinquish their role to the government, nor to outside organizations as if these are better qualified under God. Occasional pulpit messages are not enough.

2. *Make the evangelistic outreach culturally appropriate and attractive*. Outdated methods should be immediately

discarded. Mass meetings and old-fashioned Gospel hymns were successful at the turn of the century, but they usually fail miserably today. We have been assigned the task of reaching this generation for Christ. Therefore, we need to use methods that will be more effective with our young but media-sophisticated audience.

3. *Discover the felt need of the group you are trying to reach.* No one should ever compromise the centrality and importance of the gospel message, but it is important to know with whom you are dealing. Nearly all of America's youth are lonely and will respond to anyone who genuinely cares about them—someone who is willing to spend time listening and encouraging them on a consistent basis. Show them that you care. Look for ways to relate to their needs and problems. Help them see the need for spiritual reality in their lives, and then explain the message of the Gospel to them.

4. *Explore the variety of evangelistic helps available.* Literature, videos, and other ideas for reaching this crucial age group abound. Sports, afternoon clubs, special tutoring, summer ranches, camps or farms, clubs, or other groups can all be highly effective, if the main purpose for these groups remains the propagation of the Gospel. If the intent of spreading the Good News of Jesus Christ is diluted, the outreach is doomed to failure, and the workers will usually find themselves disillusioned.

STOP AND APPLY

Put a *T* for True and an *F* for False:

_____ 1. God intended for families to incorporate His Word and plan for their lives into every aspect of child-rearing.

_____ 2. The gospel of Matthew tells of Jesus warning His disciples that all believers must become like little children.

_____ 3. You can't genuinely accept Christ until age fourteen.

_____ 4. Evangelistic outreaches for children should use old traditional methods that have been tried and tested.

_____ 5. Nearly all of America's youth will respond to anyone who genuinely cares about them.

List at least two ideas that your church can use in child evangelism:

1) _____

2) _____

III. EVANGELISM AND YOUR CHILD

A. God's Plan

From the beginning, God planned for children to learn of Him through the teaching of their parents. Some of the earliest written instructions to the nation Israel speaks to this topic. In a well-known and often-quoted passage of Scripture from the Book of Deuteronomy, God commands His people through Moses:

> *Hear, O Israel: The Lord our God is one. Love the Lord your God with all your heart and with all your soul and with all your strength. These commandments that I give you today are to be upon your hearts. Impress them on your children. Talk about them when you sit at home and when you walk along the road, when you lie down and when you get up. Tie them as symbols on your hands and bind them on your foreheads. Write them on the doorframes of your houses and on your gates [Deut. 6:4–9].*

God's plan is clear. His word and the reality of His presence should pervade the daily existence of His people. The children of Israel would learn to love and obey God not just on the Sabbath but every moment of the week, because His presence would be constantly before them.

Christian families should strive for the same goals. Children raised in a home that habitually and readily places the Lord at the center of all family goals and activities will naturally grow up with an intimate knowledge of Jesus. When the person and work of Jesus is clearly and logically presented, children are instinctively drawn to Him. Evangelizing our own children should be of paramount importance to all Christian parents. Christian leadership and nurture should begin in the home. This is a solemn and God-given duty of all parents.

Unfortunately, many Christian parents feel that it is enough to simply take their children to church and assume that contact with Sunday School and morning services will lead their children into a true relationship with Jesus Christ. Such an assumption is not only misleading but dangerous. God holds parents responsible for teaching their children about faith, and such instruction must include proclamation of the Gospel in the most appealing and attractive of ways.

Our homes should be places of Christian nurture where children will not only learn to love the Lord, but also to respect and obey Him. God should be visible and indispensable to all that happens throughout the day. Children should observe that He is indeed the true head of the house and a part of all daily decisions. When God becomes a real person to the children, they will naturally form habits that are pleasing to Him because they will want to obey Him. The Book of Judges warns of the consequences for those who neglect their duty as spiritual parents—"another generation grew up, who knew neither the LORD nor what he had done for Israel" [Judges 2:10].

B. The Role of the Parents

1. Parents must be believers

In Joshua's "farewell address" to the people of Israel, we find one of the oldest and most enduring guidelines for families of God. Standing before the entire nation, he challenged them with the stirring words:

> *"...if serving the Lord seems undesirable to you, then choose for yourselves this day whom you will serve, whether the gods your forefathers served beyond the River, or the gods of the Amorites, in whose land you are living. But as for me and my household, we will serve the Lord" [Josh. 24:15].*

Obviously, family evangelism must begin with parents who are believers. If the parents are only halfheartedly following the Lord, then it is foolish to assume that they will be wholeheartedly committed to this task of evangelism. Evangelism begins with "me," as Joshua so succinctly proclaimed. He not only clearly knew and trusted the Lord, but he boldly announced his conviction to all of Israel. His children could not fail to see that their father not only spoke God's words, but that he also lived them. Family evangelism presupposes that either the father or the mother—or ideally both—

have a deep desire to see their children learn the truth about Jesus and trust Him as their Lord and Savior.

2. Parents need to pray

Early in the Book of Samuel, we read the oft-quoted words of Hannah as she takes Samuel to the Temple and tells Eli: "I prayed for this child, and the Lord has granted me what I asked of him. So now I give him to the Lord. For his whole life he will be given over to the Lord" [1 Sam. 1:27–28]. Long before Samuel's birth, Hannah discovered the importance of prayer. On her own, she failed to solve her seemingly overwhelming personal problems, but through prayer she proved the victor. The lesson remains the same

**Pray for
Future Generations**

today. If we want children who will be totally dedicated to the Lord, then we need to be parents who pray, even before these young ones are born. It is never too early to pray for your children or grandchildren!

3. Parents must be an example to their children.

Furthermore, the lives of Christian parents must be consistent with their words or their children "won't hear them because they see them." If the children see a godly witness in their parents on a daily basis, then they will be prepared to accept the truth of the Gospel message when it is presented.

STOP AND APPLY

Fill in the blanks:
1. God holds _____ responsible for teaching their children about faith. Therefore our _____ should be places of Christian nurture.

2. Parents must be an _____ to their children and must be _____ with their words and actions.

3. Prayerfully take a few moments and evaluate your example to your children. Ask God to reveal to you any wrong attitude, tone of voice, or action in which you need His help to change. Confess these to Him and ask for His strength to live a godly life.

C. Principles of Child Evangelism

The following principles in child evangelism can be adapted easily to single adults, childless couples, grandparents, Sunday School teachers, and many other relationships to children.

1. Treat each child as an individual.

Belief in a living Savior is a personal matter between Christ and an individual. No matter what our age, each person must make this decision for herself. Stuart and Jill Briscoe understood this principle and did not view their children as a "clump" to be evangelized, but as individuals with special needs and interests. As the story of Judy Briscoe's conversion illustrates, they must also realize that becoming a Christian requires a change of lifestyle from that of sin to one of obedience to God. Judy's mother, Jill, recalled this momentous event in the life of her daughter. Children do not need a clear grasp of theological doctrine, but they must realize that they are sinners who can only be saved by Jesus (who died for them on the cross).

> Judy was... four years of age. And I remember wishing the children would all wait a little bit, so that I could really be sure they understood. And yet, all of them insisted on finding Jesus at a very young age. And Judy was no exception. I remember standing at my baking board in my kitchen... I was being domestic at that point, and cooking some English cookery, and I really did have my hands full of the dough.
>
> Suddenly, Judy, who had been playing in the little room off the side, came running in, clutching a toy, and her little hands came up on the baking board, and I was suddenly aware that she and I were in a little still-point because her big, blue eyes asked me a question. Then the question came out in words.
>
> "Mommy, if I ask Jesus into my heart, will I have to put my toys away?"
>
> And that was a very deep question for a four-year old. Because, however the Holy Spirit had been speaking to her in the middle of that very domestic occasion, she had understood that if she asked Jesus into her heart, a change is necessary. And she didn't like putting her toys away. And so, I did what good Christian mothers should do, I said, "Oh, yes, Judy, if you ask Jesus into your heart, you'll have to put your

toys away, because Jesus will ask you to be obedient to mommy."

Whereupon she replied, "Oh, then I won't."

And I remember standing there thinking, "Oh, no, now I've blown it! She'll go on drugs, leave home, you know, I was into the whole thing." [Then] I remember praying fervently, "Lord, how silly of me! Why didn't I get her into the Kingdom, and tell her all about Your rules afterwards!" And yet I knew that Jesus never did that, and that even at a very early age, children need to know very little to enter the Kingdom of God, but they do need to know that repentance means turning away from selfishness and turning your face towards Christ.

And so thinking all these thoughts through, I was delighted to see my daughter come back with the same toy clutched in her hand, and she said to me, "Alright, I will." And I remember just moving, with my hands still full of dough, into the living room, and we knelt down, and Judy came to Christ.[4]

2. Help the child to see Christ as a living person and not a rigid theology.

As with adults, the primary focus is to introduce the child to the Person and claims of Christ—not to a doctrine or set of beliefs. Sometimes in our zeal we make the mistake of reducing the Gospel to a set number of points, and then we try "to maneuver" or force someone else to accept the validity of our arguments. A decision that is made under force is worse than none at all, because it places Christ in an unfavorable light and usually results in a counterfeit conversion. This often disillusions and hardens the person to the real nature of Christ and the Gospel. No one wants to voluntarily place themselves under the authority of someone that they associate with "scare" or "strong arm" tactics. Children often have a keen sense of intuition, and they will either quickly rebel (if they are being forced against their will), or they will appear to acquiesce (while secretly vowing to "get away quick and never come back").

3. Look for opportunities to plant seeds about the Gospel.

Parents have hundreds of contacts daily with their children. Jill Briscoe calls this daily life "Nazareth Living" or "Nazareth Days," and she urges parents to remember that their home is holy ground because God is present there. God is not limited to church or other "spiritual places." The home of believing parents is holy ground. That is why it is important to look for opportunities to share the gospel or to disciple our children through the everyday situations that we encounter. Never compartmentalize the spiritual nurture of your children. This training should be incorporated into all aspects of your family life.

Sometimes the urgency of accepting Christ is expressed in rather unusual settings, but wise parents are always open to the stirring of the Holy Spirit in the life of a young child. As Judy Briscoe Golz remembers:

> I have a younger brother called Pete, and he was young, too, when he came to know the Lord. He was four years old. He and mom were driving home from shopping one day, and my mother is not that good a driver. She doesn't mind me saying it; we all know it. In fact, her driving would put the fear of death into anyone or everyone.
>
> So, mom wasn't at all surprised actually, when Peter all of a sudden said, "Mom, stop the car! I want to ask Jesus into my tummy."
>
> Mom said, "No, Pete, why don't you wait until we get home."
>
> And he said, "No, Mommy, you've got to stop right now, right now." And so they did. And he asked Jesus into his heart.[5]

a. Have consistent family devotions. The fast pace of life in most American families leads many to forego a daily Bible time or period of family devotions. Yet these same families would never dream of sending their children to school in pajamas or to bed without brushing their teeth. Each person and each family has priorities, and we find time for what we consider to be important. When we omit time with God each day, we send a clear message to our children: things of this world are more important than time with God. Christian parents need to let their children know that spending time with God is the most important thing we do each day, and they should try to plan a regular devotional time for the family.

Start when your children are young. Most families prefer to have devotions at night, but if this is not a good time for your family, consider doing them at breakfast. You might read a portion of the Bible or a Bible story and then all discuss how it might apply to each member of the family. Follow with a time of prayer for each person;

encourage your children, no matter how young, to pray for other family members. Remember to ask God specifically for the needs of the day ahead.

If your spouse is not a Christian and a time of family devotions is not possible, think about reading Scripture or a Bible story to your children before nap time or after school. Again, follow the reading with a brief discussion and then a time of prayer.

Christian bookstores are full of books for children of all ages, and choosing an appropriate one can be confusing. The following guidelines should help you with this process:

1) Always read the book yourself before you read aloud to your children. If you are selecting a book for an older child, read the beginning and end in the bookstore and skim the middle. Consider the explicit theology as well as the morals or relationships that are portrayed. Are they consistent with what you are teaching your child?

2) Make sure that the book accurately presents the Word of God and does it in a manner that is age-appropriate for your child. When selecting a book for a younger child, remember that words are more important than artwork. Endearing pictures will not mask a flawed story in the mind of your child.

3) Some books are written to teach a moral, such as clean your room, be nice to siblings, or do not fight with friends. There is nothing wrong with such a book, but they should not be confused with Bible stories. The goal of Bible stories should be to teach your child about her relationship with God. If you are selecting a Bible story, consider carefully what message the author is stressing.

4) Christianity is centered on our relationship with God. Because of Jesus we no longer live under the law of *do's* and *don'ts,* but rather in a relationship of loving obedience to a loving God. Do the words of the story teach this concept to your child?

5) Does the book accurately present the Bible story, or does it add non-Scriptural embellishments?

6) Does the book hold the reader's attention?

b. Spend some quiet time with your children before they go to bed. Try to put them to bed early enough so that you can spend 10–20 minutes with them. Children are very receptive to parental input just before they fall asleep. Encourage your children to pray out loud with you for all of their needs as well as for lost friends. Use this time to communicate genuine love by looking them in the eyes and verbally telling them you love them and that you are glad that Jesus died on the cross and rose from the dead for them.

c. Pray consistently with them and in different types of situations. Prayer should not be limited just to times of daily devotion. There are hundreds of opportunities for prayer each day—e.g. for safety to and from school; for freedom from fears or worries; for wisdom to know God's will in various situations; for the ability to be a friend to another child who is "difficult"; for how to handle playground problems. The list can and should go on and on. No situation is too little to pray about. It has been said that if it is big enough to worry about, it is big enough to pray about.

d. Model how the Scriptures can help handle day-to-day situations. The daily obstacles and difficulties faced by each family member provide an ideal starting point for searching Scripture. The wise parent uses these opportunities to help her child learn about God's word. Look up passages that relate to the problem, and then look for ways to help your child apply the lessons learned.

e. Tell your children how Christ has changed your life and how He affects it daily. All children love stories, especially those about their parents. Each of us has "milestones" in our pilgrimage. Recall those times when God acted powerfully or directly in your life and share them with your children. Help them to look for similar milestones in their lives. Enable your children to see that a relationship with God affects *all* aspects of your life and theirs. Also, be transparent with them about ways Christ is helping you deal with current struggles and problems.

f. Use discipline in a godly manner. No one enjoys discipline, but the wise person acknowledges its necessity. Your children will naturally look for ways to avoid facing the consequences of their actions. Yet the Bible is full of injunctions to parents. The Book of Proverbs says that a lack of discipline results in death. "Do not withhold discipline from a child; if you punish him with the rod, he will not die" [Prov. 23:13]. Loving parents are sometimes reluctant to punish an errant child, but undisciplined children grow to be self-centered adults who often rebel against the Lord and His discipline. This verse and others from Proverbs should be taken very seriously. Parents will be held accountable on judgment day for the spiritual and earthly training of their children. Such a solemn task should never be taken lightly.

On the other hand, parents should be very careful when they administer discipline. Most children base their idea of God on the example they see in their earthly parents. Discipline needs to be fair, firm, and consistent. Make certain that the child understands the reason why his or her actions are unacceptable. Help the child to see that while you disapprove of his or her actions, you don't waver in your love. Teach your child that God feels the same way about us—He hates our sin but never ceases to love us. Finally, parents should take great comfort and hope in the promise that is also found in Proverbs. "Train a child in the way he should go, and when he is old he will not turn from it" [Prov. 22:6]. Sometimes it is not easy to know how to handle a difficult child. If you need more help in the area of discipline, consider reading one or more of the following books: Dr. James Dobson's *Dare to Discipline, The Strong Willed Child,* or Dr. Kenneth Leman's *How To Make Children Mind Without Losing Yours.*

g. Show your child how you handle failure. Everyone, even parents, makes mistakes. Admitting your shortcomings and asking your children to forgive you can be a powerful witness. Explain to them that God holds you accountable to Him for your actions. Let them see that you take the commands of God very seriously and that you expect them to do likewise.

h. Look for opportunities to ask probing questions that will help you discuss the message of the Gospel. Look for Christian books, puppet shows, videos, theaters, concerts, or other media presentations that will help your child "grow in the grace and knowledge of our Lord and Savior Jesus Christ" [2 Peter 3:18]. Likewise, programs such as Sunday School and Vacation Bible School will naturally stimulate parent/child discussions.

Judy Briscoe Golz recalled a simple conversation between her father and brother that led to an eternal change.

> My older brother, David, was five years old when
> he started really questioning Mom and Dad about
> God, about **why** Jesus had died on the cross, and been

raised again from the dead. And one Easter Sunday morning, he and Dad were sitting at the kitchen table talking, and [David] was asking Dad some very, very poignant questions about Jesus and God.

So Dad turned to him and said: "Dave, do you want to accept Jesus as your Lord and Savior?"

And he said: "Yes, Dad—I do." And at the age of five, my father led my brother to the Lord.

Now, my older brother is a pastor in the upper peninsula of Michigan, and he has a five-year old son, and a few months ago, this five-year old son—the same age as Dave—started asking the same questions, and Dave had the joy of leading him to the Lord.[6]

STOP AND APPLY

1. Treat each child as an _____. Help the child to see Christ as a living _____ and not a rigid theology.

2. Look for opportunities to plant _____ about the Gospel.

3. Write a brief paragraph explaining how you could plant seeds in your children's lives and encourage their faith; use the suggestions from this chapter.

4. If you are a parent, list everything you have done in the past week to help your children see the truth about Jesus. Resolve to add at least one "new seed" this week.

_____

_____

_____

_____

4. Be alert to respond.

The Briscoes were alert and ready to respond when the seeds they had sown began to bloom in each child's heart and mind. Even though the parents might have preferred the children to wait until they were older and more capable of fully comprehending the importance of their decision, the Briscoes wisely encouraged each of the three to make a decision when the child felt the time was right. Each conversion conveys an urgency—a need to get it sorted out and settled with God. *Wise parents bow to the leading of the Holy Spirit and His timetable.* Children do not need to be biblical scholars before they become Christians.

5. Stick to basic theology.

Unfortunately, many involved in child evangelism are confused about this point. A thorough comprehension of biblical doctrine is not what God requires, but rather a knowledge of His love and a sense of one's sin which results in separation from God. Children also need to understand the meaning of the death and resurrection of Jesus and be willing to place themselves under the Lordship of Jesus Christ. No one—child or adult—can become a true Christian if they do not adequately understand what they are committing to believe and follow.

Explain the Gospel in terms understandable to children. Remember that the goal is not to stuff information into children, but to discover whether their thoughts are biblically correct. If not, then your job is to lead them gently to an accurate understanding. You will want to present only the relevant biblical truths in a simple, straightforward manner which is easily grasped by the child, and then check to be certain that your hearer understands properly.

The evangelist Sam Jones said the greatest compliment he ever heard about his preaching came from a small boy on his first preaching circuit. The little boy said to his father: "I want Brother Jones to come back to our church. I can understand everything that he preaches!"

6. Don't ask "yes" and "no" questions.

Questions that can be answered with a simple "yes" or "no" do not adequately reveal much about a child's understanding. However, ones that require children to explain their faith can be an effective means of guiding parents so that you can lead them to a greater level of understanding.

Children frequently misunderstand what is being told them, and it is important that we ask questions that will give us accurate insight into their thoughts. Try to avoid questions that merely require a one-word answer. Think about the difference between these two sets of questions.

Don't Ask "Yes" & "No" Questions

Amber, do you really believe that Jesus is God's Son who died on the cross for your sins? Do you know you are a sinner and that Jesus wants you to stop sinning and ask Him to help you to be a good girl?

Instead, rephrase the question, and ask:

Amber, why do you think Jesus died? Does His death on the cross mean anything for your life?

7. Make sure you diagnose the real spiritual need.

Sometimes children who are looking for an assurance of salvation appear to be interested in making a first-time profession of faith. If no one understands the real problem, they might make several "professions of faith" but never receive the assurance that they seek and need. Parents and other Christians sometimes question the sincerity of child conversions among the young. They worry that there is no way that a child of four or five could fully grasp the message of the Gospel and be saved. The wise Christian will take the extra time to ask pertinent questions that will help diagnose the real problem. Consider the following dilemma:

> *Two weeks ago Jean's Mom prayed a sinner's prayer with her, but three times since then Jean told her mother that she is still praying that Jesus will take her sins away and let her into heaven when she dies. Because Jean is only nine years old, Mom wonders if Jean really understands what it means to be a Christian, and she secretly doubts the veracity of Jean's "conversion."*

Since Mom is unsure about the authenticity of the conversion, she should ask questions that will reveal the real need. "Jean, what do you think happens when you honestly ask Jesus to take away your sins?" If Jean answers that Jesus does it, then Mom might ask: "Do you believe that Jesus did this for you?" If Jean is unsure, Mom might ask her to read aloud John 3:36. [Having Jean read the verse will help her to appropriate the truth contained in it.] Then Mom might ask Jean to tell in her own words how one knows if they have eternal life. If Jean still can't answer the question, then Mom needs to review the plan of salvation and check to be sure that Jean knows how to apply it to her life. On the other hand, if Jean immediately grasps the meaning of the verse and says that believing in Jesus gives you eternal life, Mom should ask her if she really meant it when she first prayed for Jesus to forgive her sins and to begin to work in her life. If so, then she should help Jean to conclude that she does indeed have eternal life.

8. Conversion is only the beginning.

Finally, remember that the job is only begun when a child makes the decision to allow Jesus to be the Savior and Lord of his or her life. Now begins the slow and sometimes frustrating task of helping this young convert to surrender all areas of his or her life to the Lordship of Jesus. Discipleship is an ongoing process that should cease only at the death of the believer. Up to the point of death, we are each required to be continually conformed to the image of Jesus.

STOP AND APPLY

1. Be alert to _____.

2. Stick to basic _____. Children do not need comprehensive Bible doctrine.

3. Do not ask _____ and _____ questions.

4. Make sure you diagnose the real _____ _____.

D. A Sample Outline of How to Present the Gospel to Your Children

In his book *The Effective Invitation*, R. Alan Street offers wise guidance for parents who would like some practical suggestions for sharing the Gospel with their children. Adults tend to think in abstract terms, while children think in concrete terms. Therefore, it is of primary importance that the words used convey the meaning that is intended. For instance, "saved by the blood of the Lamb" or "being washed in the blood of Jesus" might sound very scary to some children. Others could imagine that "taking a stand for Jesus" means operating a lemonade or hot dog booth. If not properly explained, a child might think that asking "Jesus into your heart" meant somehow fitting another human inside yourself.

1. Begin with the fact of God's love.

Even small children can understand that God loves them and wants to be their friend. Most will readily accept that He made them and cares about them in a special way. Explain that God will always care, even when we cannot see Him. You might use the analogy of the sun which is not seen at night but is still there. Or explain that after you leave the room, the child can no longer see you, but you are still there if he or she needs you.

2. Present the issue of sin.

When speaking to a child, "speak of lying, kicking, biting, disobeying mother, grabbing toys or books out of baby brother's hands, selfishness, fighting, or throwing a temper tantrum when not getting one's own way. They are sins a child understands because they are acts of rebellion he commits daily."[7] Even if she did not know to call it a sin, Judy Briscoe understood that not putting away her toys was displeasing to God. She knew that she was choosing her own way over God's way, and that He would not be pleased with her decision.

3. Explain that sin leads to a drastic consequence—punishment.

Even though God loves us, He cannot leave sin unpunished. If the child is old enough, allow him or her to read Romans 6:23 aloud. Remind the child of a time when he or she did something naughty and was punished by you. Ask why he or she was punished, and make sure that he or she sees the punishment is a result of disobedience and that it did not indicate a change in your love.

4. Share the main points of the Gospel.

Briefly and concisely explain that even though we deserve to suffer for our sins, God wants to help and love us. That is why He sent Jesus to earth. Jesus left heaven and became a man so that He could take our punishment for us. Jesus loves us so much that He paid for all our sins when He died on the cross.

5. Tell your children that God expects them to respond positively to the message.

Even a child must repent and believe. The theologian, George B. Eager, believes that repentance should be explained to children as "being sorry enough for your sins to want to stop doing them." Children must also understand that unless they repent, they will be held accountable for their sins.

As far as faith, it is easy for a child to trust Christ as Savior. Children respond to love. "Because of a child's early capacity to trust, it is not difficult to lead him to Christ."[8]

One idea is to use John 3:16 and personalize it "For God so loved Kristi, that He gave His one and only Son, that if Kristi believes in Him, Kristi shall not perish but have eternal life."

6. Give your children the opportunity to respond.

a. Make sure they understand they should not do this just to please you. Their motive for coming to Christ should not be to gain your acceptance.

b. Do not manipulate by offering rewards or special privileges in return for their decision.

c. Never embarrass your children.

> ### *STOP AND APPLY*
>
> **1.** Number the following statements to reflect the proper order when sharing the Gospel with children:
> _____ Tell them God expects them to respond positively.
> _____ Explain that sin leads to punishment.
> _____ Tell of the fact of God's love.
> _____ Give the opportunity to respond.
> _____ Present the issue of sin.
> _____ Share the main points of the Gospel.
>
> **2.** Prayerfully consider making it a goal to present the Gospel to a child God has placed in your life, whether it is your own child, a grandchild, a niece, a nephew, or neighbor.

IV. CONCLUSION

God's plan for evangelism is to begin with the family. When parents are deeply committed to being disciples of Jesus, they will naturally communicate this to their children (who will see the wisdom of following in the same path).

Now if you haven't already done so, listen to cassette tape #2B in the series which begins with an excerpt from a message by Henrietta Mears. Also on the tape are excerpts of messages from Martha Wright, Ann Hibbard, and Karen Mains. The tape concludes with the first part of *Evangelism and Family* by Jill Briscoe and Judy Briscoe Golz.

ENDNOTES

[1] "Politicians Discover Children," *Christianity Today* (Mar. 17, 1989), p. 34.

[2] *Chicago Tribune*, Mar. 19, 1991.

[3] R. Alan Street, *The Effective Invitation* (Old Tappan, NJ: Fleming H. Revell, 1984), p. 209.

[4] Jill Briscoe, Talk given in Wheaton, Illinois, Mar. 19, 1991, pp. 4–5 of transcript.

[5] Judy Briscoe Golz, Talk given in Wheaton, Illinois, Mar. 19, 1991, p. 3 of transcript.

[6] Street, p. 209.

[7] *Ibid.*, pp. 211–212.

[8] *Ibid.*, p. 216.

SESSION FIVE
Evangelism With Spouses and Other Family Members

GOALS FOR THE CHAPTER:

After reading this chapter, you should be able to:

1. Examine some suggestions and principles which are applicable for a person who is married to an unbelieving spouse.

2. Understand that it is important to recognize that successful evangelism with spouses begins with ourselves.

3. Explore some different ways of witnessing to parents and other family members.

I. INTRODUCTION

The first couple, Adam and Eve, give Bible readers a vision of what God originally intended for spouses. Before the fall, life in the Garden of Eden was perfect in every way. Not only did harmony characterize the relationship between the first two caretakers of nature and the environment, but it also flowed freely between the husband and wife. God planned for spouses to base their marriage on a mutual commitment to Him and obedience to His word. Before the fall, Adam and Eve were at peace with themselves, each other, and their surroundings.

Unfortunately, the same is not true in many homes today. Discord rather than harmony often characterizes the relationship between husband and wife. Suspicion and mistrust have replaced the love and support that starry-eyed newlyweds once thought would be theirs. Such battlegrounds are not part of God's plan for this most intimate of relationships.

II. EVANGELISM WITHIN MARRIAGE

Many wonder how a marriage between a believer and unbeliever can occur. Sometimes it happens that a young Christian thinks she can disobey "just this once," marry an unbeliever, and still live happily ever after. Other times a person becomes a

Christian after they are married, and their unbelieving spouse is either disinterested or hostile to the faith. Still others believe they are marrying a Christian, only to later discover that this was not true. Regardless of the circumstances, marriage between a believer and an unbeliever is always less than perfect. Paul's advice to the Corinthians is equally applicable today: "Do not be yoked together with unbelievers. For what do righteousness and wickedness have in common? Or what fellowship can light have with darkness?" [2 Cor. 6:14]. An unbeliever will naturally follow his secular instincts and desires with no thought to holiness or obedience to God. His goals all involve this life because his perspective is limited to this world. The believing wife will just as naturally set her sight on God and heaven and will find herself walking a path that is different from her earthbound husband. Although some marriages survive this tension, it is usually a difficult task.

A. God's Purpose For Marriage

God's plan for man and woman to become one flesh includes a provision for spiritual unity and harmony as well as emotional and physical oneness. When this dimension is missing, there is an obvious void. Even a cursory look at most "secular" marriages will quickly point out the truth of this observation. Most secular couples spend a good part of their lives searching for "happiness," "meaning," "the good life," or whatever name they

Unity and Oneness

want to apply. What they do not understand is that we are all created to have fellowship with God. When this is missing, there is a deep inner craving that might not be understood consciously, but nevertheless compels us to either search for "deeper meaning in life" or to find some toy or diversion that will momentarily distract us from our hurt.

B. How to Begin

Sharing faith with an unbelieving spouse can be difficult, but there are some guidelines that apply to nearly all cases.

1. Begin with yourself.

Examine your motives for wanting your spouse to become a Christian. Do you merely want the comfort of having someone to go with you to church? Are you hoping that a "saved" spouse will be less quarrelsome and perhaps more generous with time or money? If your motives are self-centered, in other words, "I want Dick to become Christian because life will be easier for me," then recognize your sin and ask God to forgive you. Evangelism is *never* to be based on self-centered desires.

However, if you truly want your husband to become a Christian because you recognize his great spiritual need and you are worried about the fate of his soul, lay your concerns openly and honestly before the Lord. Set out to make yourself an attractive Christian woman who will reflect the love of Jesus to her spouse. Become so appealing that you will arouse in your spouse a natural curiosity and attraction to the Gospel.

Many wives resist this step because they reason that they are already more attractive than their spouse, and it should be up to him to take the next step. This logic, however, is self-centered and runs counter to the Christian truth that each of us should follow the example of Jesus. He remained obedient even when he was betrayed and deserted by those closest to Him. We are called to follow the example of Christ and measure our performance against His. Jesus, not our husband, is the standard for our conduct.

Once this fact is firmly established, the wife will begin to examine her own life and look for ways that she can change to bring harmony into the home through her example and presence. This, in turn, allows the Holy Spirit more freedom to turn the eyes of the unbeliever to the One who is the answer.

The Bible contains a wealth of advice for wives who want to better understand God's plan for their attitude and behavior. If you have never systematically studied these passages before, get a concordance and a good study Bible with a chain reference and begin to look up all the references to wives. You will soon have a well-rounded picture of the kind of woman God is calling you to be. You are not responsible for saving the soul of your husband. Conversion is the work of the Holy Spirit. But someday you will stand before the Lord Jesus and answer for your own behavior. On that day, you will feel prepared and happy if you have done all in your power to meet the expectations that God has for you, even in the midst of a less-than-perfect relationship.

If you are a mother as well as a wife, you will also be assured that you have fulfilled your role as the spiritual guide and leader to your children. In all families the spiritual role of the mother is vital, but it is even more important when the father is not a believer. The mother then needs to assume spiritual leadership for her children as she seeks to undertake the job that God originally intended for both parents to share.

2. Pray and then pray more!

Prayer is your greatest ally. Wives need it so that they have the strength to continue to grow into the women Christ intends for them to be. Husbands need their wives' prayers because "the unbelieving husband has been sanctified through his wife" [1 Cor. 7:14]. Living with an unbelieving spouse is often a difficult and demanding task. Prayer enables the Christian spouse to maintain her poise and confidence in the face of adversity because of the knowledge that God stands with her in each trial or temptation. The assurance of Christ's presence brings a peace to situations that otherwise would escalate out of control. Unbelieving spouses may pretend not to notice, but they do! It cannot be missed. Some will react strongly against such supernatural power, but deep in their heart they will acknowledge the "rightness" of godly behavior. Concentrate much of your prayer time on yourself. Where can you improve that you might be a better wife? Ask Jesus to show you how you can better model His love to your husband and children. "Grow in the grace and knowledge of our Lord and Savior Jesus Christ" [2 Peter 3:18] so that you will have the wisdom to handle any situation in a manner that will bring glory to the Lord.

STOP AND APPLY

Ponder the following questions if you are married to an unbeliever:

1. Am I truly trying to reflect the love and understanding of Jesus to my spouse?

2. Do I look for ways to encourage and support him with my words and actions?

3. Does my behavior toward him convey acceptance or rejection?

4. Am I as quick to forgive him as I want him to be with me?

5. Following the example of Jesus, am I willing to serve him even if there is no apparent reward for myself?

C. Principles for Living with an Unsaved Spouse

Every marriage is unique because each human differs at least slightly from everyone else. Consequently, there is no way to illustrate or discuss the myriads of problems that will be faced by each spouse who is unequally yoked. However, the following story is meant to illustrate some of the principles which will be discussed, and to give encouragement to those who have been waiting and praying for something to change their husband's spiritual status.

A Husband's True Story

For you married women whose husbands are not Christians, I want to tell you about part of my spiritual pilgrimage. I pray it will encourage you to be hopeful about the conversion of your spouse. I know that my experience will differ from yours but many of the principles involved will remain the same.

Although I was taken to church from the time I was an infant, God seldom, if ever, seemed real to me. Church and Sunday School were weekly ordeals that I dreaded, and when I went to high school I found plenty of excuses to avoid these tedious hours of boredom on Sunday morning.

Going away to college was joyously freeing in many ways— not the least of which was the liberty to skip church every Sunday, away from the watchful eye of my worshipful parents. Also, I found my agnostic and atheist professors' verbal attacks on Christianity to be especially stimulating.

Marriage, career, children, and home ownership occupied the next several years and kept me far too busy to reconsider my fashionable anti-religious presuppositions. But a few years after our marriage my wife's life changed dramatically. She became a Christian. Lillian not only claimed that Jesus was now real to her but she began to take the teaching of the Bible seriously. Someone gave her a "Living Bible" and, to my utter astonishment, she not only read the bulky book, she seemed to enjoy it. Indeed, I can still recall how she sat up in bed and exclaimed over many passages, "this is fascinating."

The event of Lillian's conversion was significant, but the process of her life being transformed before my eyes was at once astounding and threatening. The woman I had married was changing before my eyes and I was not at all pleased with what I saw. Rather quickly her taste in movies changed. Furthermore, she lost all interest in going to night clubs and staying up late just to drink wine and get high.

In brief, the woman I had married was gone and in her place was someone interested in her spiritual life; she even talked about Jesus as if He were real. I was increasingly jealous of God, and I especially resented the hours Lillian invested in church-related activities even though I pretended not to care.

However, if Lillian's new-found faith became a wedge between us, it also became a bit of a magnet. As her values and interests were transformed, she became increasingly peaceful and fulfilled. Indeed, we weathered a couple of family crises and she sailed through the storm with relative stability and tranquillity. I, on the other hand, increasingly turned to alcohol for my anchor in these tempests of life. Lillian later recalled that God spent those years revealing the rough spots in her own life that desperately needed work. Often when she would cry out to him about my behavior, the Lord gently but firmly reminded her to concentrate on her own shortcomings before she tried to tackle mine. This process of focusing her reforming tendencies on herself served two purposes. It made her more attractive as she became the sure and stable anchor of the family. It also kept her from nagging me which would have only made me more hostile to the very message that she was trying to help me see.

During the next few years, I sank deeper into alcoholism. Lillian, on the other hand, was truly getting her life together and in the process making me feel insecure, resentful and angry. She wasn't perfect and I loved to catch her short-tempered or nasty. I enjoyed being able to remind her that she wasn't currently acting like a "real Christian." Although she sometimes lost her temper with these snide remarks, she usually took my criticism to heart and even apologized for her outburst. That reaction really baffled me. But despite my apparent antipathy, I surrendered my life to Jesus just a few years later after a prolonged and unsuccessful struggle to quit drinking.

Lillian played a key role in my spiritual surrender and regeneration. Perhaps learning what she did will help you. First of all, she continually prayed for my soul, asking the Holy Spirit to soften my heart and point me to Jesus Christ. To be sure, Lillian did not often mention that she prayed for me, but after I surrendered to Christ she admitted that prayer was the focal point of her evangelism strategy.

Besides prayer, Lillian firmly, yet lovingly, refused to be intimidated by my criticism of her Bible reading, church attendance, and ever-growing Christian service. Although she faith-fully performed her role as a wife and mother, she insisted that her prayer times and church-related activities were important to her and the children and they quietly went on with them when they didn't interfere with our time together as a family.

Even though her commitment to new things often made me jealous, I was impressed with her demeanor of peace and her ever-growing ability to cope with life's problems. To put it bluntly, she was living much more sanely and gracefully than I. It could neither be denied nor ignored.

Besides prayer and an attractive life style, Lillian did not flinch from opportunities to witness and confront at the appropriate moment. Although she never preached at me, she did mention from time to time that she found some of my behavior unattractive. Likewise, she made it clear that my drinking was a horrid example for the children, and she implored me to stop drinking in our home.

There were times when I drank to excess, made a fool of myself, and then felt guilty and regretful. Frequently, I swore off of drinking, but eventually the temptation to imbibe once more would be all-consuming. When I would cry out, "I'm so sorry, I really do want to quit," she would calmly yet confidently tell me that Jesus Christ could free me from this bondage if only I would surrender to Him. Her gentle and timely reminder that Jesus Christ could set me free were words that echoed through my mind on numerous occasions.

Lillian was not the only person witnessing to me during those difficult years. Her faithfulness, however, was the most constant and transparent factor. One morning, after an all-night drinking spree, I awakened with desperation in my soul. I cried out "God, if you are there, please help me." Lillian had said He could. No doubt my feeble plea for His assistance was in large part inspired by her forthright assurance. In the final analysis, she was the key person that God used as He pursued me during those times of turmoil and darkness.

God did rescue me that morning. It's been almost twenty years since I cried out for help and I have never again had a drink of alcohol. Lillian and I have grown much closer to Jesus during those years and as a result we have drawn much closer to each other.

<table>
<tr><td>

STOP AND APPLY

Before proceeding, identify in your own terms some of the principles which are at work in this illustration.

</td></tr>
</table>

Several principles are illustrated in this story, but for the sake of clarity, they need to be re-emphasized and expanded. The following are keys to working with an unsaved spouse:

1. Do not Preach.

When one spouse is growing spiritually but the other remains unresponsive, some tension is bound to occur because the two are moving in opposite directions. At this point, the temptation to try and "preach your spouse into the kingdom" is great. Rather than producing the desired results, this almost always clarifies the battle line and the war begins. Some angry mates grow silent, cold, and sarcastic. Others erupt in heated, passionate outbursts. The common denominator remains the underlying premise: "Don't try to change me because I don't want what you have."

The rejection hurts because the believer knows that what is being offered will bring peace with God and an end to that empty, aching void. Books have been written to advise wives how to "win their husbands to Christ" and a variety of methods are introduced. Yet all share at least one common command that *wives should refrain from preaching to their husbands*. "Wives, in the same way be submissive to your husbands that, if any of them do not believe the word, they may be won over without talk by the behavior of their wives" [1 Peter 3:1]. Not only is this advice Scriptural, it is eminently practical. Seldom is there any gain when Christian wives consciously or unconsciously behave in a manner that is "superior" to their husbands. "Preaching" implies such an attitude because it says: "I have some truth and *you* need to hear it." When this happens, the wife usually sounds condescending or dictatorial. Christ is neither glorified nor made attractive to her unbelieving spouse—usually the opposite occurs.

Does that mean that a wife should never speak of her faith to her husband? Certainly not! The wife is not to behave as if she has been "gagged" and never mention God or her faith to her spouse. When it is appropriate, she should openly and freely explain what faith in Jesus means to her and how He is helping her to change her life for the better. But always speak in such a way that will bring glory to Jesus. She should answer questions about Scripture or faith. Freely talk about spiritual issues when the conversation naturally presents opportunities. She might consider inviting her spouse to share in her spiritual journey, but never nag or preach! For the most part, her actions will speak louder than her words. Concentrating on becoming a better wife and a more loving and supportive partner will naturally help build more bridges to her husband and help him to be more open to the message of the Gospel.

2. Live a Changed Life—Become More Christlike.

Your goal is to help your husband to see that you are changing because Christ is at work in your life. Concentrate on your goal of becoming more Christlike. Resolve to root out sin in your life. The multitudes in Israel could not be held back from Christ; they were strongly attracted to Him because He was compelling. When Christ lives in us, we take on this same compelling characteristic. The better we know Him, the more we can reflect His image to the world around us.

Give Christ the credit for changes or improvements in your personality, but never imply that you are now "perfect." In their eagerness to help their husbands see what a difference Christ can make in their lives, many wives unconsciously fall into this error. The result usually is that the husband takes great delight in pointing out his wife's mistakes—sometimes quite derisively—and both Christ and the Gospel are discredited.

Family life at Ted and Molly's house is often turbulent, and they find it easy to lose control of their tongues when disciplining their children. About six months ago Molly became a Christian, and now Ted has noticed that she no longer screams at the children. When he mentions this observation, Molly delightedly informs him that "Christians keep their tempers under control." Molly said this because she wanted to underscore the power of the gospel to change lives, but Ted felt put down. He heard Molly self-righteously saying "Unlike you, I can keep my temper." However, after a particularly trying day, Molly lost her temper with the children, and Ted was right there to point out her hypocrisy.

This problem could have been avoided if Molly had explained to Ted that Christ wants wives and mothers to be gentle and loving—not loud and quarrelsome. Molly could explain that she is pleased that Ted sees some improvement, but the credit must go to Christ who wants to teach her new ways. Molly could further convey that this is an ongoing process about which she has much to learn and that she is not suffering from any delusions about being perfect. Such an explanation gives Christ the credit for the improvement, but does not create a barrier of resentment between the spouses.

3. Look for Bridges.

Christian wives should look for bridges or ways that they can "act out" the Gospel for their husbands, and thus make Christ attractive to them. When Christ gets credit for the improvement in the house, He naturally becomes more interesting and appealing to the husband. Think about your husband and the things that he really enjoys. Then set out to fulfill his expectations in one or more areas. If you have become somewhat careless about mealtime, resolve to make an extra effort to prepare and serve meals that are not only nutritious but attractive. Make his favorite dinner or dessert. Perhaps your husband would really like it if you took bike rides with him on Saturday afternoon, but you would rather meet a friend for lunch. Surprise him by cheerfully changing your plans and go out with him. When your husband inquires about your efforts, let him know that you are merely obeying Christ and trying to be the best wife that you can be.

If your husband is absolutely opposed to your attending church on Sunday morning, then prayerfully consider whether the Lord is leading you to an alternative. Various authors and authorities differ on the proper response to this behavior. Some say that it will help to abstain from Sunday because this demonstrates the wife's submissiveness to her husband and prevents him from developing a resentment toward Jesus and Christians. Others disagree in certain instances, but all tell the wife to pray before she acts and seek the counsel of the Holy Spirit for this sensitive area.

If Sunday church attendance is driving a wedge between you and your husband, then it ceases to be a positive in your marriage. Wives are to be submissive to their husbands in all issues that do not contradict the commands of God, and Sunday church is not a direct command for Christians. If this is a problem in your marriage, you might want to look for creative ways to have fellowship and study at times when your husband is at work or otherwise busy. Perhaps you could join a weekday Bible study or attend midweek services. Find a friend who is willing to pray and hold you accountable for Christian growth and meet at a mutually convenient time. If you feel that God is leading you to forego Sunday worship, it is vitally important to read and study the Bible daily and set aside a time for private worship. Christian lives need constant nurture or else they begin to wither. If you atrophy as a Christian, you will significantly reduce the chance for your spouse to see and hear the message of the Gospel. Keeping your spiritual life vital and growing benefits not only you, but your spouse and entire family.

4. Give Respect and Encouragement.

Paul makes it clear that marriage partners are to be accorded respect whether they are Christians or not. "Wives, submit to your husbands, as is fitting in the Lord" [Eph. 5:18]. Often Christian wives make the mistake of thinking that this command for submission is to be applied only to believing husbands, but that is a mistake. As long as the wife is not asked to violate a God-given command or principle, she should accord her husband honor and respect. No one should ever be forced to cheat, lie, or perform any action contrary to God's will, but Scripture indicates that a believing wife should be submissive to her husband's leadership in other matters.

> *For three years Marcia struggled with this principle. As a new Christian herself, she often rebelled at the idea of submitting to Bill's leadership. "After all," she reasoned, "he's not reliable and he seldom carries his fair share of family responsibilities. If I am going to have to assume the role of both mother and father to our children, why should I then accord Bill respect, as if he were doing his job?" Yet the Biblical passages continued to convict her.*
>
> *After much agony Marcia finally collapsed before the Lord, confessed her wrong attitude, and prayed to love Bill as Christ asked her to do. It was then that the changes began. Nothing spectacular occurred at first, but slowly Marcia began to see Bill's good points and she worked on encouraging him in those areas. Much of the tension in the house disappeared as a result of her efforts and Bill became more tender toward his wife.*
>
> *It took two years before Bill could acknowledge the need for Jesus Christ in his life, but what a joy it was for Marcia to then hear him tell others that her acceptance of him had been the turning point. Marcia's acceptance and respect convinced him that it was possible for Jesus to accept him too.*

D. Encourage the Discouraged Spouse.

Having said all this, it would be unrealistic to close this section without including a word for wives who have faithfully and lovingly followed all these suggestions and more, but who still live with unregenerate husbands. Only a person in your place can truly know the heartache with which you live. Each marriage is different and there is no one "right" answer that will fit all situations. Your first loyalty is always to God. You are never required to do anything which breaks His law. If your husband asks you to participate in immoral or unethical situations, you must refuse because God has instilled in you a higher calling for your behavior. Your eternal life belongs to the Lord who saved your soul, and He will never ask you to do anything which compromises His pure standards for holy living.

Again it needs to be said—prayer is your best defense and ally. To those caught in abusive situations, one can only counsel you to seek the help of trusted Christian friends who will pray with you for guidance and support you in times of crisis. In general, Christians agree that no one should remain in a situation that is habitually abusive and risks the well-being of the spouse or children. This applies to emotional, as well as physical, abuse. The point at which a situation becomes emotionally abusive is not always clearly defined, but the Holy Spirit will guide those who seek His guidance. Some women feel that leaving their husbands and living in a secure and emotionally stable environment is God's will for themselves and their children. The alternative to leave should always be the last resort of the Christian wife, but it would be unfair to end this discussion without saying that it is sometimes the best one for all concerned. Indeed, sometimes a wife who is being abused by her husband moves into safe quarters and then discovers that her action causes the husband to repent and seek God. In other cases, of course, the unregenerate spouse grows even more angry, but at least the wife and children [if they are involved] are safe from physical harm.

On the other hand, if your situation is tolerable, then decide to make the best of it and enjoy the good things that you can share with your husband. Some women grow so discontented when their spouses refuse to convert that they look for any reason to leave. They do this because they assume that a good marriage can only happen when both spouses are believers. They then become discouraged with all the good things that they have, and concentrate instead on what is not perfect. They make the mistake of believing that all Christian marriages are always lovely and harmonious. They are not! Christian spouses disagree over money, in-laws, and children just like their secular counterparts. Wives who have loving but unbelieving husbands should learn to be "content whatever the circumstances" [Phil. 4:11]. Look for the good in your mate and concentrate on what you can do to develop that part of your relationship. Find hobbies or shared interests that will draw you closer to each other and improve your relationship. Your mate is closest to the Kingdom of God when he is closest to you. You and your prayers for him may be the only things in his life which bring him near to the presence of God. Continue to work on improving your relationship as a wife and pray that God will become as real to your spouse as He is to you. But you must place the answer to that prayer in God's hands and leave it there.

E. Suggestions for further reading

Although some common and practical suggestions have been offered, most women living with unbelieving husbands will want to read more on the topic. Jo Berry, author of *Beloved Unbeliever* [Zondervan, 1981], offers much practical advice that most will find helpful and encouraging. In 1989, Focus on the Family [Pamona, CA 91799] published a pamphlet by William Deal titled, "Living with an Unsaved Spouse." Although not as comprehensive as the Berry book, it offers a good introduction to the topic. C.S. Lovett's *Unequally Yoked Wives* [Personal Christianity, 1968] presents a step-by-step plan for seeing your husband converted that some might find helpful if their situation is conducive to the approach. Marion Beaver's *Becoming a Loving Witness...to an Unsaved Mate* [Broadman Press, 1988] chronicles her experience and offers encouragement to wives in similar circumstances. Nyla Witmore's book *How to Reach the Ones You Love* [Here's Life Publishers, Inc., 1981] is not limited to the topic of spouses, but there is a wealth of practical and applicable advice that will be useful to anyone involved in any type of evangelism to family members.

STOP AND APPLY

Fill in the blanks:

1. God planned for spouses to base their marriage on a mutual _____ to Him and _____ to His Word.

2. Begin by examining _____ when evangelizing your spouse.

3. _____ is your greatest ally.

Circle the answer that best describes the principles related to evangelizing your spouse:

4. Do not:
   a. Preach.
   b. Forget to wear makeup.
   c. Talk about anything spiritual.

5. Your goal is to help your husband see that:
   a. Your life is far better than his.
   b. He is a sinner.
   c. You are changing because of Christ's work in your life.

6. Look for:
   a. Opportunities to read Scriptures to him.
   b. Bridges to act out the gospel.
   c. Opportunities to point out his faults.

7. Give him:
   a. A Bible.
   b. Respect and encouragement.
   c. A copy of your goals for him.

8. Begin to pray daily for your spouse (if you do not already).

9. Whether or not you are married to a Christian spouse, look for three ways to compliment and encourage him this week.

   _____

   _____

   _____

10. Humbly pray and ask to have a godly attitude toward your spouse. Resolve to change any area of your behavior that is not Christlike. Select one or two areas at a time and really concentrate prayer and effort on them.

III. EVANGELISM WITH PARENTS AND OTHER FAMILY MEMBERS

No one knows you as well as your family. Your virtues and vices are familiar ground with them. This intimate relationship offers the new Christian many unique avenues for sharing with her family. Especially when one has experienced a rather spectacular conversion from a life of sin to one of faith, the temptation is to try to reach out and corral your loved ones and drag them to the feet of the Savior. Such tactics seldom work. The Bible records all sorts of conversion experiences, but never do you find an example where the evangelist actually forced someone else into belief. Real faith is based on a voluntary acceptance and belief in the claims and commands of Jesus. Christ attracted people to Himself because His example was compelling. Christians who witness to family members need to follow the example of the Master and win them with loving actions, as well as timely words.

A. Mistakes To Avoid

New converts, especially young adults, often make some rather common mistakes when talking about faith with their parents or other family members.

1. Do not act superior to family members.

Jane is a sophomore at State College, and she is excited to be coming home for spring break because a dynamic woman from a campus Christian ministry has been leading a Bible Study in her dorm. As a result, Jane has realized, for the first time in her life, that she is a sinner in need of a Savior. Since she was a baby, Jane's parents faithfully took her family to Sunday School and church. Jane remembers that the pastor often preached about God's love, but it was done in such a remote and universal way that she had never applied what was said to her life. Now she realizes that just going to church doesn't make you a Christian.

Jane's excitement about this new-found spiritual life erupts from her the moment she rushes in the door. "Mom, Dad, guess what? I've become a Christian and it's so wonderful." For the next twenty-four hours, Jane continues to gush about her faith. Unfortunately, she fails to see that her parents have gone from being perplexed to being dismayed; now they are becoming angry. Her siblings write her off as a "nut case," while her parents quietly pray that she will quickly come to her senses and stop acting like a fanatic.

For the moment, Jane stands little chance of helping anyone in her family to see the truth about Jesus. Her family feels confused and betrayed. Jane appears to placing herself above them spiritually. From their perspective, she seems to be saying, "I've got it together spiritually but you don't!" After all, her parents have been attending church for more years than she has, and they are well-respected for their moral lifestyle. Unfortunately, Jane's words put her family on the defensive and closed their ears to her message.

2. Do not ignore your family.

Other young Christians "turn off" their families because they become totally absorbed in "Christian activities." Retreats, Bible studies, prayer groups, quiet times, church meetings and other activities demand their attention and leave the family feeling forgotten and unimportant.

The oldest of four children, Abby used to be the one her younger sisters turned to when they needed help. Likewise, her parents trusted her judgment and often depended on her help. Then Abby started spending all of her time in church or locked up in her room where she read her Bible and memorized Scripture. She ignored her sisters and "forgot" her chores because she always needed more time for her church responsibilities. Abby's family knew that she had changed, but they weren't sure that it was for the best.

Both Jane and Abby meant well. They wanted their families to share in their new-found faith and relationship with Christ, but unfortunately they did not coordinate their actions with their words. A positive Christian witness springs from a combination of action, word, and the power of the Holy Spirit. Jane and Abby would have fared much better if they had been more careful in their approach to their families.

B. Principles to Remember

1. Family evangelism, like all other types, should begin with prayer. Intercede daily intercede for those members of your family who do not know the Lord. Ask Him to bless and protect them, to melt the opposition to His word that is in their hearts, and to raise up workers who will take the message to them. God might give you the joy of allowing you to introduce your loved one to Him, but in some cases, He uses others to do the harvesting while He allows you to plant the seeds and water them. Remember that your goal is to see your family come to know Jesus in a personal way, and it does not really matter who has the privilege of being the final harvester.

2. Be sensitive when sharing your faith with family members. More than one Christian has offended a family member by speaking too soon or without sensitivity. Knowing the need, it is difficult to restrain ourselves, but conversion happens according to God's timing. Paul reminded the Corinthians of this when he said, "I planted the seed, Apollos watered it, but God made it grow" [1 Cor. 3:6]. "Dumping the whole Gospel" on family members who aren't ready to hear it can be just as disastrous as never sharing the faith at all. In all your family encounters, wait for God's time to share. Let the Holy Spirit guide your words.

3. Let your actions abound with love. Look for ways to build common ground with your family. Show them that "Christ living in you" has changed you for the better and that they will reap some of the benefits. If you live at home with your parents, do your chores without reminders. Encourage and support your siblings. Be sensitive to special needs or problems that your family might be facing. If you live away from your family, remember to write or phone often and tell them how much you appreciate them. Look for other ways to send the message that you really care about each of them.

Mark's Gospel tells us that "Even the Son of Man did not come to be served, but to serve, and to give his life as a ransom for many" [Mark 10:45]. If Christ could willingly give up the pleasure of heavenly fellowship with the Father while He was on earth, then we should joyfully look for ways to serve those that we love (even if this means skipping a prayer meeting to go on an outing with your mother or sister). Spending quality time with your family sends the message that you care. When someone feels cared about and respected, they are far more likely to listen when you share the message that's on your heart.

4. Keep your lines of communication open. Look for shared interests or activities and spend time with family members. Really listen to their problems, concerns, or worries. Do not feel a need to "dump" the whole Gospel message each time you meet. Let the Holy Spirit guide as to the appropriate time to raise the issue of spiritual life. Make certain that they know how much you care about their well being. Sometimes unbelievers feel like a "project" or a "mission," and they instinctively rebel and put up defenses. Good communication reassures the other person that you care about her as a unique individual.

Sometimes good communication is blocked because of past hurts or conflicts. Old resentments can build into walls that separate us and hinder the communication we desire. When this happens, examine your past actions and determine if you are at fault. If so, resolve to do all in your power to improve the situation. First, go to God and ask His forgiveness for your sinful actions; then go and confess to the one you have wronged. Humbly ask for forgiveness. Most people in our society have a hard time admitting mistakes. Consequently, some Christians fear that confession will bring disrepute to the Gospel, but the opposite is usually true.

5. Be patient. Finally, remember that even Jesus met with opposition and misunderstanding from His family. During His time on earth, the Master Teacher, Communicator, and Lover of our souls was rejected as the Messiah by His own family. It was only after His death and resurrection that they finally understood the truth about Him. Family evangelism often moves slowly. Do not despair. Continue to live your life in such a way that your family will be confronted daily with the truth of the gospel through your actions. Speak when the Holy Spirit opens opportunities. Pray diligently, and leave the time for harvesting in the hands of God.

STOP AND APPLY

Fill in the blanks:

1. Two mistakes to avoid when witnessing to family members are not to act _____ to them and not to _____ your family.

2. Family evangelism should begin with _____.

3. Be sensitive as to _____ and _____ you share your faith.

4. Let your actions abound with _____.

5. Keep lines of _____ open.

6. Be _____. Family evangelism often moves slowly.

Student Discipleship Ministries of Fort Worth, Texas, has put together a booklet entitled, *Everyone Everywhere* which gives some practical ideas for family evangelism. In the appendix on "Family Tree Evangelism," the author suggests that you chart the names of your immediate family—aunts, uncles, cousins, and grandparents, and then:

A. Select two unsaved relatives for whom you have a burden.

   _____

   _____

B. Analyze where your relatives are spiritually:

1. What are their felt needs?— guilt, loneliness, fear of death

2. What are their current attitudes?— rebellious, angry, bitter

3. What are their needs?— health, financial, counseling, fellowship

4. What are their misconceptions about Christianity?— it is a crutch, it is based on works, it is a way—not the only way

5. What is keeping them from knowing Christ?— immorality, Scriptural ignorance, lack of conviction, confusion between religions

6. What common interests do you share?— sports, hobbies

Using the above guidelines, resolve to pray for the two relatives you have selected and do all that you can to open their eyes to the truth of the Gospel.

If you have not already done so, listen to cassette tape #3A in the series featuring the second part of *Evangelism and the Family* by Jill Briscoe and Judy Briscoe Golz. Also on the tape are excerpts of a broadcast on the Moody Broadcast Network about being unequally yoked and a message by Marta Alvarado.

SESSION SIX
Relationship Evangelism

GOALS FOR THE CHAPTER:

After reading this chapter, you should be able to:

1. Define relationship evangelism.

2. Discuss why we should build relationships.

3. Examine the quality of your life.

4. Understand the principles in relationship evangelism.

5. Apply the principles in a specific relationship.

I. INTRODUCTION

A. What is Relationship Evangelism?

This true story illustrates one answer to the question:

Tools of Relationship Evangelism

One day I was sitting at the kitchen table, wondering how I could make more contact with non-Christians, when the garbage collector drove up to my house. It dawned on me that he came to my house every week, and I didn't even know his name, let alone his spiritual condition. Since the garbage is picked up on my day off, I began to plan to be outside doing yard work when he came by. I learned his name and began to pray for him specifically. In hot weather I greeted him with a glass of iced tea, and in cold weather with a cup of hot chocolate. I threw the trash while he drank and had a break. One day Claudia baked cookies, and we invited him in. Soon he rerouted his pickups to stop at our house for lunch. After several months, we finally had an opportunity to share Christ.[1]

Relationship evangelism is a way of life centered around the Lordship of Christ. It is showing a genuine interest in other people and getting involved in the lives of those we want to reach for Christ. Relational evangelism builds bridges to people by discovering their needs and learning to love them. While not neglecting "strangers," it seeks to focus our energy and efforts on those within our circle of influence: that is, family members, relatives, friends, neighbors, work associates, acquaintances, or perhaps our garbage collectors! People are starving for love, and often seek it in a variety of ways. Recently a physician with many years of experience wrote:

> "I have been practicing medicine for over thirty years. I have prescribed many things. But in the long run, I have learned that for most of what ails the human creature, the best medicine is love."
> "What if that doesn't work?" the woman to whom he was talking asked.
> "Double the dose," he replied.[2]

One of the most important Christian responsibilities is to love other people. On the night before He died, Jesus instructed His disciples: "If you love me, you will obey what I command" [John 14:15]. A few moments later He reiterated His thought: "My command is this: Love each other as I have loved you" [John 15:12]. Relationship evangelism is not a method or an activity but rather an overflow of love for the Lord and for people.

The effectiveness of relationship evangelism has been underscored in a study done for the Institute for American Church Growth. The statistics, as compiled by Win Arn, tallied the results of a poll of eight thousand church members from different denominations. The survey asked what first attracted them to the church where they were now members and respondents reported:

Walk-in's:	4–6%	Visitation:	1–2%
Programs:	2–4%	Sunday School:	4–6%
The pastor:	4–7%	City-wide mass crusades:	.001%
A special need:	2–4%	**Friends and/or relatives: 70–90%!**

There is no doubt that relationships are a key element in evangelism! Happily, the ability to love people does not depend on gifts, experiences, emotions, or feelings. Loving people is best shown through caring actions and unselfish giving of ourselves to others. "Do nothing out of selfish ambition or vain conceit, but in humility consider others better than yourselves" [Phil. 2:4]. "Be devoted to one another in brotherly love. Honor one another above yourselves" [Romans 12:9–10].

The Great Commission's "go ye therefore" is best translated "as you are going." We are to be making disciples *as we are going* about our normal business, and relationship evangelism is one way to carry this out. "As we go" and as we relate to people we can have an impact on their lives.

B. Biblical Examples

The concept of sharing with those in our immediate circle of influence is by no means new. The New Testament contains numerous stories about relationship evangelism. When Jesus met people in the Gospels, He became their friend. He enjoyed people. People were not just "projects" to Him, but rather a very important part of His life.

The apostle Andrew provides a perfect example of relationship evangelism. After first meeting the Lord, he did not start his own evangelistic organization. He simply went and told his brother, Peter. This is the basic pattern for all evangelism: one person finds forgiveness, love, new life, and purpose through an encounter with Jesus Christ and then brings another person to experience that same relationship with Christ. The Bible is full of examples of relationship evangelism including: Philip and Nathaniel [John 1:40ff]; Lydia and her household [Acts 16:15]; the Philippian jailer and his family [Acts 16:34]; Timothy, his mother, and grandmother [2 Tim. 1:5].

Evangelism is most effective when it is accompanied by love and care. We need to be a channel through which God's love can flow to those around us. God has chosen to use people to communicate His love to nonbelievers, and showing true concern for others means spending time with them and building closer relationships. The apostle John's words are as timely today as they were two thousand years ago: "Dear children, let us not love with words or tongue but with actions and in truth" [1 John 3:18]. We need to respond to the cries of loneliness, frustration, and despair by personally investing our lives in others.

C. A Needed Caution

Relationship evangelism has many strengths, but there is also a potential weakness to this approach. Because the focus is on relationships, there is a tendency to rely on our lifestyle instead of our lips to get the message across. It is not enough merely to live a good life in front of people—you must also share the gospel verbally.

In the previously cited examples of relationship evangelism, notice that one person took the initiative and clearly shared the truth about Christ with another. No believer's life is good enough by itself to lead people to salvation. People must hear and respond to the *message* of the Gospel. "How shall they believe unless they hear?" [Romans 10:14]. Bill Bright, author of *The Calling of an Evangelist,* shares this story:

> *A dear friend in Singapore...shared with me the story of how for years he "witnessed" by his godly life, and how he prayed daily that God would use his life to be a model to those with whom he worked, so that they would take the initiative and ask him what made him different. Then as a result, he would have the opportunity to be a witness of Christ to them.*
>
> *The weeks and the months passed. A couple of years later, he was still praying, ""Lord, help me to be such a model of you in my life that this man will want to know you, too."*
>
> *One day, the man said to him, "Fred, I've been watching you."*
>
> *My friend said, "Oh Lord, thank you. At last, you have answered my prayer."*
>
> *"I have observed that your life is different."*
>
> *"Thank you, Lord, he sees the difference in my life."*
>
> *"I want to ask you a personal question."*
>
> *"Thank you, Lord, now this is the moment that I have been praying for."*
>
> *His friend asked, "Fred, are you a vegetarian?"*
>
> *At that moment, my friend said he realized that he needed to do more than to live a good moral life. He needed to be a vocal witness for Christ.[3]*

Or consider the following illustration from Leroy Eim's *Winning Ways* and note the need for a verbal witness as well as an exemplary life:

> *A Christian businessman in Seattle confessed how he had unknowingly discouraged a business associate from coming to Christ for years. One day the friend told the Christian businessman he had met the Lord the night before through a Billy Graham meeting. The longtime Christian was elated and said so, but the new Christian replied, 'Friend, you're the reason I have resisted becoming a Christian all these years. I figured that if a person could live a good life as you do and not be a Christian, there was no need to become one!' This Christian businessman had lived an exemplary life but he had not revealed the Source of strength for living it. Immediately he asked the Lord's forgiveness and His help to tell what and whom he knew that made the difference.[4]*

II. WHY BUILD RELATIONSHIPS?

There are several reasons why building relationships is effective.

1. Relationships *provide a natural network for sharing the gospel*. It is natural to tell those closest to us about what Christ has done in our lives. Whenever we have good news, we immediately want to tell our friends and family.

2. People with whom we have a relationship *are more receptive*. They will accept what we, as a friend, have to say much more readily than what a stranger tells them. Relationship evangelism deals with persons, not strangers.

3. Building relationships helps us to find and focus on *stressing the points of similarity* rather than differences with a non-Christian. We cannot expect the non-Christian to fit into our environment. We need to build bridges to her in spite of different beliefs and practices.

4. When we build relationships, there are *many opportunities to share* with the person. Whether at a backyard barbecue or over a cup of coffee, our frequent contact provides numerous opportunities to discuss spiritual things.

5. Relationships provide a *natural means of support and follow-up* when your friend does accept Christ. You are there to help her grow and learn to live as a disciple.

STOP AND APPLY

Put a **T** for True and **F** for False in discussing why we should build relationships:

___ 1. Establishing a relationship guarantees we will share the Gospel.

___ 2. People are more receptive when we build a relationship.

___ 3. It helps us stress points of similarity rather than differences.

___ 4. It provides many possible opportunities to share with the person.

___ 5. It provides a natural means of support and follow-up.

Unfortunately, few Christians have meaningful relationships with nonbelievers. Studies have shown that the average Christian loses contact with her non-Christian friends after two years. Consequently, we need to learn *how* to build relationships with unbelievers and set out to change our world.

III. HOW TO BUILD RELATIONSHIPS

A. Your Quality of Life

Before discussing some steps for building relationships, we need to examine the *quality* of our own Christian life. Are our lives really any different from our non-Christian friends? Are we at peace in the midst of stress and crises? Are we content with our circumstances in life?

Relationship evangelism develops when people are attracted by the difference Christ has made in our lives. According to Ephesians 2:12, the main difference between the Christian and non-Christian is hope. The hope that is within us then produces other qualities such as joy, peace, purity, self-control, and endurance. As the non-Christian observes this and comes in for a better look, our genuine love and care breaks down the barriers and we are able to freely explain our faith to her.

Though our love and concern for people is certainly an important motivation in sharing, it should not be our primary motivation. Our *primary* motivation for telling the world about the Lord stems from our love for Jesus. We need to be sure that we continue to pursue the lordship of Christ in our lives and that we continue to deepen our love for Him.

We also need to be persistent in our prayer life to ask Him to lead us to those He wants us to befriend. As many have observed, "Prayer is not preparation for the battle, prayer *is* the battle." We should begin each day by asking God to show us the people He wants us to love, and then pray for opportunities to share about Him.

As well as a persistent prayer life, we need to daily study God's Word for ourselves and strive to live in obedience to Him. We need to have a genuine concern for people, have infinite patience, and be willing to live according to God's timetable. An anonymous writer sums it up quite clearly:

The Gospels of Matthew, Mark, Luke and John
Are read by more than a few,
But the one that is most read and commented on
Is the gospel according to you.
You are writing a gospel, a chapter each day
By the things that you do and the words that you say.
Men read what you write, whether faithless or true,
Say, what is the gospel according to you?
Do men read His truth and His love in your life,
Or has yours been too full of malice and strife?
Does your life speak of evil, or does it ring true?
Say, what is the gospel according to you?

This is not to say that we have to be perfect—we never will be this side of heaven—but we can have the sincere desire and make conscious efforts to live a life pleasing to Him. Take encouragement from Acts 4:13: "When they saw the courage of Peter and John and realized that they were unschooled, ordinary men, they were astonished and they took note that these men had been with Jesus." Peter's and John's confidence did not depend on theological degrees or upon being perfect—they simply had been with the Lord. Our friends should be able to see a difference in our lives and our confidence in God's Word.

STOP AND APPLY

1. Ask yourself these questions: Would a non-Christian see any difference between my life and theirs? How am I perceived by those I am trying to win? Do I complain about my circumstances, or do I let Christ's peace flow through my life?

2. On a scale from 1 to 10, how would you rate your devotional life?

   1   2   3   4   5   6   7   8   9   10

3. What can you do to strengthen this?

B. Principles in Building Relationships

Meaningful relationships seldom happen by chance. Successful evangelism follows a plan. Bringing lost people to Christ means involvement and risk. If we really love God (who so loved the world that He sent His only Son to die for us), then we must be willing to lay our lives on the line as well. We need to *accept*, *love*, and *care for* those we hope to reach. As we plan to do this, the Holy Spirit will guide and enable us.

Ann Kiemel Anderson had a unique way of using chocolate chip cookies to accept, love, and care for those she hoped to reach as the following incident in her life shows:

> *Oh God, it's so ironic—it's so ironic that the people living closest to us are almost always the ones we overlook and fail to really love— i was out to love my neighbors to Jesus. Everyday i would pray— "Jesus, what can i do to share you with them?"*
>
> *It was a Saturday night and it had been several months of praying when i looked up into the cupboard and saw a package of chocolate chips. Now i'm not a special cook or anything but i can make some pretty good toll house cookies, and i said to myself, "i'll bake them some toll house cookies."*
>
> *And i threw everything together and put the cookies in the oven and when they were done i threw them on a plate and ran downstairs.*
>
> *"Sir, hi. My name is Ann. And sir, i baked some cookies for you and your wife. i'm your neighbor from upstairs.*
>
> *"Well, i baked them for you, sir, because i love you and i ... well, what i mean is, sir, i love you because Jesus loves me and i don't know why, He just makes me want to love you and your wife."*
>
> *He looked blank and shocked and sort of helpless. And suddenly i couldn't think of anything else to say and i felt foolish and stupid and sort of helpless, too.*
>
> *And so i kind of shoved the cookies into his hand and said goodnight and tripped up the stairs and ran in my apartment and burst into tears.*
>
> *Oh, God, i blew it. i really blew it. What a ridiculous thing for a twenty-six year old girl to do. Take homemade cookies to the man downstairs and tell him i love him. He'll think i'm weird.*
>
> *But God, you know what my motive was. i was trying to tell him, Jesus, that he is a part of my world and his wife is and i wanted to befriend them and love them to You.*

Jesus, can you make something out of this mess? If you will, God, i promise—i will never do anything irrational again. i'll think it through clearly.

For three days i was heartsick. i mean they didn't tell me they liked the cookies, they didn't return the plate, they didn't do anything. But at the end of the third day i was running up the stairs to my apartment when there on the carpet in front of my door was an empty plate with a note taped to it. i've never been so happy to see a plate in my life. i ran in the door, dropped my books and picked up the note and began to read.

"Dear Ann—Thanks a lot for the cookies. We never heard anyone talk about God the way you did. I was in a convent studying to be a nun when I met Mike and we've wandered from God. Could you come down and have coffee with us sometime and share your God with us? Thanks a lot.

Mike and Kay."

> *i see people—*
>   *warm faces,*
>   *a running tear,*
>   *a small child's hug,*
>   *an old man's gnarled grip of love.*
> *Saroyan said,*
>   *"People is all there is—*
>   *and all there was—*
>   *and all there ever will be."*
> *People—*
>   *that's all that matters to me*
>   *that Jesus be Lord*
>   *and people.*[5]

Joseph Aldrich, in the booklet "Friendship Evangelism," suggests that before you do anything, you should visualize the readiness of others to receive Christ. Believe that the Spirit of God is working in your neighborhood, workplace, or school. The fields are white unto harvest. God will lead you to these people.[6] The following practical principles provide concrete guidelines for getting started:

1. Identify the people with whom you come into contact on a regular basis.

Make a list of all the relatives, friends, neighbors, co-workers, people that you see often. Oscar Thompson, a professor who taught at Southwestern Baptist Theological Seminary, maintained that there is a certain order of concentric circles of relationships that we need to be concerned about.[7] It would look similar to the diagram to the right.

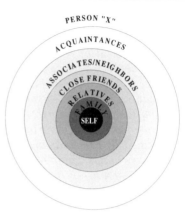

Relationships in Your Ministry

Christians sometimes jump from self to person "X," bypassing family and friends. This may happen because there are ruptured relationships between the "family" and "acquaintances" circles, or it may be because we are embarrassed about a lack of consistency in our Christian life. We know that with person "X" we can talk and be on our way, but relating to family and friends requires a time-consuming involvement in their lives. However, if we are sincerely interested in sharing our faith, we will see the wisdom of taking the time and effort to build relationships with those near to us.

2. Narrow your list to a realistic number of people.

Given the other responsibilities in your life, you may find that you can only focus on one person, or you may have the time and energy to work with several. Start collecting facts about those on your list: birthday, anniversary, important events in their lives, job, leisure activities, and names of other family members. Perhaps you will even want to keep an information sheet on each of those you are seeking to reach.

3. Establish additional points of contact.

One of your immediate goals is to find ways to improve or strengthen your relationship. Try to really understand what motivates your friend. Ask about her profession, hobbies, sports, family activities and interests, vacations, children's activities and accomplishments, current news, home improvements, books, and films. Be genuinely interested in her. Try to put yourself in her shoes. Your friend's first glimpse of Christ can begin with what seem to be very inconsequential things. A casual conversation can be turned into a significant step forward.

For example, be the kind of family your neighbors would want to know. Simple acts of kindness and pleasant attitudes can be powerful instruments when under the control of Christian love. Our neighbors will not believe we are truly concerned about them if we never have them over or if we do not take the time to speak to them in their front yards. We have to know our neighbors before we can meet their needs. Borrowing and loaning things among neighbors, conversing over the fence, doing small favors, taking cookies to new neighbors, and sharing your list of baby-sitters grow into larger acts of friendship.

Simple acts of kindness and pleasant attitudes will also be noticed among your work associates. Co-workers usually observe your life more than you realize. Lunches or coffee breaks often afford opportunities to express genuine interest in all aspects of their lives.

4. Deepen the relationship with her.

a. Be sensitive to specific needs and opportunities where you can serve. Jesus gave us one of the greatest examples of One who was a servant. "For even the Son of Man did not come to be served, but to serve, and to give his life as a ransom for many" [Mark 10:45]. Take the initiative to help out when appropriate. Look for specific things you can to do meet specific needs. For example:

- provide transportation if a person's car is getting repaired
- baby-sit to allow for a special night out
- clean the house for a new mother or elderly person
- mow the lawn for a neighbor who cannot do it
- help to meet a material or financial need
- take a meal to a sick or grieving person
- help a neighbor move in
- water the lawn, get the mail, or feed a pet while a family is on vacation
- send a card if you know someone is feeling down
- offer to help paint a house

"Therefore, as we have opportunity, let us do good to all people" [Gal. 6:10].

b. Concentrate on being a good listener. Everyone needs a good listener in her life. Listening means giving up the right to talk about yourself. When you listen, look your friend in the eyes, pay close attention to what she says, ask pertinent questions, nod, smile, and comment briefly along the way. Sincere listening is one way to say "I care about you."

There was a lady at one of the places Holly worked who was rather unpleasant and critical. Usually Holly just ignored her and tried to stay out of her way. But one day she was convicted of her lack of love for this woman and Holly made a conscious effort to start a conversation with her and really listen to her. The woman broke down and cried and shared how her marriage was breaking up and her family was falling apart. She was waiting for someone to show a real interest in her life.

c. Cultivate common interests. Build a reservoir of shared experiences. Discover what interests her and then plan to do one of these things together. Let her know that you enjoy spending time with her. Some ideas are that you could invite your friend to:

go to dinner	play tennis	go jogging
a PTA meeting	go to a rodeo	a knitting class
get coffee	play bridge	an aerobics class
play golf	go fishing	a sewing class
go boating	go bowling	go to a movie
go to a concert	go to lunch	go ice skating
play racquetball	go skiing	go bicycling
	go for a walk	

d. Talk about her needs. Meaningful conversations naturally spring from a deepening relationship. She may be dealing with loneliness, lack of purpose, loss of self-control, low self-esteem, financial problems, or wayward children. If this is the case, your friend needs you. She needs your steadfast love that stands with her in difficult moments.

e. Be transparent with your friend. When appropriate, relate her struggles to your own experiences and share how your faith in Christ has given you answers for problems. For example, if you have a financial need, tell her of your concern and then explain how you are relying on verses such as Philippians 4:19. If you have an ongoing struggle with needless anxiety, share with her how you are learning how to rely on Philippians 4:6–7. If you are battling self-control in your diet and weight control, tell her of your desire to overcome that weakness in your life. When you are vulnerable, it makes it easier for your friend to be open.

STOP AND APPLY

1. List some specific ideas you have to deepen a relationship in light of the people who are in your circles of concern.

_____

_____

_____

_____

_____

> **2.** Write down one time in your life where your personal relationship with Jesus Christ gave you strength and guidance in a particular situation. Think of how this can be used as an evangelistic tool.
> _____
> _____
> _____
> _____
> _____
> _____

5. Use hospitality to help build your relationships.

a. Definition of hospitality. "In Webster's dictionary, the definition for hospitable is wedged between the word 'hospice' which is a shelter, and the word 'hospital' which is a place of healing. Ultimately, this is what we offer when we open our home in the true spirit of hospitality. We offer shelter; we offer healing."[8]

The Greek word for hospitality is *philoxenos*, which is a combination of two words that mean "love" and "stranger." If we put this together with "evangelism" (meaning the sharing of the good news of Jesus Christ), then "hospitality evangelism" is sharing the good news of the gospel through hospitality and deeds of love so that our friends and relatives will see their need for a relationship with Jesus.

Practicing hospitality is a way to show love for another person and offer genuine warmth and acceptance. It is one way to turn love from theory to a practical application. Our home is a wonderful tool through which we can minister. However, hospitality is also a duty. Romans 12:13 commands us to "practice hospitality." 1 Peter 4:9 exhorts us to "practice hospitality without grumbling." 3 John 7–8 says for us to "show hospitality... so that we may work together for the truth."

Hospitality defined in a practical way is cheerfully opening our homes and lives to friends or strangers. Hospitality is not trying to impress people, but rather making people feel welcome. It encourages us to develop the attitude of a servant and is a way of ministering to lonely people. Nothing leaves a better impression on someone than a friendly invitation into a Christian home.

b. Goal of Hospitality. Hospitality is not just entertaining others.

> Entertaining has little to do with real hospitality. Entertaining says, "I want to impress you with my beautiful home, my clever decorating, my gourmet cooking." Hospitality seeks to minister and serve.

> Entertaining always puts things before people. Hospitality puts people before things. Entertaining looks for a payment—the words "My isn't she a remarkable hostess" and esteem in the eyes of friends. Hospitality does everything with no thought of reward, but takes pleasure in the joy of giving, doing, loving, and serving.[9]

The story of Mary and Martha illustrate the danger of placing priorities on impressing rather than ministering. They lived with their brother Lazarus in the village of Bethany, and Jesus frequently stayed with them. On one occasion, Martha wanted him to have the best possible meal and spent all of her time preparing it. Overwhelmed by all the work, her attitude grew worse and worse as she thought of her sister Mary, who did not help with the preparation. In exasperation, she complained to Jesus. "Jesus gently chided Martha, but not for exercising hospitality. She was right to serve her guests. He did scold her [however] for placing a priority on an impressive meal."[10]

One of the main goals of entertaining for evangelism is to create a social atmosphere where friendships can be made and strengthened. This can be done in a variety of ways. You could consider having a youth group fellowship, Bible study, or campus meeting at your house. College students might make their rooms available for study and talk times, or a neighbor might keep a cup of coffee ready to share. Some families may invite a church visitor home for a meal after the service. Jo Ann Cairns, author of *Welcome Stranger, Welcome Friend*, suggests a wide range of ideas for offering hospitality: welcoming a person or family to your neighborhood; offering friendship to employees or fellow members of an organization; providing a loving setting for the family and close friends of the deceased following a funeral; interacting with other believers about the Christian life; providing a sympathetic ear to persons experiencing difficult times; and getting to know new people in your church and making them feel welcome.[11]

"Although we want to see people enter into a personal relationship with Jesus Christ, we should not make their salvation an end in itself. Hospitality must be an outworking of genuine Christian love, no strings attached."[12] A person does not have to have a lot of money to practice hospitality. Serving soup and salad or cooking hamburgers and hot dogs on the grill can be just as nice as cooking a gourmet meal. Remember that your goal is not to impress, but to serve. Nor does a person have to have a big home in order to be hospitable, as is proven in this example of a seventy-seven-year-old lady:

She lived in a one-room efficiency apartment on the fifteenth floor of a senior citizen building. She continually shared hospitality with a cup of tea or coffee, a few raisins and mixed nuts, perhaps some banana bread or cookies. Her guests always felt special, sipping tea in real china cups with a flower or rose in a drinking glass and many times a candle on the table. These simple touches say, "Welcome, I care."[13]

Dawson Trotman, founder of the Navigators, and his wife, Lila, determined to make their home a center of hospitality from the beginning of their marriage. As a result, within three or four years, a sailor from every state had come to know Christ as Savior in their living room.

c. Practical Suggestions. If you want to start inviting people into your home, consider adopting one or more of the following suggestions:

☑ Set some hospitality goals for yourself. You might decide to invite someone new over once a month so that you can become better acquainted.

☑ Clean the house the day before so you can enjoy your company. Plan your work so that, if possible, most of it is done ahead of time.

☑ Make a "to do" list and a corresponding timetable.

☑ Strive to make the guests feel comfortable. Make it a point to listen to your guest and ask about her interests and experiences.

☑ Keep it simple. Elaborate meals are fine when you have the time, but most people are just as happy with soup, a casserole, or coffee and dessert.

☑ If someone volunteers to bring a dish, offers to clear the table, or to wash dishes, let them. It can help them feel more involved and can lighten the load for you.

☑ Have fun. Try not to be so busy in taking care of things that you don't have time to get involved with your guests.

☑ Look for areas of common ground. Listen for felt needs in the conversation, but do *not* feel pressured to turn the evening into a serious conversation about Christ. This is not necessarily your immediate goal.

☑ If you want specific suggestions for meal planning and house cleaning tips, check the resources at your local library.

6. *Share spiritual things and eventually present the gospel.*

a. Keep your focus clear. Never lose sight of your evangelistic aim of reconciling your friend to God through Christ. The ultimate goal is not to help your non-believing friends feel more comfortable with their secular lifestyle or merely to impose Christian morals on friends, but rather to introduce them to Christ and His lifestyle.

b. Look for open doors. Be assured that the Lord will prepare hearts—yours and hers. Keep your eyes and ears open for the appropriate moment to tell your friend in simple, everyday language what the Lord means in your life. When you look at your friend, remember that she has the potential to have the same relationship with the Creator of the Universe that you have, but she needs to hear the gospel presented in words she will understand.

Your faith in God is an important part of your life, and your friend should allow you the freedom to talk about that area of your life. As your friendship deepens, begin looking for open doors to share with her about Christ. Ask about her own religious background. Try to determine her spiritual condition.

There are certain signals and symptoms in a person's life that may indicate that your friend is ready to hear the gospel. For instance, you may find that your friend has a low self-image and constantly compares herself with others. Share how she can become a new person in Christ and how God fashioned her in a unique and special way. A complaining and unpleasant spirit are symptoms of restlessness and a lack of contentment with circumstances. Real contentment begins with inner peace. Philippians 4 speaks eloquently to this problem. Many in our society feel rejected, and they need you to tell them about God's unconditional love.

c. Take advantage of appropriate materials and outreach opportunities. Be alert for opportunities to share quality Christian literature with a seeking friend. For example, if your friend is struggling in the area of parenting, give her a book based on solid

Christian principles such as Dr. James Dobson's *Dare to Discipline* (Bantam Books) or Dr. Kenneth Leman's *How to Make Children Mind Without Losing Yours* (Revell Publishing Company). If she is struggling with her marriage, Gary Smalley's books, *For Better or Best* and *If Only He Knew* (Zondervan Publishing House) might be of interest to her. Verna Birkey's book, *You Are Special* (Revell Publishing Company) speaks to those struggling with self-image. If you don't know of a particular book for a need, ask for suggestions at your local Christian bookstore.

Most churches or Christian organizations sponsor evangelistic events where the Gospel is clearly presented. The choices are endless. Evangelistic dinners, Christian business breakfasts, Christian movies or concerts, conferences or retreats, and church sports programs provide a wide variety of opportunities for your friend to hear the gospel.

Len Andyshack, author of *A 30-Day Evangelism Plan,* recounts the story of Levi throwing a party so that all of his tax-collector buddies could meet Jesus, and it appears that a lot of them came [Luke 5:27–32]. "One of the advantages to an invitation like this is that you are not asking a person to make the final leap to conversion. It just gives them a chance to take a step closer in the safety of your friendship."[14]

C. Use Spiritual Bridges As a Means of Sharing

The following illustrations, taken from Richard Sisson's *Evangelism Encounter*, may be used to begin a meaningful discussion of the gospel message. Study each example carefully and then determine how you might adapt it to sound like you.

Church bridge: *You're right, Jessie. I am excited about our church. I think it is because we are trying to meet people's needs. Our pastor has been teaching us that the purpose of our church is to show people how they can have a fulfilling life in this world and have eternal life in the next.*

My life has not always been fulfilling, but since I started trying to straighten it out, it has taken on new meaning and purpose. What about you, Jessie? Do you feel your life has any real significance?

Personal experience bridge: *Tammy, do you realize that we have worked together for two years now? We have talked together about so many things, yet there is a very important part of my life I have never shared with you. Could I share with you now how I found meaning and purpose?*

Philosophy bridge: *Lori, we have been friends for years and we have done a lot of things together and have talked about a lot of things. But there is one thing of interest to me that I don't think we have ever discussed. Do you mind if I ask you a rather philosophical question? Where are you in your own personal search for meaning?*

Current issues bridge: *Yes, Hope, the threat of nuclear war seems like such a real possibility. I just wonder what is going to happen in the next few years with all the latest war technology. What about you? Does the thought of nuclear war ever scare you or make you think about the meaning of your life? How do you deal with your fears about the future?*

Loneliness bridge: *Yes, Courtney, I sometimes feel lonely, but not nearly as much as I used to. I used to wonder if anyone would miss me if I died. I asked myself if I thought my life had any significant purpose or meaning. I'm glad now that I asked the question. Here is what I discovered.*

Love bridge: *Allison, I appreciate your trusting me enough to share with me that you feel very unloved. Everybody needs to feel loved. We need to know that others realize that our lives have value. Do you think your life has any value?[15]*

No matter what the outcome of your discussion, be sure that you continue your relationship with that person. Let your friend know that your love and concern for her is not based on her response or on her decision, but is unconditional. Leave the door open for further opportunities. But at the same time, keep your eyes open for other people God may want to put in your life. The fields are white for harvest. Do not abandon the relationships God has given you. Just keep praying, fishing, and expecting God to work.

IV. CONCLUSION

Bringing people to Christ is not an impossible job. It only seems impossible when we try to do it in our own strength rather than Christ's. If you genuinely seek courage for witnessing boldly, God will give it to you. He has given us His Holy Spirit for that purpose. Paul said, "Pray also for me, that whenever I open my mouth, words may be given me so that I will fearlessly make known the mystery of the gospel, for which I am an ambassador in chains. Pray that I may declare it fearlessly, as I should" [Eph. 6:19–20].

As we try to share good news with people, we need to remember that *evangelism is a process.* God may use you at various places along a continuum of a person's life. He may choose to use your witness only to plant seeds in another's life, to water seeds planted by a previous witness, or He could choose you to reap the fruit by being the one to actually lead her to Christ. Each stage along the continuum is vitally important, and we must remember to be faithful and obedient to His command to share the Gospel.

We need to be patient and always keep in mind that not all fruit ripens at the same time. We are not God—He has his own timetable. Note what Paul says in 1 Corinthians 3:6–8, "I planted the seed, Apollos watered it, but God made it grow. So neither he who plants not he who waters is anything, but God, who makes things grow. The man who plants and the man who waters have one purpose, and each will be rewarded according to his own labor." The Holy Spirit is the One who converts an individual. His work in a person's life sometimes takes days; sometimes it takes years. Our job is to keep loving, sharing, and remembering that "The one who calls you is faithful and He will do it" [1 Thess. 5:24].

Dawson Trotman used to pray that God would use him in the life of every person he met. Following his example, we should pray that we can help every person we meet to move just one step closer to Christ—whether it is through sharing a smile, doing a kind deed, listening, sharing an answered prayer or a verse with them, or sharing the whole gospel. Be ready to take advantage of those relationships that may briefly come into your life.

Now stop and take a look at your own unique world. No one knows the same combination of people. That is exciting! Ann Kiemel affirmed this fact in her life when she shared:

> *I could tell you many stories from my life. I could tell you of taking children to Israel to watch me run my first marathon. I could tell you of those children today, and where they are. I could tell you of God giving me the idea of building a gymnasium in the heart of Boston for ghetto children who had no place to play and of using all my money to build a gym in Boston. Dr. Ken Taylor from Tyndale came and dedicated the gym for me on Easter Sunday the day before my first Boston marathon. I could also tell you of things that are happening in Idaho Falls. But basically, it has been built around the Holy Spirit taking my simple prayer every morning: "Jesus, I'm yours. I'm so inadequate. I'm so imperfect. But make me creative today so that the world will be different because you live in me—that somehow may that*

power in my life today extend to others around me."
I've truly seen that happen and I challenge you today
to try and make Jesus creative where you live. Begin
to pray for creative ideas that fit who you are, how
you feel and what you do. Pray for creative ideas that
God will take your one life. If you live in the smallest
house on the most ordinary block, and drive an old
Dodge Dart, I want you to know that you have all the
power in the world to make a difference. If you really
care enough to say, "Yes, Lord, I will let you plant a
dream in me," God will do it—a dream that is bigger
than you, a dream that is greater than you, a dream
that will take all of you and all of God to really live.[16]

God has a special and unique role for you in this world!
Prayerfully consider Ann's challenge: "Let Him plant something in
your heart that will make you stand on your tiptoes and reach for
something bigger and greater than you've ever experienced before." Expect God to give you opportunities to share and the
boldness and wisdom needed for that moment. "Not by might nor by
power, but by my Spirit, says the Lord Almighty" [Zech. 4:6].

STOP AND APPLY

1. Arrange the following six steps used in relationship
   evangelism in the proper order:
   ___ Use hospitality to help build your relationship.
   ___ Establish additional points of contact.
   ___ Deepen the relationship with her.
   ___ Share spiritual things and eventually present the
   gospel.
   ___ Identify the people with whom you come into con-
   tact on a regular basis.
   ___ Narrow your list to a realistic number of people.

2. In sharing spiritual things and presenting the gospel, it
   is important to keep your focus _____, look for
   _____ _____, and take advantage of appropriate
   _____ and _____ opportunities.

3. Look at the practical suggestions for inviting people into your home. Plan now to do this, and share with your mentor how you plan to implement those suggestions which are most appropriate to your situation.

4. Make a conscious effort to pray for this person and about the possibility of applying the six steps discussed in this chapter.

Now if you haven't already done so, listen to cassette tape #3B in the series featuring *Evangelism and Relationships* by Ann Kiemel Anderson. Also on the tape are excerpts from Roberta Hestenes, Joanne Shetler, and Judy Streeter.

ENDNOTES

[1] Jerry and Claudia Root, *Friendship Evangelism* (Wheaton: Shaw, 1990), p. 38.

[2] Herb Miller, *Actions Speak Louder Than Verbs* (Nashville: Abingdon Press, 1989), p. 69.

[3] Bill Bright, *The Calling of an Evangelist* ("The Evangelist's Personal Witness," Worldwide Press, 1986), p. 28.

[4] Leroy Eims, *Winning Ways* (Victor Books, 1980), p. 48.

[5] Ann Kiemel, *I'm Out to Change My World* (Nashville: Impact Books, 1974), pp. 109–112.

[6] Joseph Aldrich and Sterling Huston, *Friendship Evangelism* (Minneapolis: Billy Graham Evangelistic Association, 1988).

[7] Oscar Thompson, *Concentric Circles of Concern* (Nashville: Broadman Press, 1981), p. 21.

[8] Karen Mains, *Open Heart Open Home* (Elgin, Illinois: David C. Cook Publishing Co, 1976), p. 18.

[9] *Ibid.*, p. 15.

[10] Jo Ann Cairns, *Welcome, Stranger: Welcome Friend* (Springfield, Missouri: Gospel Publishing House, 1988), p. 30.

[11] *Ibid.*, pp. 45–46.

[12] *Ibid.*, p. 46.

[13] Emilie Barnes, *Things Happen When Women Care* (Eugene, Oregon: Harvest House Publishers, 1990), p. 217.

[14] Len Andyshack, *A 30-Day Evangelism Plan* (Downers Grove, IL: InterVarsity Press, 1986), p. 11.

[15] Dick Sisson, *Evangelism Encounter* (Wheaton: Victor Books, 1988), pp. 137–138.

[16] Ann Kiemel Anderson, talk given at Wheaton College, Wheaton, Illinois, March 26, 1991, pp. 3–4 of transcript.

$\mathcal{U}$NIT THREE:

Community
Evangelism

SESSION SEVEN
Evangelism and Bible Study

GOALS FOR THE CHAPTER:

After reading this chapter, you should be able to:

1. Present an overview of the reasons why evangelistic Bible studies are important.

2. Take the steps necessary to begin a well-organized, small group, evangelistic Bible study.

3. Analyze some of the issues involved in the selection and presentation of materials.

4. Recognize cautions in order to avoid potential problems.

I. INTRODUCTION AND DEFINITION OF AN EVANGELISTIC BIBLE STUDY

Evangelistic Bible studies are an important tool for outreach. Because they usually meet in homes, these groups often attract people who are hesitant to attend a formal church service. Consequently, it is important that Christians know how to organize and lead such a study. An evangelistic Bible study is one where believers and nonbelievers meet to discuss in an open and nonthreatening way the claims of Jesus Christ. The goal of an evangelistic Bible study is to present the Gospel message in a clear and compelling fashion. The study seeks to give the unbeliever an opportunity to discover for herself the person and work of Jesus Christ. The facilitator of these studies will seek to raise questions or guide discussion in such a way that all who are present will encounter Jesus. This is not the place to debate creeds, theologies, or doctrinal differences between various denominations. All of these are important topics and should be addressed by believers, but not in this setting. The evangelistic Bible study should focus on the greatest need of our life—our need to know Jesus as our Lord and Savior.

II. THE NEED FOR EVANGELISTIC BIBLE STUDIES

Many people in today's world view churches as hopelessly out of touch with their needs and realities. Unsure whether God really exists, the thought of attending a formal church service never occurs to them. Furthermore, their view of Christians and Jesus is often formed by what they see of deceitful televangelists or other fraudulent Christians whose stories contribute to the secular desire for sensational news. Sadly, this false view of Christianity deprives them of the saving grace needed for eternal life.

What is worse, many nominal Christians never truly hear the message of salvation. Anne Graham Lotz lays the blame for this omission at the door of many evangelical groups that should be offering the bread of eternal life.

> In our evangelism efforts, we have everything. I mean everything. We have seminars, and conferences... and videos, and audios, and books, and magazines! We have dramas; we have musicals; we have libraries; we have outreach banquets; we have Evangelism Explosion; we have Master Life. You name it—we've got it! But do we have everything except what is needed for life?...God's Word. The Creator, through the power of His word, creates change."[1]

Nonbelievers need to hear and study the Word of God if they are to be transformed into useful disciples for advancing the Kingdom.

A neighborhood or small group Bible study offers non-Christians a realistic alternative. The atmosphere is a familiar one. Sitting in a living room produces much less stress than attending a church service (where the unbeliever fears she will make a mistake or become the object of attention). Furthermore, if other neighbors or acquaintances are invited, the study will seem like a friendly gathering rather than a formal class. The casual setting fosters an honest, open discussion of the material, because the participants will feel more relaxed and less threatened by the surroundings.

Moreover, the study will probably meet the longing of many in our society who feel alienated or lonely. The small group will provide each member with a form of support and caring that may be unavailable to them in their daily lives. The leaders or Christian participants may be the only ones who daily pray for these precious lives. For those who are used to the competitive and often hostile environment the world offers, their first exposure to the consistent, loving care of Christian fellowship can be a life-changing experience.

Much of the secular world is looking for meaningful friendships; people feel isolated and uncared for even in the midst of large cities. Too often marriages falter almost as soon as they begin; partners that avoid divorce need help in developing a deeper, more enduring bond in marriage. Christians who live according to the standards set by Jesus for these relationships have much to offer from both Scripture and example. Those in the secular world desperately seek alternatives to their empty, shallow lifestyle; their hunger provides an open door.

Christians should be offering alternatives to these prevalent problems. However, fulfilling the Great Commission gives disciples an even more important reason for starting an evangelistic Bible study. As many Christians have pointed out, Jesus told us to "*go* and make disciples of all nations" [Matt. 28:19], not to "*wait* until all people come to you and then tell them about Me." An evangelistic study *takes* the message to unbelievers in a format that encourages them to feel open and expectant about the meeting and the material. Melody and Keith Green, whose Christian music ministry has touched millions of people, are two examples of people who were converted because of a home Bible study. Both were open to the idea of Jesus, but not to the thought of attending a formal church service.

STOP AND APPLY

1. Define an evangelistic Bible study:

2. Put a **T** for True or an **F** for False before the following statements about the merits of doing an evangelistic Bible study:

___ a. It provides a familiar atmosphere.

___ b. It gives an opportunity to conduct a formal class in a home.

___ c. It helps to provide friendship for lonely people.

___ d. It fosters an honest and open discussion about the material.

___ e. It takes the message to unbelievers, rather than waiting for them to come to church.

___ f. Participants feel threatened by the small group and will listen more closely to the discussion.

III. HOW TO START AN EVANGELISTIC BIBLE STUDY

To be successful, the Bible study needs to be well-organized. The leader(s) need to make some preliminary decisions about intended participants and some vital logistics. A number of these issues must be considered in connection with each other. For the sake of clarity, the following section has been subdivided into three major topics. To be properly understood, however, the material must be considered as a unit.

A. Pray

Even though it has been said many times, it needs to be reiterated—prayer is the most effective ally. Prayer is to the Bible study what gasoline is to a car—the power that drives it. Without prayer, do not expect to see a ripe harvest. Prayer is the cornerstone of evangelism because it invokes the power of God in the battle against Satan. Only someone very foolish or very ignorant would suppose that human power can fight and win against the forces of evil.

If possible, begin by gathering a group of other believers who will support the endeavor with prayer. Ask God for wisdom and direction about a time and place. Let God direct the invitation of potential members. Ask Him to open the hearts and minds of those who are invited so that they will respond favorably. Pray for His guidance in the selection of the material, and then seek to present it in the most compelling manner possible (see the Resource section at the end of this chapter for ideas).

Pray before the planning. *Pray* during the planning. *Pray* for those invited and the leadership of the group. Finally decide to *pray* daily for all the members. There is no such thing as too much prayer. All great soul winners will acknowledge that prayer is the great secret of their success.

B. Organize

After prayer, next decide whether the teacher will work alone or with another Christian woman. Then set the place, time, and length of study. Obviously, these specifics need to be established before the invitations can be extended.

1. Decide If There Will Be a Co-Leader.

Some women feel comfortable leading and hosting a study by themselves. However, most find that it is nice to have a co-leader who will share the responsibility for prayer, setup, and other duties. Those who feel uncomfortable leading a study should consider asking another Christian woman to facilitate the discussion, while the hostess assumes the tasks of inviting friends, providing the setting, and making sure that everyone feels welcome each time they come. Any Christians that are involved should spend their time talking to newcomers—not to each other. Avoid the look of a clique! Work on learning names and some details about each member. People feel flattered and loved when called by name or when they are remembered in a personal way.

2. Choose a Place.

When considering the place, look for a location where everyone will have a comfortable place to sit, preferably in a circle. Group dynamics work better when members can all face each other and the discussion leader does not seem more prominent than anyone else. If baby-sitting will be provided, make certain that the home or facility will adequately and comfortably accommodate the special requirements of the children.

If the meeting will be held in a public building, look for a quiet room where disturbances will be unlikely. In most instances, it is better to avoid church buildings, since some unbelievers will feel less comfortable there. However, one church in Illinois reached out to the community by starting an hour-long story time for older preschoolers. Mothers were then invited to a coffee time and study during that hour. Participation by the mothers was not necessary for the child to be enrolled, but many mothers were intrigued and elected to continue.[2]

If your study will meet in a home, do everything possible to make the guests feel comfortable. Pets should be out of sight and, if possible, out of earshot. Plan to take the phone off the hook, or have someone who can answer it quickly and unobtrusively. Look around the room. Try to notice any distractions and deal with them ahead of time.

3. Set the Time.

One-and-a-half to two hours should be sufficient if the group numbers twelve or less. If it goes on too long, the members will become bored or drop out because they cannot afford to commit themselves to such a large block of time. It is imperative that the sessions *begin and end on time*. Some in the group will have other things to do, and it is not fair to ask them to constantly readjust because someone else is late or careless about punctuality. Once the group realizes that the schedule will be followed, they will make the effort to arrive on time.

Most groups spend a few minutes either at the beginning or end, (or both) in fellowship. Simple refreshments give nervous hands something to hold and also break the ice as the group gets to know each other. It is nice to spend about fifteen minutes at the beginning around the coffee table. This gives the members a chance to catch up on the news of the week and should limit distracting questions during the study. It is wise to set a schedule for the meeting right from the first. Consider breaking a ninety-minute block into the following sections:

---

15 minutes *coffee and fellowship*
➡ **60 minutes** *for discussion*
➡ **5 minutes** *for summary*
➡ **10 minutes** *for informal sharing
or another cup of coffee*

Ideally the leader and hostess should be available for a while after the study to answer questions or talk more privately with members who are hesitant to share more personal issues with the entire group. Be prepared to listen carefully and be open to opportunities to sharing the complete message of the Gospel if the occasion arises.

When selecting the date and time of day, try to consider the schedules of others. The small group Bible study has the potential of meeting at a time that should suit most schedules. Do not waste this great advantage.

4. Determine the Length of the Study.

Given the busyness of society, few are willing to make open-ended commitments to something new. People are much more likely to attend if they know that the sessions will only last for a set period of time—usually six or eight weeks. If interest remains high when the end is reached, a further commitment can be made.

5. Arrange for Baby-sitting.

If the group includes young mothers, child care may be needed. Some groups hire a teen to take care of the children; others look for a volunteer from their church who will view it as a ministry. Sometimes the women rotate the responsibility among themselves, but this is not the best option, because it means that someone will always miss the lesson. When providing for this vital need, look for a place where the children will be well cared for but will not disturb the study. Consider renting a video or providing some other special activity so that the children will look forward to being there.

C. Invite

1. Whom to Invite

Once again, the key to inviting people begins in prayer by asking the Lord to reveal the ones who are most open. It is not only the job of the Holy Spirit to prepare hearts to hear the message, but to direct the feet (and invitations) of the messenger. Remember, too, that some people will refuse the invitation. The excuses they offer may be genuine, or they may be a cover for their uncertainties or preconceived notions. Their refusal is not necessarily a dead end. When someone declines the invitation, accept their refusal graciously but keep them in prayer. When another opportunity presents itself, cordially extend another invitation but do not try to manipulate. Often people will come when asked a second or third time, because they were given a chance to become comfortable with the idea.

There are numerous possibilities when thinking about potential group members. Consider colleagues at work. Scout around your neighborhood. Young mothers will find that others in a similar situation will often welcome such an opportunity. Fellow members of the PTA, the health or garden club, or friends who share an interest in crafts need to hear about Jesus too. Look around; souls are dying while they wait to hear.

Sometimes the decision is complicated by an overabundance of prospective members. For instance, should everyone on the block be invited or just those that might be ready? Opinions are divided on this issue—some women reach out only when they feel led by the Holy Spirit; others will invite the whole neighborhood to a "kickoff" event. There are no definitive answers to this question, but never let fear of attracting too many people become the primary concern. If ten is the target number and thirty women show an interest, go back to the Lord and intercede for more leaders. Should this occur, rejoice that so many are willing to seriously examine the state of their spiritual lives.

Most authorities agree that a small group should not exceed twelve participants (a few go as high as fifteen), and many find six to eight to be an ideal number. Recognize that not everyone who starts will stay to the conclusion, so it may be wise to begin with a slightly larger gathering than the ideal.

Make sure that there are far more unbelievers than Christians. Imagine the group from their perspective. One or two unbelievers surrounded by six or seven Christians will feel trapped and maybe a trifle hostile. Some experts on this subject feel that only Christians who bring an unbelieving friend should attend, while others find that a mix of two believers with six or seven seekers to be a good ratio. In any case, do not overwhelm the group with "authorities" (Christians) who might intimidate newcomers. It will be far easier to facilitate discussion when people feel that they are on an equal footing with the rest of the group. When it becomes obvious that most are not familiar with the teachings of the Bible, the timid members should gain confidence about adding their own ideas or opinions.

2. How to Invite Prospective Members

Consider the following invitations and evaluate each one.

Hi Carol. I know you're terribly busy with your work right now; so I don't suppose you'd want to come to an informal Bible study with some of the other women on the block, would you?

Hi Carol. I'm so glad to have a chance to talk to you. I know you're busy but I wanted to be sure and let you know about a neighborhood study that some of us are having at our house. I know that you are vitally concerned about the disintegration of families in America and so are we. That's why we decided to meet for the next eight weeks and see if the Bible and its traditional view of the family still has any solutions to offer. I know that your input would enhance our discussions.

Hi, Carol. Could you come over for coffee Thursday at 10 am? I've invited all the neighbors on these 2 blocks to get together and get acquainted. A couple of us are interested in the idea of a neighborhood Bible Study. I thought you'd like to know how women are doing this. Just come meet the neighbors and hear about the idea.

Without a doubt everyone will find the second or third invitation preferable. The first invitation is negative in its tone and almost encourages "busy" Carol to refuse it. If the leader is not confident and excited about the study, the invitation will not be attractive.

The second one starts off with the same acknowledgment of Carol's full schedule, but emphasizes the positive and then goes on to give some important information that should help Carol make up her mind. She now knows that the group: (1) will be made up of neighbors, (2) will meet for a specific length of time—eight weeks, and (3) will study the Bible's view of the family. Finally, the inviter complimented Carol by assuring her that her ideas would be of value to the group. No matter what her decision, Carol will feel encouraged to know that she has something positive to contribute. If she cannot or will not come this time, the door has been left open for a future invitation.

The third invitation represents a pre-evangelism or "middle ground" area which is not as descriptive as the second, but is still an effective approach in certain circumstances.

Some people prefer to prepare a written invitation that they send to perspective members and then follow it up with a visit or phone call. When choosing this alternative, remember to make the invitation as attractive as possible and include all relevant information: place, dates, time, length of study, topic under discussion, general information about the make up of the group, baby-sitting (if applicable), and who will be leading the discussion.

The lunch hour can be ideal for meeting with co-workers. If this seems best, try to reserve a quiet, out of the way room in your building where the meeting will not be easily observed or interrupted. If necessary, clear the room and time with the boss or the person in charge. Be honest and upfront about the activities so that a positive image of Christians and Christianity is presented.

No one likes being put on the spot, especially in front of others; so be extra sensitive when inviting colleagues. If possible, do it privately so that they can feel free to ask questions and accept or refuse without peer pressure. The same guidelines will apply when inviting club members or anyone who is part of a large group. Sensitivity to their feelings will help them to have a positive opinion about the group as well as Christianity in general. Some have found that it is better to give each person a response card which allows her to check one of three options. Take a look at the sample of an invitation to a study held in the work place. The wording can be easily

Lunch-Time Discussion

Place: The Quiet Conference Room
Time: Wednesdays from 12 - 1 pm.
Bring: A Sack Lunch - beverages provided
Format: Discussion of the claims of Jesus as stated
           in the Bible. Is He just a historical figure
           or someone with advice for today? [Nancy
           Niceperson will be leading the study]

Dates: March 6 through April 24
           [We will meet a total of eight times]

RSVP: Please respond by February 25

Name:

Extension number:

☐ Thanks for the invitation. I'd love to come.
☐ It's a great topic, but I'd like some more
  information before I commit myself.
☐ I really appreciate the offer, but my schedule has
  exceeded its limits and I won't be able to join you.

A Sample Invitation

adapted for a neighborhood study. If young mothers will be included, be sure to mention that child care will be provided.

A potluck supper, morning coffee, or afternoon tea can also be used as an avenue to issue the invitation. When choosing this route, plan to have someone share about her experience in a small group Bible study. Be sure to pick a woman who is enthusiastic and articulate. It is best to have someone else speak, because it allows the guests to decline the invitation to the study without appearing to turn down the hostess. Everyone will be more comfortable with this, and the door will remain open to include them at a future date.

Be certain to emphasize that this will be a discussion, not a class. Let them know that their input is valuable and that the group will look for answers together. Help them to see that this is not a school where one is expected to perform in a certain way, but rather is a group of interested people who are all searching.

STOP AND APPLY

1. Which of the following lists properly orders the steps used in organizing an evangelistic Bible study: _____
   a. Invite; Organize; Pray   c. Organize; Pray; Invite
   b. Pray; Organize; Invite   d. Pray; Invite; Organize

2. In organizing the study, you need to establish the following:
   Decide if there is to be a _____.
   Choose a _____.
   Set the _____.
   Determine the _____ of study.
   Arrange for _____.

3. If you were to start a group, list whom you would invite:

   _____   _____
   _____   _____
   _____   _____
   _____   _____

IV. THE LEADER

A. Born or Made?

Although some women assume the role naturally, most gain confidence with practice. Anyone who feels led by the Lord to begin a Bible study can learn the techniques. For the most part, they require patience and practice rather than great knowledge or wisdom. The ideal leader should want to introduce every person in the study to Jesus, and she should know how to present the steps to salvation in a clear and appealing fashion.

B. Studies Scripture

Obviously the leader must possess an overall knowledge of Scripture, if she is to ask relevant questions and keep the discussion focused on the passage. Nevertheless, seminary training in theology is not a requirement, and in some cases it can be a hindrance. Most non-Christians are not concerned about in-depth discussions of esoteric issues that captivate theologians. The leader needs to relate to the group at their level of understanding and interest.

Ideal leaders need to be committed, enthusiastic Christians who are willing and capable of studying their Bible, asking meaningful questions, and guiding a discussion. The leader's goal is for each person to discover the truth of the claims and person of Jesus in such a real way that the participants will be eager to surrender their lives to Him.

C. Loves Others

Good leaders are those who genuinely care about others. They enjoy people and feel comfortable talking to others. Like Jesus, the leader will look past the exterior and see the heart need of each individual. Following the lead of her Master, she will view herself as a physician who offers good and healing medicine for the heart that is plagued with sin. She will reach out to each newcomer in such a way that everyone will feel welcome and valued in the study. Learning and using the names of the participants will help create a sense of community and make each person feel appreciated and noticed.

D. Communicates Clearly

Members of the group need to understand the message, but they also need to feel comfortable with the discussion process and to be accepted for who they are. This kind of loving communication manifests itself in the leader as she:

1. Maintains good eye contact when talking and conversing with members of the group. Concentrating attention on the one who is speaking helps to make the person feel accepted and encourages her to speak honestly with the group.

2. Listens with eyes to the body language, ears to the words, and spirit to the "real" message being spoken by the participant. The leader tries to hear the heart as well as the words.

3. Encourages shy members with a smile, glance, or comment that will help them feel comfortable.

E. Leads the Discussion

A lively discussion keeps interest high and promotes active participation. The leader sets the pace at the first session and then keeps the group on target. The following guidelines give an overview of these responsibilities.

1. *Establish the ground rules at the beginning and then repeat them as necessary.* For instance, the leader should explain that the Bible will be accepted as the authority for the group. The purpose, after all, is to see what the Bible has to say on certain topics, and this can never be accomplished if the group is constantly debating what they think of it. The group does not have to accept it as the inspired Word of God, but they do need to examine carefully what it says about life and truth. Most people buy a guidebook when they take their first trip to a foreign country. Traveling through the country, they will begin by following the advice given in the book. If they find it to be helpful and true, they will increasingly trust the author. He becomes their authority for the trip. In a similar way, non-Christians will increasingly trust the Word of God—and God Himself—as they experience the truth of the Bible in their own lives.

2. *Help the members to discover Biblical truth for themselves by asking appropriate questions rather than just "telling" them the relevant facts.* (Remember that people remember 10% of what they hear but 90% of what they say.) The goal is to help others discover the truth for themselves.

3. *Learn to be comfortable with silence.* After asking a thought-provoking question, the leader must refrain from answering it herself if the group does not immediately respond.

4. *Encourage questions from the group but refrain from answering them.* Instead, refer them back to the group.

5. *Deal with inappropriate or incorrect comments in a positive manner.* Acknowledge the speaker without approving of the comment and then move on. Avoid saying or responding with "No, that's not correct," or any response which may appear to put a person down. For instance, "Thank you, Martha. I wonder, does anyone else want to speak to this point?"

6. *Keep the discussion moving.* Tangents need to be avoided, and so do in-depth discussions about unimportant details. Never let one person monopolize the session or others will rapidly lose interest. Likewise, the lesson needs to be seen as relevant to the lives of the members, or they will soon tire of it and drop out.

7. *Summarize or restate the important points at the end of each session.*

8. *Avoid any sort of pressure tactics to manipulate a decision.* Instead, focus on the material and discourage overly emotional testimonies or appeals from Christians which usually make seekers nervous and uncomfortable. The group is on a fact-finding mission. The Holy Spirit is the one who will cause these discoveries to become real and alive in their hearts. It is not the job of the leader to press for decisions, but to present the material and then wait for the Holy Spirit to quicken hearts.

STOP AND APPLY

Check the qualities of a good leader:

❏ Studies Scripture   ❏ Loves others
❏ Dominates discussions   ❏ Has all the answers
❏ Communicates clearly   ❏ Lectures well
❏ Asks appropriate questions   ❏ Restates important points
❏ Is comfortable with silence   ❏ Has good eye contact
❏ Helps members discover biblical truths   ❏ Deals with wrong answers in a positive way

---

V. PRACTICAL CONSIDERATIONS

A. Methods

Most experts on the topic of evangelistic Bible studies agree that the Inductive Method of study is preferable to one where participants merely listen to a lecture. Since the Inductive Method requires no previous knowledge of the material, it is ideal for those who are beginners. Participants read over the section of Scripture until they can answer the three basic questions used by the Inductive Method:

1. What does the passage say?	[observation]
2. What does the passage mean?	[interpretation]
3. What does this mean to me?	[application]

Before each session, the leader needs to read the passage as many times as is necessary to feel completely comfortable with it. Although some passages might require additional information to properly understand the cultural or historical setting, those familiar with the Inductive Method discourage the use of commentaries or other Bible Study tools until the text has been properly assessed for itself. In all cases, the use of outside references should only occur after the leader has thoroughly reviewed the material by using the three questions. The group should always be encouraged to think through the lesson for themselves. The Bible is perfectly capable of speaking for itself and needs no outside authorities or commentators to defend it.

Most veteran Bible study leaders who follow the Inductive Method recommend a study that focuses on material found in one of the Gospels, because Jesus is most clearly seen when He speaks for Himself. Other leaders offer a strong case for using a topical study that includes a clear gospel presentation. In either case, the goal should be an appealing presentation of the steps to salvation and discipleship.

A discussion that is relevant will hold attention and naturally encourage participants to keep returning. The leader should try to help the group view the passage in contemporary terms. Begin with the details of the Scripture and then move to the concept that underlies it. For instance, when teaching the story of Jesus and the Samaritan woman at the well [John 4], Joseph Aldrich, a well-known spokesperson for Relationship Evangelism, asks the following four questions to stimulate discussion:

1. *Describe the physical appearance of the woman at the well. What did she look like?*

2. *Describe the emotional condition of this woman (rejected by five men and living with a sixth).*

3. *What did Jesus offer as a solution to her problem?*

4. *Does His solution have any relevance to the needy people in our world? If so, how does it become operational in our experience?*[3]

The questions are designed to get the group thinking and talking. They do not have simple right or wrong answers and people should feel free to offer their opinions. There are no snapshots or home movies of the woman at the well, but thinking about the first question will force the participants to try and visualize the scene. They will begin to identify with this woman as they ponder the second question. The last two questions will help them to see the relevance of Christ's message to each person alive today. Jesus becomes compellingly attractive as the group discovers the answers for themselves. The leader's love and knowledge of Scripture will be apparent by the way that she asks probing questions and helps the group discover the unconditional love of the Savior for each person.

B. Bibles

Some leaders prefer to supply each member with an inexpensive copy of the Bible such as the ones offered by the Bible Society. If everyone uses the same Bible, the leader can instruct members to turn to a certain page rather than referring to a chapter and verse. Looking for a page rather than a citation will remove the discomfort experienced by someone who is unfamiliar with the Bible. Furthermore, when one person reads aloud, everyone else can easily follow along and the discussion will not bog down on the relative merits of various versions. On the other hand, some leaders prefer to offer a Bible to those without one, and allow everyone to bring and use her favorite translation. They find that some folks are more comfortable with their own Bible, and sometimes the different wording in various versions affords valuable insight.

C. Common Mistakes

First-time leaders sometimes make one of the mistakes listed below. If this happens to you, keep the incident in perspective. Leaders should readily and graciously admit mistakes as soon as possible and then get on with the session. In most instances, the group will find such humility attractive, and it may even be used to help them see the true character of Jesus more clearly. Although not an exhaustive list, the following points should help leaders avoid the more obvious or common pitfalls.

1. Avoid Cross-Referencing of Scriptures

Christians who are familiar with the Bible love the interconnectedness of many passages because it adds to the overall richness and depth of God's word. However, newcomers will find cross-referencing to be a confusing distraction which intimidates those who don't know how to look up the citations. Unless another reference is vital to understanding the passage under consideration, cross-referencing should be avoided.

2. Never Criticize Other Churches or Denominations

Disparaging remarks about any church or denomination have no place in the discussion. The leader should keep the discussion focused on the passage and tactfully but firmly make it clear that unkind or derogatory comments about other Christians are unacceptable.

If someone asks about a cult group such as the Mormons or Jehovah Witnesses, the leader should clearly explain the differences between the theologies, but she should never slander or belittle anyone.

3. Recruit Christians—Not Church Members

Furthermore, the Christian members of the group should be sensitive to the unbelievers by not spending the fellowship time "promoting" their own church. If asked what church they attend, a member should feel free to respond and may even extend an invitation to the questioner, but no one should feel pressured into visiting or joining a church.

4. Sidestep Arguments

Never argue—not even with a person who is obviously in error. Remember that the group gathered to discuss and not to debate. Do not agree with an erroneous opinion, but merely keep the discussion moving and emphasize the truth. Remember that winning the argument might lead to alienating the opponent and forfeiting an opportunity to share the Gospel.

5. Remain Humble

Never pretend to have all the answers or bluff your way through a question. When stumped with a difficult question, a good leader readily admits that she does not have the answer. She might respond, "That's a good point, Hannah, but I must confess that I will need some time to look up the answer. I'll make a note of it and we will plan to discuss it next week." No one expects the leader to be perfect or omniscient.

D. The Difficult Person

Every small group leader can share stories of persons who presented them with difficult situations. Learning how to handle such members tactfully is a skill acquired through prayer, reflection, and practice. Nearly all the books dealing with the topic of small group Bible studies include helpful suggestions for handling these common problems. For instance, the following illustrations highlight three common personality types that most leaders encounter. Most experts agree that the leader should:

1. Draw out shy persons carefully, if at all.

If overwhelmed, they usually retreat or withdraw—sometimes permanently. Try asking them a question that requires general knowledge rather than a deeply personal response. Sometimes a smile, nod, or other sign of encouragement will help them to gather courage and timidly offer a suggestion. Your goal is to help them feel comfortable in the group.

2. Discourage the overtalker before the group feels overwhelmed by the volume of her comments.

Asking questions of specific people (not the talkative one) will help to slow the overtalker; for the most part, try to avoid eye contact so it will be more difficult for her to volunteer every time a question is asked. If it becomes necessary to talk with her, do it privately. Explain that her frequent contributions discourage the more timid members who need time to think before they volunteer. Be tactful and affirm her; try to enlist her help in allowing others equal time.

3. Deal gently but firmly with the ones who regularly introduce a tangent.

Do not argue with the person, but merely ask if the question can be deferred until later because it is not central to the issue being discussed. Sometimes tangential questions will be answered later in the study. If they are not, be sure to discuss the issue with the person during an individual meeting after the group or during the week.

VI. IMPROVING THE GROUP

A. Fellowship

Whenever refreshments are served or time is allotted for fellowship, the Christians must carefully avoid the appearance of being a clique. Look for the person who appears to be lonely; engage the newcomer in conversation about herself; follow up on a previous conversation with another member of the group. The person who hesitates to raise a question or concern during group times needs to know that the leaders will be available at certain times for individual conversations. A woman who is ready to profess faith in Christ as her Savior will normally be more likely to take the step during a quiet conversation rather than in the middle of a group discussion.

If time permits, build relationships with the women at other times. Briefly call, write an encouraging note, plan an informal outing, or schedule a meal together. Extending interest beyond the confines of group time will help dispel any notion that non-Christians are merely viewed as targets for conversion. When appropriate, ask for their advice about issues where they can offer expertise.

B. Evaluation

A careful evaluation of the study will help to correct mistakes and point to areas that could be improved. Any Christians involved in the study should plan to meet at a separate time and discuss the presentation. The following list of questions, by no means comprehensive, may help to get the evaluation started:

- ☑ Was the leader prepared? If not, what steps need to be taken to correct this situation?

- ☑ Did the leader refrain from giving answers? Was she able to keep the topic focused, or was time wasted on tangents?

- ☑ Did everyone participate? If not, how can this be corrected? Decide on some questions for the next session that will draw out the more reserved members without making them feel self-conscious.

- ☑ Was the discussion interesting and practical? Did the women apply it to their own lives?

STOP AND APPLY

1. What are the three questions used in the Inductive
    Method of Bible study? Explain their purpose.

    1) _____?

       _____

       _____

    2) _____?

       _____

       _____

    3) _____?

       _____

       _____

2. Read the first chapter of the Gospel of John and use the
    inductive study questions. Be sure and write down
    your answers.

VII. RESOURCES

Christian bookstores carry a wide variety of inductive Bible study
booklets to get you started. Among others, InterVarsity, Harold Shaw
publishers, and Neighborhood Bible Studies produce many excellent
guides for evangelistic Bible Studies. If your budget will allow it, buy
two or three different guides that deal with the book of the Bible or
the topic selected (especially if the leader does not expect or require
individual preparation by group members). Take them home and
study them carefully. Consider not only the questions they ask but
the way they are phrased. Visualize future members of the group
and try to anticipate which study will lead to the best discussions.
Pray for the Holy Spirit to guide the choice.

There are many books that help potential leaders learn the
practical aspects of beginning an evangelistic Bible study. For
instance, try to find a copy of:

Bob and Betty Jacks, *Your Home a Lighthouse,* NavPress, 1986.

Ada Lum, *How to Begin an Evangelistic Bible Study,* InterVarsity
Press, 1971.

Marjorie Stewart, *Women in Neighborhood Evangelism*, Gospel
Publishing House, 1978.

Gladys Hunt, *You Can Start a Bible Study*, Harold Shaw.

The above list is merely intended to get women started. Books
with information on this topic are numerous and readily available.
They will give the nervous or novice leader step-by-step instruction
and encouragement. There is more than enough available material
to help anyone who is inclined to reach out in this way.

VIII. CONCLUSION

In conclusion, remember that the goal is to use the vehicle of a
Bible study to introduce people to Jesus Christ. Although the Bible
is God's inspired word and His special revelation of Himself and His
will for us, seekers are neither able nor ready to grasp this. It is of
utmost importance, then, to keep looking at the goal. Through an
examination of the Word which comes from God, pray that the
seekers meet Christ, learn of Him, and choose to become His
disciples. When the focus is misplaced, it becomes easy for a social
club to develop. When this happens, eternal fruit is usually lost.
Success comes through pointing them to Jesus—His promises,
warnings, and commands. Lost souls will be saved and disciples
developed only when they meet Jesus.

Now if you haven't already done so, listen to cassette tape #4A
in the series featuring *Evangelism and the Bible* by Anne Graham
Lotz. Also on the tape is an excerpt from a message by Martha
Reapsome.

ENDNOTES

[1] Anne Graham Lotz, Talk given at Wheaton College, Wheaton, Illinois, March 26, 1991, p. 3 of transcript.

[2] Al Vander Griend and Neva Evenhouse, *Evangelism Through Bible Discovery Groups* (Discover Your
Bible, Inc., 1976), Chapter Six.

[3] Joseph C. Aldrich, *Life-Style Evangelism* (Portland, OR: Multnomah Press, 1981), p. 191.

SESSION EIGHT
Evangelism and the Creative Arts

GOALS FOR THE CHAPTER:

After reading this chapter, you should be able to:

1. List and discuss some ways that music, drama, art, and the media can aid evangelism.

2. Explain the mechanics of starting a drama ministry in a church.

3. Know how to set up a craft fellowship for ladies.

I. INTRODUCTION

God the Creator blesses His people with talents that are expressed in infinite variations. Although the whole of God's character can never be perceived by the human mind, the diversity of humanity highlights the endless and ever-changing creativity of our Lord. Because of His great love, God does not crush and mold humans into robot-like Christians on an assembly line, but instead showers them with compassion, individuality, and unique gifts. Earlier chapters have defined the role of the evangelist as a person who carries the Good News of Jesus Christ to those who need to hear it. Therefore, the ministry of evangelism should extend to the creative arts. Music, drama, art, films, and crafts can each be used as an effective evangelistic tool.

The Bible must always remain the authority for Christians, but "properly considered, the arts are inestimable gifts of God. They can enrich our lives. They have a spiritual dimension and can enhance our relationship to God and to our neighbors."[1]

The Bible echoes with the strains of creative arts, and music plays a prominent role throughout much of it. The Old and New Testaments both have numerous examples of the purpose of music to "teach and admonish one another in psalms, hymns and spiritual songs" [Eph. 5:18].

The evangelist, Rev. Orson Parker, commented that he believed "that there is as much conviction lodged in the mind by singing as by preaching. It keeps the people together more than preaching. The melody softens the feelings and the sentiment of the hymn leaves its stamp upon the melted heart and ripens into fruit."[2] Music is also a fruit of revivals as the Holy Spirit blesses the church through a special outpouring of inspired Christian song.

In addition to music, the modern church is currently rediscovering the dramatic arts. Ironically, the history of western drama traces its roots to ancient liturgies of the church (where the first actors were clergy and the first scripts were Scripture). The refrains of the Latin liturgy expanded into dramatic dialogues and eventually led to simple plays. These dramas consistently attracted large crowds, and the church recognized in them an effective tool for teaching and worship.

In a similar manner, an abundance of resources for drama (as well as dramatic events) are contained in the pages of the Bible. The Bible has a wealth of material for skits, plays, monologues, pantomimes, and other dramatic events.

The Bible also validates the arts: "The Bible itself sanctions the arts, describing the gifts God has given to artists and recounting in loving detail works of art that were ordained by God to manifest His glory to enrich His people."[3]

Creative arts serve several useful purposes in an evangelistic service. They can:

1. *Carry a definite message to the hearts of unsaved individuals.*

2. *Attract attention and then focus that attention on the sermon or the rest of the service.*

3. *Provide a blessing to the Christian listeners.*

4. *Utilize the talents and abilities of many Christians in creative service for the church.*

Even so, Christians must be careful that these creative and different expressions are only used in a manner that will draw attention to spiritual things. We must also make certain that the presentation does not idolize the people involved, but rather Jesus Christ. "He must increase, but I must decrease" [John 3:30].

STOP AND APPLY

1. The use of creative arts in an evangelistic service can:

    a. Carry a definite _____ to the hearts of unsaved individuals.

    b. Attract _____ and then _____ that attention on the sermon or the rest of the service.

    c. Provide a _____ to the Christian listeners.

    d. Utilize the _____ and _____ of many Christians in creative service for the church.

2. If possible, list at least one instance where you have seen a creative art used in an evangelistic way.

    _____

    _____

    _____

II. MUSIC AND EVANGELISM

A. Power of Music in Evangelism

"Music has charms to soothe a savage breast" says the old expression, but science has also proven it to be true. The powerful influence of music over the human personality has been demonstrated time and time again in the lives of men and women. Music has been used to soothe insane people and to prevent attacks of epilepsy. Dentists and surgeons have long understood that certain types of music help patients withstand pain. Music can also break across barriers of race, sex, and age with a message either subtle or blatant.

The power of music is seen in every stage of life: from babies to the elderly; in homes of rich and poor; in war and peace; in the church and school. It is present everywhere. For centuries, souls have been won to Christ or empowered in Him through music. It has also strengthened weak Christians, uplifted the discouraged, and softened hardened unbelievers who sensed in it the power of the Holy Spirit. Sacred music can create a powerful emotional stimulus, leading men and women to make an eternal decision.

L. R. Scarborough, a former president of Southwestern Baptist Theological Seminary, once remarked about the power of music in evangelism that:

> Sermons have been spoken to enraptured audiences, printed in tracts and books and have gone out to bless the world, but what sermon has gone further or reached as many souls and inspired and enabled as many lives as have many of the great songs of Zion? 'Amazing Grace,' 'How Firm a Foundation,' 'Rock of Ages,' and many others sound out today their gospel message to stir and inspire lives to noble deeds in a fashion never known by the sermons of any of the world-famed preachers... Only the records of heaven will be able to measure the value of songs in the lives, worship and spiritual work of God's people through the centuries as they have wrought for Christ. Spiritual song has ever been the inspirational handmaiden of gospel preaching and teaching.[4]

Likewise in the history of the church, the creative arts have played an important role. Numerous spiritual awakenings gave rise to many of our greatest hymns (such as those which Martin Luther penned during the Reformation). Other lyrics and melodies also had a far-reaching effect on church and personal renewal. Charles Wesley's music encouraged the revival in Great Britain and did almost as much as the sermons of his brother, John Wesley, to spread awakening in England and to spread Methodism worldwide.

B. Purpose of Music in Evangelism
Evangelism is frequently more effective when coupled with music. However, evangelistic music should never become an end in itself. Rather, its primary purpose in the ministry of evangelism is to prepare the heart and mind of the seeker to hear God's Word and also to remove any wrong attitudes that would block the message.

> An Ohio woman wrote to Bev Shea [a member of the Billy Graham team], telling him that she had turned on the gas jets, plugged the cracks in her kitchen door, turned on the radio, and lain down on the floor to end her life. As she drifted into unconsciousness the radio program changed to "Hour of Decision" and Bev's voice singing, "Known Only to Him," was used by the Spirit of

God to arouse her. She found enough strength to turn off the jets and she wrote Bev, "My life has been spared, and I have given it to Christ, and I owe it to the Spirit singing through you."[5]

When they attend a church service, many Christians find that their greatest spiritual blessing comes through song. The emotional element in music provides a close union with the Spirit of God, and that relationship leads individuals to outward expressions of worship to God.

Music plays many roles in evangelism. Worship, education, and evangelism are three expressions of the function of church music, but it can also:

1.   Create an evangelistic atmosphere and prepare the heart for worship.

2.   Unite the congregation in bonds of fellowship.

3.   Give expression to common doctrinal and religious beliefs of the congregation.

4.   Serve as a vehicle for bringing the individual or whole congregation into the presence of God.

5.   Teach and preach the truth of God and His Word.

6.   Lift and encourage people.

7.   Melt and break down hearts.

8.   Enrich the life of the preacher.

9.   Provide a medium for congregational testimony.

10.   Help to center the attention of the audience on spiritual things.

11.   Provide an opportunity for conviction of sins.

12.   Powerfully attract non-Christians to a worship service.

Moreover, music provides an effective cultural tool for breaking down barriers and preparing hearts on the mission field. At the turn of the century, W. G. Bagy (ministering in Santos, Brazil) reported with great interest:

> Our songs always attracted the multitude, and they came flocking around from all sides. The members of our band. . . were greatly cheered by this first attempt at open air preaching in Santos, and so last Sunday they eagerly joined me in another meeting in the same place, and this time fully three hundred persons soon crowded about us as we sang, and listened eagerly to the message of life.[6]

What a remarkable place music has in evangelism! Cliff Barrows, a crusade musician for the Billy Graham Association, eloquently acknowledged the unique role of music in evangelism when he wrote:

> I submit to you that music employed in evangelism, which can be used by the Spirit of God to motivate and inspire an individual so that he commits his heart and life in complete surrender and dedication to Jesus Christ as Saviour and Lord, is one of the highest forms of music and worship. It also is one of the noblest uses that can be made of the musical arts.[7]

C. Preparation for Using Evangelistic Music

When using any of the creative arts, remember to consider carefully the people you hope to reach. Take into account their social and economic background, their geographical location, and their knowledge and appreciation of hymns.

Careful rehearsal is a requirement for effective evangelistic music. It should always be played with the best technical skills possible. God is not honored (nor the church uplifted) when the music reflects inadequate preparation.

Furthermore, the hearts of musicians need to be in harmony with the message they plan to share. Purity of life and motive are prerequisites for the proclamation of the gospel. Spiritual songs will only be produced by spiritual singers. The choir member, as well as the soloist, must lose all consciousness of self and be absorbed in the song. The message, not the messenger, should command the congregation's attention. The emotional content of the music should be meditative, and contribute to an atmosphere which prepares individuals to worship a Holy God.

D. Practical Uses of Music in Evangelism

"Congregational singing is an important means of expression. As masses of people join simultaneously in singing songs of prayer, praise, commitment, edification and testimony, believers encourage, admonish and inspire one another."[8]

Perhaps the most effective music used in evangelism are the songs of personal experience. Testimony in song is often more powerful than that which is spoken, because the melody carries the text in a moving rhythmic pattern and appeals to the emotions. This is not to say that testimony in song should replace the spoken word, but rather that it can strengthen the message of the speaker.

> *One young woman recalls how she was driving to work one day when she heard the song "The Old Rugged Cross" on the radio. She had not attended church since she was a child, but the words to that old hymn came back to her. She found herself in tears over the words; hearing and remembering that song led her to give her life to Christ.*

Effective evangelistic music is certainly not limited to its role in the Sunday service. There are numerous opportunities for using music in both formal and informal settings throughout the week.

Music can be invaluable in working with children's groups, Vacation Bible Schools, Backyard Bible Clubs, and other special events to teach important doctrinal truths and plant seeds in children's minds. It does not even have to be a major production. Simply singing songs or using cassette tapes around the house, in the car, or at bedtimes instills in children a love for God and His Word. It is very refreshing and exciting to hear a toddler walk around the house or sit in a grocery cart singing songs such as "Jesus Loves Me," "Jesus Loves the Little Children," or "The B-I-B-L-E." "For out of the overflow of the heart the mouth speaks" [Matt. 12:34].

Jamie went to a vacation Bible School where she learned a song that went like this:
"He paid a debt He did not owe,
I owed a debt I could not pay.
I needed someone to take my sins away.
And now I sing a brand new song 'Amazing Grace.'
Christ Jesus paid a debt that I could never pay."

She was singing this as she was playing with her dolls. Her mother overheard her, listened to the words she was singing and felt her heart stirring with the need for someone to take her sins away. She decided to take her children to church and several weeks later accepted Christ as her personal Lord and Savior.[9]

In trying to reach young people, contemporary Christian music nearly always attracts a large number. There are numerous contemporary Christian musicians who provide a wide variety of music and styles. Concerts utilizing these performers can be arranged as an outreach event, or they can be part of a youth retreat or special weekend.

If an evangelistic concert is planned, the young Christians should be specially trained to present the gospel effectively. The Christian young people need to be active and intentional about inviting friends and acquaintances from schools or the community. The steps to salvation must be clearly shared during the evening with an opportunity offered to accept Christ. After the concert, those who made decisions need someone to follow up and teach them the basics of Christianity. (See the chapter on Evangelism and Disciplemaking.) Those who did not respond positively should be included in other appropriate activities at the church, and should be offered continual hospitality and friendship.

With young and older adults, a variety show, madrigal dinner, or concert can offer an avenue for making contact with nonbelievers. As a pre-evangelism event, First Baptist Church of Libertyville, Illinois once held a Valentine's Dinner with a 1950s musical theme for the evening. After a catered meal, different lay people from the church shared their musical talent by singing secular songs popular in the '50s. It was a fun night and provided a good opportunity to build relationships with many of the adults in the community.

STOP AND APPLY

Circle the best answer:

1. Three different functions of Christian music are:
   a. encouragement, worship, and teaching
   b. worship, education, and evangelism
   c. entertainment, testimony, and education

2. Perhaps the most effective music used in evangelism are songs:
   a. that are fast
   b. that are contemporary
   c. of personal experience

3. Testimony in song:
   a. should always be slow and pensive
   b. can strengthen the message of the speaker
   c. replaces the spoken word

4. Music is helpful for teaching evangelistic truths to:
   a. children   c. adults
   b. youth   d. all of the above

Fill in the blanks:

5. When using any of the creative arts, remember to carefully consider the _____ you hope to reach.

6. Careful _____ is a requirement for effective evangelistic music.

7. Spiritual songs will only be produced by _____ singers.

III. EVANGELISM AND DRAMA

A. *Purpose of Drama in Evangelism*

Christians should be interested in drama because drama is a gift from God to help us "explore the world, enjoy it, to be moved by suffering, to laugh at the funny side of life, to provoke ourselves and others to thought."[10]

Jeanette Clift George said, "the world has been dialoguing through creativity since its beginning ... We're speaking not only the language of the nonbeliever that we might acquaint them with the acts of the person of the Lord Jesus Christ, we're also speaking the language of the believer. Entertainment is a desire for appetite, for entertainment is a healthy appetite. It has been misused. But it is a healthy appetite. We're speaking God's language. We're speaking their language."[11]

The church needs to come to terms with drama, because drama has become the most popular form of entertainment today due to television, movie theaters, and VCRs. Drama, like music, supports and enhances evangelism for a variety of reasons. Because drama presents a story, it attracts attention easily and it:

1. *Relaxes an audience.* People are not uptight about drama, and it does not raise as many defense barriers as other types of evangelism.

2. *Inspires worship.* Congregations grow spiritually through seeing Christianity in action or watching the Scriptures come alive. Providing something visual often helps people to focus attention on the things of God.

3. *Helps the preacher.* Television has shortened our attention span. Drama makes the gospel come alive. Short pieces of drama can also break up long talks and create a positive atmosphere or set a particular mood.

4. *Provides an effective means of teaching the Bible.* The Bible is full of material which is perfect for dramatization. Scripture is replete with incidents that portray ordinary men and women and their interactions with God in a format that can be easily adapted to drama.

5. *Promotes reflection of ourselves.* Drama can encourage the audience to examine their lives, feel the conviction of sin, and realize their need for God.

6. *Presents the gospel.* Drama is especially effective for sowing spiritual seeds.

Before moving on to the "how to's" of drama, Christians must make sure they maintain high artistic standards that match the spiritual message and convey an attitude of respect. If we think of it only as fun or a gimmick, it will be just that. Approached prayerfully, creatively, and with reverence, drama becomes a legitimate and effective way of communicating. Drama has the potential to affect the viewer on a deeper level than even the sermon, because it adds a visual element to the message.

Pam Hiscock, Director of Communications at Christ Community Church of St. Charles, Illinois cautions would-be drama companies to remember two primary rules:

1. *If people are going to listen to the message of the drama, the productions must be of professional quality. If lines are missed or people perform poorly, the congregation will concentrate on the mistakes, not the message.*

2. *The actors must understand that this is a ministry and they are servants. It is tempting for actors to seek the spotlight for their talent, "but a servant's heart is necessary for precisely the same reason... being on stage every week means that this person is going to be watched and noticed by the congregation and must be setting an example."*

B. How to Start a Drama Group

Willow Creek Community Church in Barrington, Illinois, has a well-respected drama ministry. Over the years, they have formulated some guidelines to help others who would like to establish a similar program. Steve Pederson, Willow Creek's drama director, suggests that you can begin with one person or a small team who has the vision, determination, dramatic and technical skills, and a call from God. This point person (and the team around him/her) will direct the major facets of the ministry. They will need to supervise the development of scripts (or find resources for them), recruit actors, direct the rehearsals, obtain props, coordinate with the worship committee or pastor, and evaluate the material, performance, and impact of the dramas presented. The key person or team should be identified and confirmed by church leaders before taking any other steps. Churches must resist the temptation to start with only well-intentioned people who do not have strong enough leadership skills or drama experience.

After the team is identified, they should begin to locate actors and actresses. Auditions, when properly promoted, will usually attract the needed people but the team should feel free to personally invite anyone who shows potential. The person who needs a nudge is often a better actor than natural "hams." Those who listen to the people who are auditioning should look for clarity, expression, and feeling.

Actors and actresses who participate in the drama ministry must be committed to Christ and to the work of the church. Participation on the team is their contribution to the church, just as Sunday School teachers or choir members freely give of their time. However, the team also needs to feel challenged and appreciated by the congregation. If they believe their contribution is significant and if they enjoy the discipline and work required, the ministry will serve the needs of the team as well as of the church.

C. Writing Sketches

Ideally, church drama groups should write their own sketches, even though this presents a major challenge for the troupe. Locally written and produced sketches can be tailored to fit the specifics of the sermon and the unique character of each congregation. However, many resources are available for fledgling programs or those who are unable to write their own scripts. (See the resource section at Appendix B for suggestions.)

Drama groups that want to write their own sketches should begin by following these steps:

1. *Pray*

2. *Brainstorm with a committee for ideas, but assign the actual writing to only one or two persons.* Possible ideas for the sketches or dramas are often found in news publications or in media dealing with issues of current interest. Modernizing the language of a Bible story or parable will give it a fresh look and spark interest. For example, a drama presented in Britain illustrated the parable of the sower by depicting actors dressed as four crates of strawberries entering a jam factory in Liverpool.

3. *Study the context and environment where the performance will be presented.* Is the context a worship service or a street drama? What about acoustics? Where are the sight lines?

4. *Keep the audience in mind.* This is a basic rule of communication. Consider the ages and groups of people that will be in attendance. For instance, the weekly dramas at Willow Creek Community Church appeal to unbelievers by raising questions that will later be addressed in the sermon. In one sketch called "Great Expectations," a couple waits to adopt a baby. At the last minute, the birth mother changes

her mind and decides not to give up the infant. The adoptive mother lashes out, calling God unfair. The audience can readily identify with her reaction, because the sketch deals realistically with the issues. The pastor then offers a Christian perspective during the sermon.

5. ***Keep the sketches short.*** Six to eight minutes is an ideal length. They should be clever, different, concise, and unpredictable. Predictability is guaranteed to kill interest.

Churches that decide to write their own material should also keep in mind what Steve Pederson labels the six "C's":

☑ **Conflict**—this drives the drama and gives it energy; it shows two ways of looking at a situation. The more conflict the sketch has, the more power it has.

☑ **Clarity**—you should be able to summarize the sketch in one sentence to make sure the message is coming across loud and clear.

☑ **Concise plot**—the drama should get started right away and only include what is necessary for the point of the sketch. Avoid covering too much material. After you write it, set it aside and look at it again in a fresh way to see if it is as concise as possible. Experienced writers say that it's important to let their scripts rest before doing the final versions.

☑ **Credibility**—ask yourself "Do I believe it?" Is it real, or is it beyond what is believable?

☑ **Construction**—a sketch needs a structure to it; that is, a beginning, a middle and an end. The opening dialogue or interplay captures attention; exciting action introduces the main conflict; the rising of tension produced by the conflict climaxes and resolution begins; finally, the receding action or wrap-up brings the drama to a conclusion.

☑ **Content**—a sketch needs to maintain interest and not repeat the same point over and over again. Employ a hook or change in the plot to help sustain interest so that it will not be predictable. Try to avoid humor that is extraneous to the plot, as this cheapens the performance. Humor should be bound up in the reality of the characters.

The ideal sketch has a simple story line with fast-paced action and utilizes humor and surprise while building to a dramatic finish. Finally, submit proposed scripts to qualified people who understand the mindset of the congregation and who also have the technical skills to evaluate the effectiveness of the material.

6. **Dramatic monologues of a biblical character offer another avenue of effective drama.** In using monologues, Jeanette George shares from one instance where she was part of a foreign mission fine arts program on the island of Grenada:

   We performed there for the natives, for the Grenadians. They came. They had music. They had drama. They had puppet shows. They had singers. I did some monologues. It was wonderful. And soon after that Grenada fell. Later I received a letter from one of the missionaries as they were asked to leave. He said that of everything that came to that island, what he thought spoke clearest to the people was the fine arts festival. And he felt that God had sent us there just in time. [12]

D. Performing the Drama

A drama should have one director whose decisions are final. Planning should be done well in advance to allow time for writing, rehearsal, and staging. Secure or construct quality sets and costumes, and utilize the stage area to the best possible advantage.

Sketches should be well-rehearsed but still seem fresh. Sometimes a brief introduction may be necessary to tie the sketch to the service. Always start on time and concentrate the action. Practice good diction and voice projection. Learn how to create character and deliver a comic line. Keep the pace lively and the dress and props simple.

Actors should be perceived as real—not staged or stiff. Look for people who are comfortable on stage and will draw the audience into the story. Keep the cues tight with no gaps in conversation. Keep the sketch moving.

E. Street Drama

Street theater offers a unique avenue for communicating the gospel. Because the audience is not captive, the drama should be exciting. In street theater, a bored audience will simply walk away.

Look for a location large enough to allow people to gather and watch or easily walk around the group if they choose not to stop. If it is public property, secure the proper permissions. The area must be large enough to accommodate the stage and still give the audience plenty of room. Avoid locations with lots of loud noises such as traffic or industrial sounds.

Gather a crowd by setting up interesting props, having costumed actors out in front, or using music with a dynamic beat. The first act of a street play should be fast moving, funny, and short. Then keep it moving—try not to go past 20–30 minutes. A good MC welcomes people, introduces the group, provides continuity between sketches and invites the audience to any upcoming events. Move from a fast, funny beginning to a serious sketch of the message, and end on a lively note. Many dramas close with an upbeat song that reinforces the message of the production.

F. Examples of Churches Who Effectively Use Drama

1. Willow Creek Community Church

Approximately twenty actors make up the drama team at Willow Creek Community Church. Not only does the church place a high priority on the quality of the performances, but also on the relationships between members of the team. Consequently, the members are encouraged to share personal needs and joys with each other. Retreats, day-long fellowships, and other community-building activities have helped foster a unique comfort level within the group. Their close relationship enables them to work and act well together.

The drama group meets every Tuesday evening from 7–8:30 p.m. for a time of sharing and acting exercises. The ones participating in services during the upcoming weekend stay to practice from 8:30–10 p.m. Casting and distribution of scripts for each drama are done a couple of weeks ahead of time so that the actors can memorize their parts before coming to the Tuesday rehearsal. Then actors involved in next Sunday's service meet again later in the week for another ninety-minute practice to fine-tune the sketch.

Designed to focus attention on the upcoming sermon, these six- to eight-minute sketches try to avoid "preaching." Instead, they attempt to present the congregation with believable characters who wrestle with everyday problems. Easy answers are avoided as the troupe strives to communicate with the non-churched.

2. Christ Community Church

Located in St. Charles, Illinois, Christ Community Church has also found drama to be an effective tool in evangelism, and they incorporate it into their weekly services.

Each month, a group of creative people get together with the Senior Pastor to brainstorm ideas for the upcoming weeks. At this meeting, the pastor shares the sermon topics for future messages and then each person spends fifteen minutes formulating possible drama themes. The team reassembles, pools their thoughts, and selects the best idea to shape into an appropriate script that will illustrate the Sunday morning messages.

Their sketches are usually humorous and are geared for a non-believing audience. For most productions, the setting is something familiar (such as a modern home or work environment). Rather than solving problems, the dramas raise issues that the sermon will address.

Selected by auditions, the drama team has fourteen members who meet each Wednesday for script assignments and rehearsal. An average script is three to five typewritten pages and requires two to four actors. Those participating in the weekend service meet for additional rehearsals on Saturday and Sunday mornings. The team also attends a quarterly acting workshop to brush up on acting techniques and to sharpen their skills.

Membership in the drama group requires a serious commitment of time and energy. Before being accepted, each actor must agree to the following specific ministry requirements:

☑ *To be available for performing periodic Sunday morning drama routines as well as acting in the annual Christmas productions, Easter services, and periodic special events.*

☑ *To promptly attend the rehearsals given for any of the above.*

☑ *To be open to contributing to the support of the Drama Company ministry through whatever abilities one can offer (props, costumes, ideas for drama).*

☑ *To attend any drama workshops that are given. These workshops are provided to improve drama skills, give evaluations, and build all the actors into a unified team.*

G. Professional Drama Groups

If starting a local drama ministry is not possible, churches or women's organizations should consider using outside groups as "special" or "occasional" resources. Explore possibilities in your area or contact one or more of the professional groups listed below:

1. Lamb's Players

The Lamb's Players, a drama group based in San Diego, California, has a year-round production schedule, and its touring companies have performed throughout the world. A pioneer in the dramatic arts, this group combines a full-time ensemble of actors, designers, directors, and playwrights with the purpose of bringing together evangelism and drama.

2. After Dinner Players

The A. D. Players are a professional drama company under the leadership of Artistic Director and Playwright-In-Residence Jeannette Clift George, famous for her film debut as Corrie Ten Boom in World Wide Pictures' *The Hiding Place*. They seek to honor God by bringing alive biblical truths.

The A. D. Players Repertory Series consists of a variety of plays ranging from five minutes to an hour in length which are perfect for church programs, college chapels, civic events or any occasion. Their ministry includes participating in Sunday services, youth programs, conferences and retreats, college concerts, evangelism outreaches, and theater workshops. They offer imaginative, inspirational, thought-provoking programming with wide audience appeal.

3. Impact Productions of "Toymaker's Dream"

Toymaker's Dream is a powerful stage presentation depicting the biblical account of man's creation, fall from God's grace in the Garden of Eden, and redemption provided by the life and death of Jesus Christ. The cast and crew use mime, jazz, ballet, modern dance, gymnastics and karate, along with creative costumes, elaborate lighting, lasers, and an original soundtrack.

The play has been seen by over a million people in the U.S. and in nine foreign countries. Over 100,000 people have made a public declaration of faith as a result of the performance.

STOP AND APPLY

1. Put a checkmark by the appropriate purposes of drama in evangelism:
   - ❐ Relaxes an audience
   - ❐ Teaches the Bible
   - ❐ Makes money
   - ❐ Inspires worship
   - ❐ Sows spiritual seed
   - ❐ Helps the preacher

2. When using drama, Christians must carefully maintain high _____ standards that match the _____ message.

3. Drama has the potential to affect the viewer on a deeper level than even the sermon can, because it adds the _____ element to the message.

Put a **T** for True and **F** for False:

___ 4. A drama ministry can begin with one person or a small team who have vision, determination, dramatic skills, and a call from God.

___ 5. You should use anyone who asks to be on the drama team whether or not they have any acting skills.

___ 6. If actors/actresses are good in drama and are willing to be on the drama team, it does not matter whether or not they are a Christian.

___ 7. The ideal sketch has a simple story line with fast-paced action and utilizes humor and surprise while building to a dramatic finish.

___ 8. A drama should have co-directors to help give necessary leadership.

___ 9. Street drama should start with an act that is fast, moving, funny, and short.

10. How could drama be used in your church?

IV. VISUAL EVANGELISM

A. Evangelism and Art

The purpose of art is not to preach, but to portray the message of the gospel in a life-changing way.

> *The young nobleman, as part of the "grand tour" of Europe that was customary for eighteen-year-olds of his rank, was going through the art gallery in Dusseldorf. He found himself staring at a painting by the baroque artist Domenico Feti. Entitled "Ecce Homo," it depicted Christ—scourged, bound, and crowned with thorns. At the bottom of the painting, Feti had added a Latin inscription: "This I have done for you, but what have you done for me?" Haunted by the expression in the painting and the accusation of the inscription, the young man proclaimed that he would dedicate his life in service to Christ. Thus began the career of Nicholas von Zinzendorf, founder of Lutheran pietism, whose emphasis on missionary work and personal evangelism was to have a major impact on American Christianity.* [13]

The gospel sometimes needs "defamiliarizing," even for Christians. Art can offer a fresh look at the message of salvation. If Scripture is clearly present in a painting, it can become an effective witness by using visual images that draw attention to the truth of Christ. According to noted art historian and critic, E. H. Gombrich: "A visual image alone cannot convey meaning in the sense that language can. Yet visual images do carry meaning, which can be interpreted according to what [is termed] their 'code, caption and context.' " [14]

The code is the set of symbols used—a type of language. When most people see a picture of a man on a cross, they will associate it with Jesus. The caption is the words that go with the art. The context refers to the setting of the art. For example, a piece of tapestry with a design on it can be an art form in itself, a flag in a battle, or a banner of praise in a church.

At the Billy Graham Center Museum at Wheaton College, more than a thousand pieces of artwork from hundreds of artists are on display yearly. James D. Stambaugh, Director of the Museum, seeks "art done from a Christian perspective that will serve the Christian community and be a vital witness to secular society as well... No other human endeavor more accurately conveys the substance of a people, a time, or a place, than its art."[15] Stambaugh goes on to say:

> For the Christian, art should never be for its own sake but as an expression of the transformed life and the singular vision which God has given the artist. The role of the Christian artist is that of a servant vessel through [whom] God's Spirit communicates his great eternal themes of holiness, judgment, grace, and redemption through Jesus Christ.[16]

B. Evangelism and the Media

Many Christians use films or videos as part of their evangelistic outreach. The feature film or full-length movies often have a compelling story which will attract a large audience. Films of sermons, lecture series, or documentaries usually stimulate discussion. These productions are normally thirty minutes or less and deal with specific issues.

Media evangelism can be used in public places or in the home. When planning for a major public showing, several factors require careful consideration. Is the film or video truly evangelistic? Not all Christian films speak to unbelievers; many are designed to edify and encourage Christians. Both types are important, but only evangelistic films are designed to reach unbelievers. *Worldwide Pictures* (the film ministry of the Billy Graham Evangelistic Association) has produced several effective evangelistic films. Refer to Appendix B for their address to get a current listing and description of their film library.

Logistics matter too. How are the acoustics in the room where the film or video will be shown? People cannot respond to a message they cannot hear. Nor will they attend an event unless it is publicized. Fliers, announcements, ads in newspapers, and word-of-mouth recommendations will help you gather a large audience. Christians trained to share the gospel should be available to answer questions following the presentation.

Finally, on the day of the film, be sure to check the lighting, power, light switches, fire exits, projector lens and projector, and make sure the screen is big enough. Allow enough time to set up the equipment so things can start smoothly.

Home video evenings offer an informal alterna-tive. Family, friends, neighbors, or colleagues can be invited. Light refreshments and a relaxed atmo-sphere create a perfect climate. Remember that the goal is discussion. There are numerous children's videos out that instill Christian character qualities and creatively express the message of the Gospel. Contemporary Christian music videos readily attract youth. See your local Christian bookstore for the latest releases.

C. Crafts and Evangelism

Something as simple as a craft has frequently become the vehicle for successfully sharing the gospel in a church or home. It can also be an effective tool at conferences and retreats to draw unchurched women, and to encourage other women to more effectively use their gifts for God's glory.

Invitations or flyers should inform the guests about the time, place, and the proposed craft. If the activity requires costly mate-rials, a nominal fee or free-will offering can help to offset costs. Provide a basket at the event where contributions can be placed. Always include an R.S.V.P. so that you will know the amount of materials to purchase.

Set up tables with designated work spaces before the guests arrive. For some crafts, it may be possible to have many of the required items placed in zip-lock bags so that everything is orga-nized and free from confusion. Be sure to have a sample of the completed craft as a model.

Serve light refreshments while the women are arriving. After a short time of conversation, begin the event with a testimony or devotion. Then have the person leading the craft explain how to do it step-by-step. Conversation and completion of the program round out the evening.

The hostess or sponsor need not teach the craft or lead the devotional. Enlisting the help of others lessens the burden on everyone and encourages more women to become involved in this creative form of evangelism. Nonbelievers are especially open to these events, which often "break the ice" and lead to fruitful conversation.

STOP AND APPLY

1. The purpose of art is not to _____ but to _____ the message of the gospel.

2. If Scripture is clearly present in a painting, it can raise visual images that draw attention to the truth of _____.

3. Feature films or full-length movies often have a compelling story which will attract a large _____, whereas films of sermons or documentaries usually stimulate _____.

4. _____ video evenings provide an informal alternative to media evangelism in public places.

5. Crafts can become the vehicle for successfully sharing the _____ in a church or home.

6. Check with your local Christian bookstore to see what Christian videos are available. Choose one evangelistic video to share with at least one person, whether it be your own child, a family member, or friend. Write down his/her name and the name of the video:

Person _____ Video _____

V. CONCLUSION

God-given talent, training, proficiency, and technical aspects are important for the creative arts, but the inspiration of the Holy Spirit is absolutely essential. Ultimately, evangelism and the arts must challenge the sinner to repent and confess the need for Christ. "As recipients of grace, our message is an independent and objective fact given from above with the command to go and tell."[17]

Now if you haven't already done so, listen to cassette tape #4B in the series featuring *Evangelism and the Use of Drama* by Jeanette Clift George. Also on the tape are excerpts from messages by Gloria Gaither and Karen Patitucci.

ENDNOTES

[1] Leland Ryken, *Culture in the Christian Perspective: A Door to Understanding and Enjoying the Arts* (Multnomah Press, 1986).

[2] Edwin McNeely, *Evangelistic Music* (Ft. Worth: Seminary Hill Press, 1959), p. 3.

[3] Gene Edward Veith, Jr., Book review: "State of the Arts: From Bezalel to Mapplethorpe" (Crossway Books, 1991).

[4] L. R. Scarborough, *With Christ After the Lost* (New York: George Doran Company, 1919), p. 115.

[5] Cliff Barrows, "Musical Evangelism" (Oct. 1963), p. 8.

[6] T. W. Hunt, *Music in Missions: Discipling Through Music* (Nashville: Broadman Press, 1987), p. 13.

[7] Barrows, p. 9.

[8] McLellan, p. 62.

[9] Jeanette Clift George, "Symposium on Evangelizing Through Music and Drama," Wheaton College, Wheaton, IL, June 19, 1987.

[10] Paul Burbridge and Murray Watts, *Time to Act* (Toronto: Hodder and Stoughton, 1979), p. 112.

[11] George.

[12] *Ibid.*

[13] Gene Edward Veith, Jr., "Art and Evangelism," *Evangelism* (Mequon, Wisconsin, Spring, 1988), p. 115.

[14] *Ibid.*, p. 118.

[15] James D. Stambaugh, "Renewing the Vision."

[16] *Ibid.*

[17] T.W. Hunt, *Communicative Method of Musical Evangelism* (Ft. Worth, TX: Southwestern Baptist Theological Seminary, 1973).

SESSION NINE
Evangelism Through Social Ministry

GOALS FOR THE CHAPTER:

After reading this chapter, you should be able to:

1. Define the terms "social ministry" and "social action."

2. Understand differing views on the relationship between evangelism and social responsibility.

3. Use social ministry as a bridge to evangelism.

4. Outline the general principles for churches interested in an evangelistically-oriented social ministry.

5. Summarize a specific strategy to begin evangelism through social ministry.

I. INTRODUCTION

More than 800 million people lack the basic necessities for life. Thousands of people die of starvation every day, while others live without adequate housing, clothing, water, medical care, and means to support themselves. Many are even denied basic human rights by dictatorial governments. People are discriminated against because of the color of their skin and their gender. More than 500 million people in the world are disabled. What can we do about these needs?

A. Definitions of Social Ministry and Social Action

Social *ministry* refers to helping *individuals* with special needs—that is, the poor, sick, aged, hurting, widowed, and bereaved. It consists of meeting practical needs through works of mercy. Social *action* refers to changing basic *conditions* that cause the hurt which affects individuals. It demands looking beyond the individual's needs to the structures which may need to be overhauled—that is, looking beyond the needs of the prison inmate to reforming the prison system, or looking beyond the poverty stricken to changing the economic system. Therefore, social *change* is the goal of social action.

Christians should be involved in social ministry to help individuals who are poor, hungry, jobless, homeless, illiterate, destitute, or elderly, but they must also work for social action to change oppressive social structures and institutions. Loving concern must be expressed to hurting individuals, but the circumstances which produce bad social conditions *need to be changed.*

B. Problems in Society

Our society reflects a multitude of problems, most of which can be grouped into general categories. These can be divided into five areas. There are issues related to:

1. **Family life**—divorce, single parents, orphans, widows, black market baby adoptions, mental illness, "mercy" killings, unwanted pregnancies, sex education, parent-child relations, child and spouse abuse, aging.

2. **Moral concerns**—AIDS, abortion, medical care, alcohol and drug abuse, gambling, pornography, prostitution, venereal disease.

3. **Community**—juvenile delinquency, segregation, housing problems, crime.

4. **Economics**—poverty, abuse of credit, unemployment, welfare programs, working conditions, job safety, inflation.

5. **National affairs**—political corruption, war, overpopulation, disarmament.

How do all of these problems relate to the topic of evangelism?

II. RELATIONSHIP BETWEEN EVANGELISM AND SOCIAL RESPONSIBILITY

Christians have struggled for years to discern the proper relationship between evangelism and social responsibility. The *Lausanne Covenant* (a landmark document written in 1974 as a result of an International Congress on World Evangelization at Lausanne, Switzerland) brought this crucial issue to the forefront. Building on two sections, which discussed evangelism and Christian social responsibility respectively, the portion titled "Evangelism and the Church" clearly announced that "in the church's mission of sacrificial service evangelism is primary."[1]

Discussion continued in the years following Lausanne, culminating in a significant meeting held in Grand Rapids, Michigan, in 1982, which produced the report entitled "Evangelism and Social Responsibility: An Evangelical Commitment." This important document examined three different aspects of the relationship between evangelism and social responsibility.

First, social activity comes about as a *consequence* of evangelism. God uses evangelism to bring persons to a new birth, and their new life in Christ should manifest itself through loving service to others.

Second, social activity serves as a *bridge* to evangelism. It can help break down walls people have erected, making them more open to hearing the gospel. Expressions of social concern which help to meet physical needs provide a powerful platform for sharing the good news of salvation available through Christ's atoning work.

Finally, social activity accompanies evangelism as a *partner*, because both express compassion for the needs of people.

The purpose of this chapter is to examine social activity as a bridge to evangelism. How can loving concern for people's physical needs be combined with a heartfelt concern to share with them the message of the Gospel and its eternal consequences? How can social ministry aid evangelism?

Reaffirming the statement in the *Lausanne Covenant* that "in the church's mission of sacrificial service evangelism is primary" (Paragraph 6), the Grand Rapids report explained that:

> … if we must choose [between evangelism and social ministry], then we have to say that the supreme and ultimate need of all humankind is the saving grace of Jesus Christ, and that therefore a person's eternal, spiritual salvation is of greater importance than his or her temporal and material well-being (cf. II Cor. 4:16-18).[2]

When Christians share the Good News, they are influencing people's eternal destiny because they are doing what no one else can do. As Anne Graham Lotz once pointed out, most of the patients that her grandfather (Dr. Nelson Bell, medical missionary to China) treated are now dead. If he had only met their physical needs without also addressing their spiritual needs, they would have entered a Christless eternity. Dealing with physical needs is essential in evangelistic outreach.

Lasting social change will only take place as people are transformed through the message of evangelism. Tony Campolo makes this point when he says:

> God's kingdom does not become a reality simply by facilitating a few positive social changes with the expectation that all will be well if we can just eliminate corrupt institutional structures. On the contrary, there will be no kingdom unless it is populated by people who incarnate the nature and the values of the King. This can't happen until the King transforms them into His character and likeness. People need to be saved from sin. They need to be converted. They need to be made into new creatures. Transformations in the lives of individuals are essential before we can have the kind of people who can effect the institutional changes which are essential if the kingdom is to come "on earth as it is in heaven."[3]

III. BIBLICAL EXAMPLES OF SOCIAL CONCERN

A. *Old Testament*

The God of justice, as frequently seen in the Old Testament, cares for the needy. Psalm 146:5–9 echoes the oft repeated sentiment:

> *Blessed is he whose help is the God of Jacob,*
>   *whose hope is in the Lord his God,*
> *the Maker of heaven and earth,*
>   *the sea and everything in them—*
>   *the Lord, who remains faithful forever.*
> *He upholds the cause of the oppressed*
>   *and gives food to the hungry.*
> *The Lord sets prisoners free,*
>   *the Lord gives sight to the blind,*
> *the Lord lifts up those who are bowed down,*
>   *the Lord loves the righteous.*
> *The Lord watches over the alien*
>   *and sustains the fatherless and the widow,*
>   *but he frustrates the ways of the wicked.*

The Old Testament is full of examples of social ministry to the sick, the hungry, the elderly, orphans, widows, divorcées, and the poor, as well as strangers and slaves. The prophets continually reminded God's people that He wants them to be involved in acts of mercy, justice, and love.

B. New Testament

Likewise, the ministry of Jesus displays a similar social concern. He Himself said, "For even the Son of Man did not come to be served, but to serve" [Mark 10:45]. Matthew 9:35 further shows how Jesus was concerned with meeting the physical, spiritual, mental, and emotional needs of people—"Jesus went through all the towns and villages, teaching in their synagogues, preaching the good news of the kingdom and healing every disease and sickness." Jesus ministered not only to the rich but to the poor, not only to the well but also the sick, not only to the young but to the old, not only to the Jews but to the Gentiles, not only to men but also to women. He ministered to the hungry, the destitute, the outcasts, the grieving. Not surprisingly, then, what He practiced came through strongly in His preaching. Indeed, social ministry should be rendered as an act of worship to the Lord:

> *"For I was hungry and you gave me something to eat, I was thirsty and you gave me something to drink, I was a stranger and you invited me in, I needed clothes and you clothed me, I was sick and you looked after me, I was in prison and you came to visit me." Then the righteous will answer him, "Lord, when did we see you hungry and feed you, or thirsty and give you something to drink? When did we see you a stranger and invite you in, or needing clothes and clothe you? When did we see you sick or in prison and go to visit you? The King will reply, "I tell you the truth, whatever you did for one of the least of these brothers of mine, you did for me" [Matt. 25:35–40].*

The early church carefully followed Christ's example and quickly became involved in social ministry. Peter and John express this sensitivity in the way they ministered to the lame beggar at Gate Beautiful. Shortly after that, the sixth chapter of Acts describes the formation of a social ministry group.

Writing to the Galatians, Paul (in accord with Peter, James, and John) urges his readers to remember the poor. Furthermore, the New Testament exhorts all Christians to express their faith through good works (James 2:14–18), which Ephesians 2:8–10 teaches is the purpose for which Christians were created.

STOP AND APPLY

1. Social ministry refers to helping _____ with special needs, whereas social action refers to changing basic _____ that affect the individual.

2. Social _____ is the goal of social action.

3. Lasting social change will only take place as people are transformed through the message of _____.

4. Briefly explain why evangelism should always retain primacy over social action.

5. Give an instance that shows how Jesus used social ministry as a bridge to evangelism.

6. Mark your level of awareness of the relationship of evangelism to social responsibility:

    1   2   3   4   5   6   7   8   9   10

IV. VOLUNTEERS IN SOCIAL MINISTRIES

Many Christians have difficulties integrating evangelism and social responsibility. Understanding the characteristics needed for volunteers in social ministries will facilitate the process of becoming socially active or involved.

A. Qualifications

Successful Christian volunteers share several common characteristics that reflect their effort to minister as Christ did. The following points highlight these distinctives:

1. Commitment and consistency

Volunteers need to be committed and consistent in their chosen ministry. Too often people start a project but drop out within a few weeks, creating a bad perception of Christian volunteers. Don Smarto, Director of the Billy Graham Center Institute for Prison Ministries, tells the story of a Christian volunteer who played his guitar to entertain the residents of a juvenile facility. They thoroughly enjoyed hearing the volunteer play and sing. He even showed one of the youths how to play a few chords on the guitar. The teenagers eagerly asked if he would be back the next week, and he enthusiastically assured them he would. However, he never returned. The youths were very disappointed and felt unworthy of the attention.[4]

2. Patience

While it is natural to want to see instant results in your efforts, recognize that it may take years to see results from social ministry projects. Trust that God is working, but do not expect immediate change. Keep in mind the word of encouragement in Galatians 6:9— "Let us not become weary in doing good, for at the proper time we will reap a harvest if we do not give up."

3. Proper motives

Your motivation for serving should spring from a desire to meet the needs of people, not to gain personal self-worth or praise from others. Be ready to accept people as they are, and do not expect anything in return, not even conversions. Expressions of gratitude will be extremely scarce, but remember the words of Matthew 10:8: "Freely you have received, freely give." Keep in mind that service is a privilege and a duty, not a performance requiring gratitude from others.

4. Teachability towards the ministry

Try to get training in the specific skills that will be required. For example, if you will be involved in a prison ministry, learn all you can about prison and jail situations; obtain training in one-on-one communication or small group skills. Make sure you can present the gospel clearly in a brief but powerful manner.

B. Principles for Individuals Interested in Social Ministry

Like Christ, the Christian involved in social ministry seeks to function holistically. The following principles present some guidelines for achieving this goal:

1. Spiritual life is the highest priority.

When a paralytic was brought to Jesus, He knew the man had physical, financial, emotional, and spiritual needs. But Jesus recognized his greatest need was spiritual. Consequently, his first words to the man were, "Take heart, son; your sins are forgiven" [Mark 9:2].

> When the healing ministry of Jesus was attracting too much attention, He said to His followers, "Let us go elsewhere into the next towns, that I may preach there also." When the crowds thronged our Lord because He had fed them, He rebuked them and showed them His cross. Our Lord's first concern was to save men from sin and to grow Christian character. That must always be the first concern of a New Testament church.[5]

2. Deal with the whole person.

Getting involved in social ministry demonstrates spiritual obedience and provides opportunities for witnessing, but not just spiritual hurts should be addressed. For instance, hungry people crave food as well as the Bread of Life; lonely individuals need companionship in addition to meeting the Lover of their souls; and the oppressed yearn for freedom and justice in *this* life and the next.

3. Treat each person with dignity.

Social ministry can easily become depersonalized if we forget to treat every person with respect. All humans are created in the image of God and should never be treated as hopeless or worthless objects.

4. People need personal attention.

People are dying from the lack of personal attention. "Cipher in the Snow," a movie based on a true incident, recounts the story of a little boy who literally dropped dead because of the complete lack of love or attention at home and in school. Jesus touched the lepers and laid hands on the sick. He cried with those who were grieving and was not afraid to be with the destitute and outcast. People need attention as much as they need food, clothing, and shelter. Never let the program become more important than the people.

Consuella York, chaplain to the Cook County Department of Corrections, displays love to the people in jail to whom she ministers. Therefore, she is able to share Scriptural truths and they listen:

Give Them the Truth in Love

> Listen, I've seen hard men break down and cry like little babies. I've seen tough women and pistol-packing men and tough men come down. I say, "You need Jesus. You need love. You need understanding. ... 'Do not be deceived. God is not mocked; whatsoever a man sows, that shall he also reap.' What you put out you're gonna get back." But you see, when you give it to them with love, they can't resist it.[6]

STOP AND APPLY

1. Volunteers in social ministry should be:
   a. committed, patient, teachable, and have proper motives.
   b. joyful, rich, committed, and patient.
   c. poor, patient, humble, and empathetic.

2. The *first* concern of a New Testament church must be:
   a. to meet financial needs of people.
   b. to save people from sin.
   c. to provide an emotional support group.

3. Christians should address:
   a. spiritual hurts of people.
   b. physical needs of people.
   c. emotional needs of people.
   d. all of the above.

4. In social ministry, remember to treat each person:
   a. like a child.
   b. as you would an employee.
   c. with dignity.

V. CHURCHES AND SOCIAL PROGRAMS

Churches often sponsor one or more social programs as part of the overall outreach of the local congregation. Social ministry keeps the congregation in touch with needs and opportunities that are readily available, provides meaningful contact with non-Christians, and aids the Body of Christ in fulfilling the commandment to "love your neighbor as yourself." Perhaps God has chosen you to help lead your church in meeting social needs. If so, the following material will apply to you.

A. Principles for Churches Interested in Social Ministry

1. Relate social action goals to evangelistic and educational goals.

Keep a balance of worship, Bible study, evangelism, Christian education, and social ministry within the congregation or in the social program. Evangelism, not humanitarian service, is the ultimate purpose. Do not lose sight of the fact that the eventual goal is to bring people into a right relationship with Christ. However, social ministry should be a gift, given in the name and love of Jesus, with no strings attached. No one should ever feel coerced to attend or join your church.

2. Lay people should take the lead.

Pastors have other responsibilities within the church and they cannot do everything. Many lay persons, on the other hand, have not only the time but the interest, skills, and contacts to start and run these programs well. As representatives of the church, these lay leaders should keep the standards high.

3. Adapt as the situation demands.

Programs, like the people they serve, need to change with varying conditions. An inflexible or rigid program will always fail.

4. Be selective.

No one church can do everything. Begin only as many programs as can be handled realistically.

5. *Cooperate with other churches and community agencies.*

This broadens your exposure to the community, your knowledge of needs, and your relationships with groups and individuals who are seeking eternal answers to daily needs.

B. *Specific Steps to Start a Social Ministry in Your Church*

1. *Form a committee.*

Begin a new social program by forming a committee made up of a small number of people who are interested in a certain social or moral issue. The committee should awaken interest in church members who have the skills and gifts to reach out. Topics for these committees will vary but might focus on any of the following: abortion/sanctity of human life, race relations, alcohol and drug abuse, citizenship, hunger, pornography, aging, child abuse, criminal justice, drunk driving, pollution, gambling, or poverty.

The simplest structure for a committee incorporates a chairperson with a minimum of three and no more than seven additional members who are genuinely interested in the same issue.

2. *Discover real needs.*

Committees benefit the church by doing research and then presenting needs and opportunities that might otherwise be overlooked. Do not rely on one or two perceptions of a problem; be thorough in your research. Gather all of the available facts. Read studies, take surveys, or make tours. Contact appropriate local agencies in your community. Consider inviting a panel of experts who represent different concerns to make a presentation on their perception of the issues.

3. *Determine available resources.*

Draw up a list of the financial resources, space, equipment, individuals, leadership, or existing programs within the community with which you have access. Then consider the most prominent or immediate problems and try to match needs with resources.

4. *Select social ministry projects carefully.*

Determine the most significant problems that affect people in your community. Seek God's guidance as you narrow the list and make the final decisions about involvement.

5. Identify your allies.

Identify those existing organizations, churches, or community groups with which you can cooperate.

6. Develop a strategy.

Successful programs work toward specific goals. Organization will depend on the project selected and the local church's size, location, resources, and leadership. The strategy may involve using committee members, forming special interest groups, or mobilizing and encouraging individual volunteers.

7. Carry out a plan of action.

a. *Pray*. Every successful Christian ministry is undergirded and protected by prayer. The whole church should be involved through corporate prayer in worship services and prayer meetings, but individuals or small groups are needed too.

b. *Inform people of social problems or concerns.* Opportunities to share about needs are plenteous: the pulpit, the educational ministry of the church, small groups, retreats, special conferences, literature displays, or audiovisual aids. Graphically present selected issues or projects to the church family, and seek their input and guidance. Use skits or drama, bulletin boards, and church and community newspapers to inform people of progress made by the committee. Raise interest and involvement by bringing the project alive. Plan a special Christian Life Emphasis Week to inform people and distribute resource materials which supplement the other educational programs of the church.

c. *Divide your plan into logical categories and assign these to qualified people.* Organize specific times and places for ministry. To avoid overworking your volunteers, divide responsibilities into manageable portions and make sure they are overseen by interested and reliable people.

8. Evaluate and make any necessary adjustments.

Hold regular sessions to determine whether current goals have been met. Assess any difficulties or problems that arose from your project and method. Evaluate mistakes and successes. Decide whether to modify your plan or continue as originally scheduled. In some cases, it will be best to discontinue the project if it does not meet a need.

C. Practical Suggestions for Ministries

☑ Food and clothing banks

☑ Supporting a crisis pregnancy center

☑ Offering classes to teach English as a second language

☑ Helping to elect Christians to various community or government positions

☑ Offering day care for single-parent families

☑ Adopt a grandparent—enlist youth to visit a nursing home (or elderly people who are alone), and then have them choose one to visit on a regular basis

☑ Tutoring ministry—offer tutoring in basic subjects, such as math and reading

☑ Involvement with prisoners and/or their families

STOP AND APPLY

True/False:

___ 1. A church should keep social action goals separate from evangelistic and educational goals.

___ 2. Lay people should take the lead in social ministry.

___ 3. A church should get involved in as many ministries as possible.

___ 4. A church should cooperate with other churches and community agencies.

Arrange the following steps for starting a social ministry in the proper order:

___ Retain available resources ___ Discover real needs
___ Identify allies ___ Select projects
___ Form a committee ___ Develop a strategy
___ Evaluate and make ___ Carry out a plan of
   necessary adjustments   action

VI. EXAMPLES OF MINISTRIES

Most people learn best by example and by doing. Therefore the rest of the chapter will present a small but diverse sample of the kinds of projects that fall under the heading of social ministry. The "Resources" section at the end of the chapter lists a broader range of existing organizations involved in this field.

A. Prison/Jail Ministry

1. Needs of Inmates

Never forget that prisoners are humans created in the image of God. Jesus died for their needs, and He bids them enter a right relationship with Him. They are lost sheep in need of the Good Shepherd.

Inmates have many emotional, psychological, and spiritual needs. They often feel bitter, angry, lonely, scared, and humiliated which gives rise to a desperate longing for a message that conveys love, hope, and forgiveness. The gospel is indeed good news to those who know the burden of physical and spiritual bondage.

Matthew 25 reminds us that ministering to those in prison is the same as ministering to Jesus. Prison ministry allows those behind bars to hear of freedom through the forgiveness of sins and the release from guilt. Those who had no hope will be offered a fresh start and a return of their self-respect and dignity.

Unlike long-term inmates, the need of those in jails are slightly different because they are usually transient and therefore more uncertain about their future. Jails are primarily used as short-term detention centers or holding facilities for those awaiting trial. Most jails have no educational or medical facilities; neither do they have programs for counseling and rehabilitation. But many local jails will welcome a well-planned and consistent program offered by a local church.

2. Opportunities for Ministry Inside the Prison/Jail

Volunteers are very important to the inmate who lacks contact with the "outside." They desperately need someone to listen, rather than condemn them. Most prisoners are aware of their guilt whether or not they admit to it. In many cases, the volunteer will be the one friendly contact in an otherwise hostile environment. Prison administrators usually appreciate volunteers, because they represent another resource working to rehabilitate the inmate.

Consistent visitation is one of the most helpful ministries and takes many forms: weekly Bible study classes or discussion groups, worship services, presentations of Christian movies, special speakers, or Christian concerts. The Billy Graham Evangelistic Team has a crusade ministry which takes teams into prisons and jails using music, drama, and preaching, but they need local volunteers to follow up with the new converts and give prisoners personal attention. Other groups such as Prison Fellowship and Bill Glass Ministries have similar programs.

Many local jails have a chaplain who can explain the necessary steps for getting involved and alert prospective volunteers or groups to any rules that must be followed. On a national level, Prison Fellowship can supply lists of needs and opportunities. Delegated to the care of area or state directors, Prison Fellowship provides information on all major penal institutions in a given region. Individuals or groups beginning a work in this area should utilize the facts and resources available through Prison Fellowship.

3. Opportunities for Ministry Outside the Prison/Jail

Ministering to the families of inmates is equally important. Most feel desperately lonely, confused, and betrayed. Volunteers can provide encouragement and information, as well as assisting in practical ways to ease the trauma. Wives often need information on visiting regulations or a ride to and from the prison. Churches located near a correctional facility might offer child care during regular visiting hours, or volunteers could perform this service on an individual basis.

Consider adopting a prisoner as a pen pal. Prisoners can read letters over and over again. There are less security precautions attached to letters than to visits. Again, the goal of writing is not to preach or to give advice, but to establish a good relationship with the prisoners. In his book *Justice and Mercy*, Don Smarto related the stories of two men eternally changed through this simple medium:

> *Former inmate Jim Tucker recalls that during his years in Soledad Prison he had forgotten when his birthday was. Ernie Hollings, who served 27 years in Canadian prisons, lost track of holidays like Christmas and Easter. Both came to believe that no one cared about them until finally someone took the time to visit and write. Eventually, both Tucker and Hollings came to know the Lord through the correspondence of Christians who cared. The unconditional love reflected in the letters they received softened their hardened hearts.* [7]

It takes less than an hour a month to get involved in this ministry. Those who are willing to make a steadfast commitment to a prison pen pal should consult Appendix D, Section III, of this manual for organizations which provide names and addresses of possible prison pen pals.

Prison chaplains often need help in the office or with projects. Many would be very grateful for extra emotional and/or prayer support.

Finally, look for ways to integrate the inmates into a local church after they are released. They need encouragement, love, help in finding a job, and a lot of time and support.

B. Ministry to the Disabled

About ten percent of the world is disabled in some way. Of the more than 516 million disabled people around the world, more than 42 million are blind and 294 million are deaf or hearing impaired.[8] As with any other unsaved person, a disabled person needs to know that Jesus died on the cross for that person, that He offers forgiveness of sin, and that He promises victory over death as well as victory in daily living. The disabled need the hope of God's help and comfort in dealing with their disability.

As we share God's message of redemption and divine help, we must be careful not to imply any promises of miraculous physical healing. Joni Eareckson Tada, a quadriplegic paralyzed from a diving accident shares:

> Shortly after I was injured, I read wonderful promises from Scripture such as 1 John 5:14: "We have this assurance in approaching God, that if we ask anything according to His will, He hears us."
>
> I prayed in faith that God would hear me and heal me, but my fingers and toes still did not move. I went back to 1 John 5:14 and read it closer. That's when it struck me. It said "if" we ask anything according to His will. I realized that was quite an "if." Not "if we ask anything we think we might like," or "anything that would make life easier," or even "anything we imagined God would want," but anything that's actually "according to His will."
>
> But friends said to me, "Why in the world would it be God's will to deny a Christian's request for healing?" That's a good question—but for every verse seeming to guarantee positive answers to our prayers for an easier, happier, more healthy life, there are countless verses about the good things suffering can bring.
>
> My disability takes my mind off of temporary enticements and forces me to think about God (Col. 3:20). Trials have a way of making

us rely on the Lord (1 Cor. 1:9). Sometimes sickness serves as God's chastiser to wake us from our sin (1 Cor. 11:29–30). And always God uses suffering to help us relate to others who hurt (1 Cor. 1:3–4).[9]

If you are holding an evangelistic meeting or are trying to reach out to disabled people through your church, here are some practical suggestions from Joni:

1. Find out where disabled people are and invite them to your meeting or church.

2. Make certain they can easily gain entrance to your church building or meeting.

3. Provide space near the front for people who are hard of hearing, or in wheelchairs, on mats or on stretchers.

4. When possible, have a Christian interpreter "sign" your message for those who are deaf.

5. Greet disabled people in a friendly, non-condescending manner, and feel free to reach out and touch. Your example will speak loudly to those watching.

6. If a person is nonverbal, ask them their sign for "yes" and "no," then simply ask questions which have "yes" and "no" answers. For those who are deaf, communicate with a pencil and pad of paper. If a person is blind, there is no need to shout—they only want to know that you are speaking directly to them; use eye-to-eye contact. For mentally handicapped people, don't use "baby-talk," but speak simply and clearly.

7. Try to get others to provide transportation to church, or even to help disabled persons get out of bed and get dressed.

8. Enlist helpers to push wheelchairs. Have them hold hymnals and Bibles for those who are paralyzed. This kind of sacrificial service will teach able-bodied Christians what real Christian living is all about.[10]

C. Angel Tree Ministries

Children suffer for crimes they did not commit. It is not their fault that Dad is in prison. Yet they're serving time, too. The doors that lock prisoners in also lock their sons and daughters out.

> *Lonely, isolated. And the hardest time of all for these children is Christmas. Inmates grieve that they can't provide gifts for their children. Children wish for presents they aren't likely to receive. The season meant for joy turns sour and sad.*
>
> *Charles Colson remembers the painful Christmas he spent in prison: "My anguish was compounded by the realization that my wife and children were suffering more. I'm convinced that the ones who are hurt most are the little children... [To them] Christmas is just another day of the year." [11]*

Angel Tree Ministries is one avenue for helping to spread the love of Christ to children at Christmas. Angel Tree began with the idea of a concerned woman who matched the needs of prisoners' families with a desire to help others at the holiday season.

Now operating on a national scale, each fall Prison Fellowship works with prison officials to collect the names and addresses of the inmates' children. Prison Fellowship then shares these names with interested churches, and volunteers phone the families to ask what each child needs and wants.

About a month or six weeks before Christmas, church volunteers set up a Christmas tree decorated with paper angels which have a gift suggestion printed on the back. Church members choose a paper angel and buy the designated presents. In mid-December, volunteers deliver the gifts which are given on behalf of the parent who is in prison.

Angel Tree plants the seeds of God's Word in needy hearts as Prison Fellowship provides an illustrated gospel tract along with each gift. Many Angel Tree families have no other Christian contact. Charles Colson, chairman of Prison Fellowship, hopes this tangible gesture will ease their pain and loneliness:

> *The children of prisoners are some of the saddest victims of crime in our society. They are separated from one, and often both, of their parents and are frequently placed in foster homes or cared for by various relatives. These children are almost always socially and economically deprived. With this separation and economic hardship, Christmas for these children can be a lonely and empty day. We're hoping to make their Christmas a bit brighter. [12]*

For more information on Angel Tree Ministries, write to them at: *Post Office Box 17500, Washington, DC 20041-0500 or call (703) 478-0100.*

D. The South Carol Stream Project

College Church, an interdenominational congregation of 1,200 attenders is located in Wheaton, Illinois. Building on a long history of social concern and involvement, the leadership of the church (with cooperation from the Social Awareness Committee) felt the church needed to be involved in the holistic outreach ministry located in the nearby suburb of Carol Stream.

The neighborhood of South Carol Stream consists of over 5,000 residents in ten apartment complexes. Ten major languages are spoken and dozens of different nationalities represented, resulting in racial tension and mistrust. Eighty to ninety percent of the residents are single mothers with children. Many of these family groups are without any support from extended family or friends; children are often neglected and left on their own. The average income is less than half the national average.

In response to the needs of this neighborhood, the South Carol Stream Community Center was established in July, 1986. The center developed five service programs:

1. Counseling programs

2. Referral services provide information and assistance with employment, housing, legal concerns, day care services, transportation, and health/medical problems

3. A volunteer program coordinates volunteers who provide transportation, child care, and other assistance

4. Big Buddy Program matches children with adult volunteers who are willing to make a long-term commitment

5. Children's programs such as Little League, Scouts, day camps, or Vacation Bible School.

In an effort to stimulate involvement and establish well-defined goals related to those of the South Carol Stream Community Center, College Church drew up a list of objectives found in Appendix C. The church formed a "dream team" to brainstorm about involvement. In their "dreams" the church envisioned reaching out through various programs such as: a sidewalk Sunday School for latchkey kids; matching churches and Carol Stream families, organizing a junior high kids' club, participating in the ongoing tutoring ministry, using church doctors, dentists, and medical personnel to open a free medical center; beginning a legal aid clinic staffed by

Christian lawyers; opening a thrift store; raising money for a new outreach center; setting up a food pantry at a strip mall near the project; and encouraging some of the congregation to move into the South Carol Stream area and live as "ambassadors for Christ."

For details or further information, you can write to *College Church in Wheaton, 330 East Union Avenue, Wheaton, Illinois 60187.*

E. Life Choice Ministries in Manhattan, Kansas

Life Choice Ministries in Manhattan, Kansas was founded in 1987 by a group of Christian families. It offers practical help and encouragement to women who are dealing with unexpected pregnancies. The ministry is totally funded by donations from supporters and churches in the Manhattan area who share a similar concern for these women.

Life Choice is guided by a director and volunteer staff and has an elected board of directors. The volunteers are trained at seminars and by community professionals.

Committed to helping each woman assess all the alternatives before making decisions, Life Choice offers a wide variety of services and encouragement to the expectant mother. (See Appendix C.) An ever-growing number of women testify to the support they received from Life Choice Ministries. Because of this support, they were able to make what they feel was the best decision for their babies.

> *Katie called Life Choice Ministries for help in her crisis pregnancy. When asked by a volunteer how far along in the pregnancy she was, Katie replied "eight or nine months!" To that point she had not seen a physician. She needed assistance in finding a loving couple to adopt her baby. Two weeks later Katie gave birth to a beautiful healthy baby. That precious baby now has a brand new set of Christian parents.*
>
> *Alice came to Life Choice Ministries early in her pregnancy. Upon her positive pregnancy test, LCM assisted Alice to inform her boyfriend and parents. While Alice considered adoption as a loving and viable option, she really wanted to keep the baby. She delivered a beautiful baby boy and is courageously raising him alone.* [13]

Life Choice offers a compassionate and practical voice to troubled girls as it seeks to fulfill its primary goal of helping these women to see their great worth in the eyes of the Lord. Being able to communicate effectively the message of salvation is an important prerequisite for the volunteers who seek to fulfill the objectives for the ministry. (See Appendix C.)

For more information on this center, write to: *Life Choice Ministries, 1433 Anderson Avenue, Manhattan, KS 66502.*

F. Clothes Closets

A clothes closet provides an opportunity for a small or a large church to participate in meeting the needs in the community. Furthermore, it offers a chance to involve many people, including youth and children.

First Baptist Church, a congregation of about 200 located in St. Charles, Illinois, is known throughout the community for its clothes closet. A willing lady in the church organizes the closet, which is actually located in half of one of the Sunday School rooms. People in the community as well as the church donate clothes all year round, while the clothes closet itself is open during the school year. Each month there is an emphasis on special items according to the need of the season—that is, in January it is mittens and hats; February, loaves of "love" (literally loaves of bread); March, bars of soap; April, New Testaments; May, vegetable and flower seeds; September, school supplies; October, candy; November, canned goods; and December, toys.

Volunteers in the church sort the clothes one morning a week, opening the closet to the public one Monday night a month. People can then come and take whatever they need. No one is turned away and no one regulates what they take. Direct evangelism is not usually practiced, unless the opportunity presents itself; but this project has provided many other opportunities to share the message of the gospel as well as to convey to others the church cares about meeting their needs.

G. Food Pantries

Hunger and malnutrition are growing problems in most communities in America. Consider the following true stories:

> Physicians investigating hunger found that Pat Jones' refrigerator contained only a jug of water, a slice of cheese and three eggs. They learned that her three-year-old son had not had milk to drink in three weeks and that he had eaten his last bowl of cereal with water. Pat Jones and her son, residents of Montgomery, Ala., were at dire risk of malnutrition.
>
> Hundreds of miles away in Roses Creek Hollow, Tenn., Letta Casey and her two boys eked out a living in the Appalachian Mountains. She eagerly waited for school to start in September so that her sons could get decent breakfasts and lunches.

"These news stories represent the ongoing reality of poverty and hunger faced by countless people at home and abroad."[14]

Food pantries are an excellent way to meet needs in the local community and they are relatively easy to start. The members of Larkin Avenue Baptist Church (a church of about 150 people in Elgin, Illinois) decided they would make a concerted effort to meet some of the physical needs of people in their community through a food pantry. The mission organization of the church assumed the responsibility for overseeing it, but the whole congregation has become involved. Members of the church bring food on an ongoing basis and deposit it in a big wooden box donated by one of the members. One of the women of the church then puts the food in a closet that they designated as their food pantry.

The church takes referrals of those in need from the local crisis center, the local crisis pregnancy center, and from others in the church. The church staff then gives the referral to a member of the missions organization, who in turn puts together a food basket and delivers it to the person in need. The person delivering the basket always gives a tract along with the food and tries to be alert to any spiritual needs they could meet along with physical ones.

STOP AND APPLY

1. List some ministries of which you are aware in your community:

   _____   _____

   _____   _____

   _____   _____

   _____   _____

   _____

2. Prayerfully consider your possible involvement in one of these ministries (Keep in mind that a person cannot do everything, and that God has certain tasks for us at different times in our lives.)

VII. CONCLUSION

Social action should be a natural Christian response to those in need. Recognizing and helping people in distress simply repeats the pattern set by Jesus. "The church is, according to the Scriptures, the body of Christ—the actual presence of Jesus in the world. As individual members of that Body, we are in fact His hands and His feet—ministering to a broken humanity."[15] Believing himself and all Christians to be called to Christian social ministry, Tony Campolo vividly recalled a prophetic and life-changing incident from a trip to the Dominican Republic.

Some years ago I was in the Dominican Republic doing research on missionary work. I had been working in the western part of the country near the Haitian border. Because I was scheduled to be flown back to the capital city of Santo Domingo in a small Piper Cub, I was waiting for the airplane at the edge of a grass landing strip. As I stood there, a woman approached me. She was carrying her baby in her arms. The child was suffering from malnutrition; its stomach was swollen to four or five times its normal size. Its hair had taken on that rust tint which is evidence of malnutrition. The pupils in its eyes were rolled back, so that only white showed. The child's arms and legs were as spindly as my thumb. This dying, emaciated child hung limp in its mother's hands as she began to beg me to take him.

She pleaded with me, "Please, mister, take my baby. Don't leave my baby here to die. My boy will die if he stays here. Take my baby. Make him well. Take my baby, mister. Don't leave my baby here to die." I turned away from her and tried to escape her pleadings, but she became all the more insistent. Raising her voice, she shouted at me, "Take my baby. Take my baby. Don't leave my baby here to die."

I tried to get away from her, but there was no evading her plea. It went on and on. I was relieved when I saw the airplane come into sight and then land. I ran across the field as quickly as I could to get into the plane and away from her. She came running after me screaming, "Take my baby. Take my baby. Don't leave my baby here to die."

I climbed into the plane and closed the Plexiglas door, but she was alongside of the plane, beating on the fuselage, still screaming at the top of her lungs for me to take her child. The pilot started up the engine and the plane pulled away from the woman, down the landing strip, and into the air.

As we circled the field, I could see her solitary figure below. And halfway back to Santo Domingo it dawned on me; I realized who it was that I had left behind on that landing strip. The name of that baby was Jesus; the Jesus who said, "Inasmuch as ye have done it unto the least of these my brethren, ye have done it unto me. And inasmuch as ye have failed to do it unto the least of these my brethren, ye have failed to do it unto me."

> *Someday when I stand before the Judgment Seat, the Lord will say, "I was hungry and you never fed me, I was naked and you never clothed me, I was sick and you never ministered to me, I was a stranger and you did not take me in."*
>
> *And I will say, "Lord, when did I see you hungry and not feed you, naked and not clothe you, sick and not minister to you, a stranger and not take you in?"*
>
> *And the Lord will say, "Just east of the Haitian border, on a landing strip, when you failed to respond to that child, you failed to respond to me."* [16]

Now if you haven't already done so, listen to cassette tape #5A in the series featuring *Evangelism and Social Action* by Mother Consuella York. Also on the tape are excerpts from Connie Fairchild and Joni Eareckson Tada.

ENDNOTES

[1] John Stott, *The Lausanne Covenant* (Minneapolis, MN: World Wide Publications, 1975), p. 30.

[2] *Evangelism and Social Responsibility: A Evangelical Commitment* (Wheaton, IL: World Evangelical Fellowship, 1982), p. 25.

[3] Tony Campolo, *Ideas for Social Action* (Grand Rapids: Zondervan, 1983).

[4] Donald Smarto, *Justice and Mercy* (Wheaton, IL: Tyndale House Publishers, 1987) p. 295.

[5] W. L. Muncy, *New Testament Evangelism for Today* (Kansas City, KS: Central Seminary Press, 1946), p. 177.

[6] Consuella York, talk given at Wheaton College, Wheaton, IL, April 9, 1991.

[7] Smarto, p. 290.

[8] Statistics from World Health Organization, International Christian Blind Mission and the National Information Center on Deafness at Galludet University cited by Joni Eareckson Tada, *What Does the Gospel Have to Say to Disabled Persons?* (Agoura Hills, CA: Joni and Friends Publications, 1991), p. 4.

[9] *Ibid.*, pp. 2–3.

[10] *Ibid.*, p. 3.

[11] Angel Tree Ministries Brochure, Washington D.C.

[12] *Ibid.*

[13] Crisis Pregnancy Center Brochure, Manhattan, KS.

[14] *Light* (Christian Life Commission of the Southern Baptist Convention, Oct–Dec, 1990), p. 3.

[15] Campolo, p. 33.

[16] *Ibid.*, pp. 33–34.

$\mathcal{U}$NIT FOUR:

Evangelism and Vision

SESSION TEN
Cross-Cultural Evangelism

GOALS FOR THE CHAPTER:

After reading this chapter, you should be able to:

1. Develop a working knowledge of the terms associated with cross-cultural ministry

2. Understand the Biblical mandate for cross-cultural ministry and the example God has given us in Jesus

3. Recognize the unique role of the Holy Spirit in this ministry

4. Identify some of the main principles involved in this difficult but important task

I. INTRODUCTION

> *How, then, can they call on the one they have not believed in? And how can they believe in the one of whom they have not heard? And how can they hear without someone preaching to them? And how can they preach unless they are sent? As it is written, "How beautiful are the feet of those who bring good news!" [Romans 10:14–15]*

In the book *Ministering Cross Culturally*, Sherwood Lingenfelter recounts the first decision faced by his family when they arrived on the tiny South Pacific island of Yap. A local Yapese man showed the young American two locations where he might build a home. One location would be considered the American dream—a gorgeous beach location with lots of nature and privacy. The second lot was located in the midst of a noisy, littered, local village. Not surprisingly Lingenfelter preferred the beach setting, but his local guide urged him to reconsider. "If you want to learn to speak our language, the other place is better for you," he explained. Realizing the wisdom of these words, the Lingenfelter family built their home in the midst of the village which proved to be as public, littered and noisy as first predicted. However, the family all quickly learned the language and soon became immersed in the culture of their new surroundings.[1]

Cross-cultural ministry has been defined by Lingenfelter and his co-author Marvin Mayers as "any ministry in which one interacts with people who have grown up learning values and lifestyle patterns that are different from one's own."[2] Using this definition, an American who leaves home and goes to live and witness to the truth about Jesus in Tibet is a cross-cultural minister, but so would be the suburban Anglo-American who decides to live and work in the midst of Laotian refugees living in an inner city in the USA. Reaching across language or cultural boundaries is not easy. By nature, most people prefer to live in an environment which is similar to their own cultural and linguistic group.

II. THE THEORETICAL AND BIBLICAL BASES FOR CROSS-CULTURAL MINISTRY

A. What is Culture?

Culture has been defined as "the anthropologist's label for the sum of the distinctive characteristics of a people's way of life."[3] From infancy on, each of us begins to absorb the culture of those around us. As babies and small children, we quickly learn what brings pleasure or discomfort. The way we relate to our primary care givers

India

and those who surround us each day provides a pattern for us to follow and teaches us what to expect from others. Culture is naturally and automatically imprinted into our being as infants. We grow up learning to watch for clues that will help us to refine our understanding of what will be required of us in different situations. In most societies parents model acceptable behavior for their children. For instance, a child of parents who are openly affectionate will usually respond to loved ones in a similar fashion. If a society or family never shows affection, even in private, the children will likely grow up and repeat similar behavior which they will accept as the norm.

Because culture is so infinitely varied and unique to each people group and locality, it presents a major hurdle when we are ministering cross-culturally. Anyone involved in such an outreach must be

Japan

willing to become like a baby and relearn
the new culture's guidelines for acceptable
behavior. This is not an easy task. It requires patience, humility, and humor.

Greece

Although some readers of this chapter
will feel called to spend their lives in a
foreign country, most will not. Nevertheless, the opportunities to
reach out to someone of another culture surround us. For instance,
more than sixty different languages are spoken in the greater
Chicago area, and even more can be heard in the greater Los
Angeles area. Most colleges and universities have a sizeable number of foreign students. Furthermore, businesses are increasingly
viewing the world as their marketplace. Opportunities to reach out
cross-culturally are endless in our increasingly cosmopolitan world.

B. Definitions of Cross-Cultural Evangelism

Just as culture contains many variations and differences, so
does the ministry of evangelism within the cross-cultural realm.
Dividing the evangelistic outreach into four "E" levels helps both
author and reader to be more precise about the task at hand, and
most people who work in this field use the following definitions
when attempting to explain it to others:

E-0—*the winning of nominal Christians in a similar culture
to personal faith and commitment.*
E-1—*evangelism within homogeneous groups.*
E-2—*evangelism of geographically close and culturally or
linguistically related groups.*
E-3—*evangelism of culturally distant groups in which the
evangelist is separated from the people to be evangelized by monumental cultural distances.*

Obviously E-0 evangelism is the easiest and E-3 the most
difficult. E-0 evangelism takes place within the local church setting.
Many people who fill the pews of American churches have no real
understanding of what it means to be a Christian. If quizzed, they
might tell you that "real Christians go to church every Sunday" or
"contribute ten percent of their money to the church," but they have
no understanding of the person and work of Jesus in their lives.
These sincere but misguided nominal Christians need to be introduced to a Savior who is very much alive and who desires to have
a deeply personal relationship with them. E-0 evangelism is consid-

ered the easiest because the recipient is not only culturally similar to the evangelist, but is normally open to the claims of the Gospel.

E-1 evangelism occurs when persons with similar cultural and linguistic backgrounds discuss the claims of Christ. A young mother who explains the Gospel to another new mother in the neighborhood engages in E-1 evangelism. Neither E-O or E-1 evangelism is considered cross-cultural.

On the other hand, both E-2 and E-3 evangelism require a cross-cultural dimension. The suburban college student who spends her summer working in an inner city ministry engages in cross-cultural evangelism. The American family who adopts an international student or family and attempts to introduce them to Jesus also participates in E-2 evangelism.

To be an E-3 evangelist, one must leave her home and travel great distances to reach a people who are distinctively different in culture and language. E-3 evangelists are what most people would consider to be true missionaries. The task would be almost impossible if it were not for the example of Jesus (who is the role model for all who want to participate in cross-cultural evangelism).

C. The Incarnation—God as Cross–Cultural Evangelist

When Jesus chose to become a baby, He provided the ultimate example of cross-cultural or E-3 evangelism. The Creator became the creature, and He took on all the limitations of human nature. Rather than just burst into the universe and take the world by force, Christ became a helpless Jewish baby who learned language and culture first from His parents and then from the rabbis and teachers. The Incarnation provides the cross-cultural evangelist with the supreme example to be emulated. Jesus, who is God, willingly laid aside His rights to deity to become a completely human man. As such, He accepted all the limitations that human nature placed on Him. This voluntary relinquishment of rights allowed Him to enter perfectly into the culture of His people and thus convey the love of God for all humankind.

D. The Need to be 150% Persons

Lingenfelter and Mayers propose that the successful cross-cultural evangelist will become a 150% person. Looking to Christ, they observe that He was a 200% person—100% God and 100% man. Such a complete identification with a foreign culture is not possible for us, but we can strive to set aside much of our cultural and national identity and seek to identify with the country to which we move. So deep is the imprint of culture that one can never totally shed it, but one can adapt to a new culture in such a profound fashion that even nationals accept the newcomer on an equal basis.

Born and raised in Northern Ireland, Amy Carmichael felt called to minister in the south of India. Leaving behind family and friends, the young woman sailed to India in 1895 and never returned—even for a furlough—to the home of her childhood. At her death in 1951, she was known and loved by thousands in her adopted country as "Amma" [Tamil for "mother"]. During her more than fifty-five years in India, she never forgot her primary goal of bringing the Gospel message to all who would listen. For most of her life, she worked tirelessly to rescue orphans who would otherwise have lived a life of degradation and extreme poverty. She became fluent in the Tamil language, dressed like a national, learned to think like an Indian woman, embraced the cultural distinctives of her adopted district, and often referred to herself in print as a Tamil. She is an outstanding example of a successful cross-cultural evangelist. By the end of her life, most of her Tamil co-workers and friends thought of her as one of their own; yet to the end, Amy Carmichael could also relate to and identify with the western culture of her early years. The goal of the E-3 evangelist, then, is to become 75% the child of the new culture while recognizing that she will always remain 75% the culture of her youth. Amy Carmichael is an excellent example of the 150% person.

E. The Goal of the Cross-Cultural Evangelist

The cross-cultural evangelist must be constantly aware of the need to accommodate the host culture in all areas that do not contradict Scripture. Nonetheless, there can be no compromise when it comes to the Word of God. Scripture is, and always will be, the highest authority for Christians.

When an American woman enters the Muslim world, there are many cultural differences that she must learn to observe, if she is to be effective. For instance, the standards of dress are much more rigid than those found in the States. Even a very modest pair of bermuda shorts would be considered indecent public attire in Pakistan. Furthermore, there is very limited contact between the sexes, and a woman needs to be very careful about her behavior in the presence of men. The easy familiarity so common to Americans would often be greatly misunderstood by an Islamic man.

It is important to recognize differences such as these and accept the standards as set by the host country. In cultural issues, the evangelist needs to be the one willing to do the compromising.

However, the Christian can never compromise the truth of Scripture. John 17:17 quotes Jesus as praying to the Father and asking that God "Sanctify them by the truth; your word is truth." In 1974, devoted Christians from all six continents met in Lausanne, Switzerland to discuss the great task of evangelizing the world. One outcome of the Lausanne Conference was its statement on Scripture which declared: "We affirm the divine, inspirational, truthfulness, and authority of both Old and New Testament Scriptures in their entirety as the only written Word of God, without error in all that it affirms, and the only infallible rule of faith and practice." A follow-up document, *The Willowbank Report*, brought further clarity to the issue by pointing out that those who accept that Scripture is "without error in all that it affirms" need to fulfill three requirements when dealing with God's Word:

1. The essential meanings of Scripture must be retained.

2. Cultural forms may require changing for communication purposes but even so, a normative quality must be attributed to them because those forms were the ones chosen by God for purposes of His communication. (For example, in primitive tribes who have never seen paper, the translation may indicate that God wrote on "banana leaves" or "pottery" rather than on "scrolls" or "parchment.")

3. Each fresh formulation and explanation in every generation and culture must be checked for faithfulness by referring back to the original.[4]

III. THE URGENCY OF CROSS-CULTURAL MINISTRY

In 1950, there were 21 non-Christians for every believer in the world. Forty-two years later, Ralph Winter of the U.S. Center for World Missions in Pasadena estimates that the gap has narrowed to 6.8 non-Christians for every believer. This phenomenal growth should be an encouragement and a challenge. These statistics underscore the possibility of reaching the world by the year 2000 (the goal of many mission groups), but success will not be possible unless more committed Christians are willing to forsake their comfortable lifestyle and relocate to the mission field.

To put these statistics into a more understandable form, Winter suggests dividing the world into ten portions. One of the ten would be a Bible-believing Christian. Two of the ten would best be called "nominal Christians." These are people who go through the motions of faith, but have never formed a personal relationship with Christ. The third group represents 1.6 billion non-Christians who live in close proximity to Bible-believing Christians. They can be reached with much less effort than the last group. The last four of the ten are the unevangelized. Winter says that there are approximately

> 2,000 peoples or nationalities in which there is not yet a vital, indigenous church movement.... There are now about 12,000 such unreached people groups within the 2,000 larger peoples, so that the task is not impossible. Yet at present only 7% of all missionaries are engaged in this kind of outreach, while the remaining 93% are working in the already evangelized half of the world. If this imbalance is to be redressed, a strategic redeployment of personnel will be necessary.[5]

The challenge is clear. World evangelization is possible by the year 2000, but it will require each of us to be fully committed to the Great Commission.

STOP AND APPLY

1. Define culture.

   _____

   _____

   _____

   _____

2. List and describe the four levels of cross-cultural evangelism.

   1) _____

   2) _____

   3) _____

   4) _____

3. When Jesus chose to become a baby, which level of evangelism did He exemplify?

4. Lingenfelter and Mayers propose that the successful cross-cultural evangelist will become a _____ person.

5. The cross-cultural evangelist must accommodate the _____ _____ in all areas that do not contradict Scripture.

6. World evangelization is possible by the year 2000, but it will require each of us to be fully committed to the _____ _____.

IV. HOW TO BEGIN? THE PRINCIPLES INVOLVED

A. The Call Should Come from God

Speaking to the topic of "Evangelism and Missions," former missionary, Elisabeth Elliot, attempted to answer the basic question that plagues so many Christians when they think about missions: "how do I know if I'm called?" According to Elliot:

> ...a call I believe is first of all, a desire. And then a conviction. And then a commitment.... The shepherd is much more interested in getting the sheep where they belong, than the sheep are in getting there themselves... He's not going to make it impossible for you to find out what He wants you to do, provided He has your heart. Provided you have set your face like a flint to do what He says, no matter what it is, and you don't ask Him ahead of time to give you a blueprint.[6]

Melody Green, co-founder of Last Days Ministries, took this challenge in a slightly different direction when she asserted her belief that "God gives us the burden as we go, as we allow Him to stir our hearts." Recounting the lessons learned on her first trip overseas, she remembered that her concern for missions first became real and then increased as she was exposed to the people and the needs in various parts of the world. In the midst of the trip, she recalls feeling the presence of God nudging her to respond to the deprivation she had encountered.

Confronted by the spiritual, emotional, and material poverty of much of the world, Green found her heart wonderfully softened. "And it wasn't out of guilt. It was because God had genuinely moved on my heart in compassion and I thought, 'This would be ... really difficult to live in,' but I could sense the reward in my spirit and God brought me to a place where in each nation that I went I loved the people there. You know, it wasn't scary." Like many missionaries, she had discovered that love for people comes when you get to know them.

The command to go has already been issued by Jesus. Our job, then, is to figure out where He can best use our labor. Every Christian has a talent which God can utilize to further His kingdom. Some will be called to foreign fields while others will work nearer to home, but we all need His vision and direction. In his pamphlet, "Who's Calling?" Robertson McQuilkin, retired president of Columbia Bible College and Seminary, reminds all Christians that the first step in any Christian ministry begins with complete surrender and obedience to the commands of Christ. McQuilkin quotes George Murray, General Director of the Bible Christian Union, who "for years ... was 'willing to go, but planning to stay.' Not until he became 'willing to stay, but planning to go' did God move him out to Italy."[7]

Having spent most of his life preparing missionaries for the task, McQuilkin cautions that many on the field today have forgotten that our first task is to make converts and incorporate them into the Body of the Church. Teaching nationals to read, healing sick bodies, or building sanitary wells are noble vocations, but they should never be the primary focus of the missionary. God is calling His people to the mission field, but many have no ears to hear because we are preoccupied with the desires and goals of our own hearts. Our view of God has dwindled so much that we limit Him to what our finite minds can comprehend. Furthermore, we ignore the clear teachings of Scripture and most Christians have only a feeble prayer life. With such neglect, McQuilkin does not find it surprising that many who are called to the mission field fail to hear the summons.

In an attempt to clarify some of the confusion that surrounds the concept of "a call," McQuilkin explains that some will receive a specific "call" from the Lord which will make it crystal clear that He wishes them to spend their lives on the mission field. For others, the "call" will come through the guidance of Scripture, the promptings of the Holy Spirit, the counsel of more mature Christians, and the circumstances of their lives. In this latter case, the person becomes increasingly convicted and assured of God's direction as all indications point to a particular ministry. Although this type of leading lacks the dramatic elements of a heavenly vision or voice, it is nonetheless a call from God to a specific form of ministry.[8]

B. Recognize the Power and Leadership of the Holy Spirit.

Once again, the supremacy of the work of the Holy Spirit cannot be underestimated. Unless He prepares the heart and mind of our hearer we will labor in vain, much like a farmer who tries to harvest a crop two months before it is ripe. The fruit of a person who tries to spiritually harvest without the guidance of the Holy Spirit is equally underdeveloped and worthless.

C. Test the Soil.

In the parable about the four kinds of soil in Matthew 13, Jesus teaches that not all people will be receptive to becoming His follower. Merely hearing the good news about Jesus does not mean that one is a Christian. Christ instructs those who will sow the seed to look for prepared soil where the crop will yield many times what was initially planted. Practically, that means that we need to look for a person or people group who displays a favorable reaction to our message. If after repeated attempts to share the Gospel message there is no interest or response, the evangelist needs to pursue the leading of the Holy Spirit actively and perhaps look in another direction where people show interest in finding the truth about Jesus.

In India, for instance, Christians have found that in general they have much greater success when they work with the poor rather than the rich. Therefore, it makes little sense to spend most of the limited time and resources on the rich at the expense of the poor, who are spiritually hungry and eager for the truth. In the States, this might mean caring for children or youth in the city (who desperately need someone to take a genuine interest in them), or to homesick and lonely international students.

D. Seek to Imitate the Incarnate Son of God

The need to imitate Jesus cannot be sufficiently emphasized. When God chose to communicate with His people, He acted in a way that could be readily understood by all of humankind. He became one of us. No human can ever completely understand God and His love for us; but in His Incarnation, Christ gave to the world a tangible demonstration of God's love. Our human limitations and difficulties were readily embraced by Christ that He might more fully communicate His message to us. Anyone seeking success in cross-cultural ministry must adopt Christ's selfless attitude and willingly put aside preconceived notions about culture and individual rights.

E. Consider a Short-Term Assignment on a Mission Field

Many churches and mission-sending agencies have opportunities for short-term involvement. The time period can be as short as a few weeks or as long as two years. The opportunities are endless, especially if you have a specific skill to offer.

Short-term assignments serve to acquaint people with the needs of the world and also enlarge the heart of the missionary. No one can spend time ministering to those in need without being changed. Short-term missionaries usually return home with a new and enthusiastic dedication for the task of world evangelism. Some go on to make a lifelong commitment, but all will find their world view to be greatly expanded.

If you would like to know more about opportunities for short-term missions, consider writing to one or more of the following agencies for information.

> **Latin America Mission/Spearhead**, P.O. Box 52-7900, Miami, FL 33152; (305) 884-8400. Opportunities for summer or up to two-year internships are available working in Latin America. Applicants must be committed Christians between the ages of 19 and 30, and they must be willing to work and live with families in the community where they are assigned. Costs range from $695 for a summer to $500 per month for longer assignments.

> **Operation Mobilization**, P.O. Box 2277, Peachtree City, GA 30269; (404) 631-0432. OM has opportunities for work in most areas of the world and primarily attracts young people for its short term (1–2 year) and summer ministries. Applicants must be at least 17 years old and have been a Christian for at least one year. OM does provide training for all who are accepted. Summer teams are primarily involved in evangelism. Long-term applicants need $700 per month living expenses, and summer applicants will need between $1600–2200.

> **Wycliffe Bible Translators**, P.O. Box 2727, Huntington Beach, CA 92647; (714) 969-4600 or 800-388-1928. This well-known agency has opportunities for Christians of all ages on five different continents. The length of service varies from a few weeks to a lifelong commitment. Costs and training vary depending on the assignment.

Youth for Christ, P.O. Box 228822, Denver, CO 80222; (303) 843-9000. Youth For Christ seeks to reach young people around the world with the message of the Gospel. Applicants for a two-week project will receive two days of orientation. Project Serve teams work in local communities doing a variety of tasks. Applicants must be high school age or older and will need between $300–2400 in funding, depending on location and length of service.

Youth With a Mission, P.O. Box 4600, Tyler, TX 75712 (903) 882-5591. YWAM works in over 400 centers located in 120 nations. Both short- and long-term assignments are available. YWAM provides training for all of its programs and offers a variety of opportunities for those interested in missions. Short termers are primarily involved in evangelism or mercy ministry, and costs vary depending on the location of the assignment.

The above names and addresses represent only a tiny portion of the agencies and possibilities available to those who are interested in missions. For additional information and a more complete list of agencies, write for a current copy of *The Great Commission Handbook*. It is published by:

Berry Publishing Services, Inc.
701 Main Street
Evanston, IL 60202

F. Decide on a Strategy.

The veteran missionary, John Robb, sharing with evangelists from all over the world at the Amsterdam '86 Conference, underscored the need for including strategy into the life of the evangelist. Defining strategy as "a careful plan, more specifically, the art of devising or employing plans to reach a goal," Robb went on to stress that "good strategy, therefore, is related to long-range planning and foresight."[9]

Without strategy, Robb and others fear that we will lose our way and end up working for something other than the salvation of lost souls. It is important, for instance, to teach people to read, but education should never become the ultimate objective for evangelists. Furthermore, strategy helps to keep our focus sharp and enables us to avoid many mistakes that might undermine the goals we are striving to achieve.

To illustrate his point, Robb told of a mistake that he and other missionaries made when they were working in Kuala Lumpur, Malaysia. After hearing reports of success with the "I Found It" in other cities, the pastors and missionaries adopted the program and invested much time and effort into bringing it to Kuala Lumpur. They enjoyed a moderate response from young people who understood English, but few of these went on to become committed disciples. Far more demoralizing than the lack of lasting fruit, the Muslims in their town (50% of the population) felt personally offended by the campaign's "culturally insensitive approach." Upon reflection, the workers involved concluded that had they:

> ...thought strategically and exercised foresight in visualizing the probable impact of the campaign as far as the likely number of disciples that would be made and the adverse reaction by Malay Muslims, we would not have employed this standard prepackaged approach to our unique culturally diverse city. We would have developed long-range evangelistic strategies for each of the distinct social and cultural groups, that took into account their uniqueness as groups.
>
> When we busy ourselves with evangelistic activities without taking the time to do long-range planning, we are applying tactics without strategy.... Strategy informs and guides tactics so that each tactical action counts.[10]

The failure of the "I Found It" campaign in Kuala Lumpur lay not with the program itself; it had been a great success in other cities. It failed because the leaders had not properly assessed the spiritual needs of the community within the context of its own unique culture. Strategic planning would have given them a clear vision of their future goals for the city and then enabled them to plan wisely for reaching their aims.

1. Make certain that you know your focus.

If God leads you to minister in India, you will need to decide whether you want to make your focus the Hindu or the Muslim people. Both groups desperately need a Christian witness, but the odds are very much against one person ministering successfully to both peoples (because they do not normally get along well).

If you attempt cross-cultural ministry nearer to your home, you will need to make some similar decisions about your focus. Do you want to reach out to internationals, to lonely children in the city, or an immigrant ethnic population (to name just three choices)? Each of these groups has enormous needs that no person can fulfill alone. Scattering your energies among several projects, no matter how important they are, will result in severely reduced effectiveness (and often discouragement) on the part of the worker. On the other hand, choosing one area for ministry will enable you to keep your focus and resources concentrated and applied to your goal.

2. Establish a clearly defined evangelistic goal.

We sometimes laugh at the person with the "one track mind," but keeping the goal of evangelism ever before our eyes should prevent us from getting sidetracked or distracted to secondary issues. Our goal needs to be clearly defined rather than vague; and it helps to write it out, even if no one else ever reads it. Committing our goal to paper helps us to plan logically and concretely. The goal can be reviewed at a later date and an accurate assessment of progress or failure established.

If, for instance, you decide to get involved with an international student, your goal might read: "Get to know at least three international students at Local Community College before the end of September. Establish a more intimate friendship with at least one in order to have the opportunity to share the gospel by Christmas at the latest."

3. Set specific goals that meet the physical, as well as the spiritual, needs of the person(s).

Even a cursory reading of the Gospels underscores the holistic ministry of Jesus. Without a doubt, He knew that spiritual needs were of primary importance; but even so, He consistently taught, fed, and healed those with physical needs. From the raising of his dead friend, Lazarus, to telling Peter that he would find the money for the Temple tax in the mouth of a fish, Jesus showed an unwavering interest and concern for the physical and material needs of those with whom He came into contact.

Now it is our turn. The Master set the example and the world waits to see if we will care as He did. Often it takes a while to build enough trust into a relationship so that people will see that you live what you teach. If you have spent time, energy, and resources caring for the physical, material, or emotional needs of your new friend(s), you can expect that they will take you far more seriously when you share your concern for the state of their spiritual lives.

Do you live in a cold part of the country and did your new international friend come from a hot climate? If so, your advice about dressing for winter will be invaluable, especially if you know garage sales or thrift shops where a student can get a good buy on a warm coat. If you are working with an immigrant family, consider their needs for tutoring or for someone to drive them to the doctor or other appointments. Do the kids need help with school work? Inner city kids need tutors, coaches, and friends who will make a firm commitment to them. Watch your new friends and look for clues about their culture. Go to the library and check out materials that will help you better understand their homeland or ethnic background.

Again, set some specific goals. In our busy world, it is easy to let good intentions get lost in the maze of daily events. Written goals help us to avoid this pitfall. Let us say you decide to minister to an immigrant family. Sit down with your personal (and family) calendar and write your new friends into your schedule. For instance, a three-month plan might look like this:

Month One:

- ☑ Visit weekly with the mother and the small children at home and establish a friendship.
- ☑ Invite the family for dinner at least once during the first month.
- ☑ Assess the tutoring needs (if any) of the older children.
- ☑ Take the mother and small children on outings that will acquaint them with facilities that can meet their needs—that is, medical centers, food stores offering specialized products, government offices.
- ☑ Learn about the religious heritage or background of the family.

Month Two:

- ☑ Include the older children in an outing with your older children.
- ☑ Try to identify areas where the family has the greatest need for assistance.
- ☑ If possible, find a project that can be worked on jointly so that your friend can share a talent or skill with you.

Month Three:

☑ Continue to deepen the friendship through regular visits.

☑ When it seems natural, discuss spiritual beliefs with your friend—seek to tell her about Jesus in a context that she can understand (be prepared to do this at any time, but resolve to bring the spiritual element into your relationship by month three at the latest).

☑ If she seems open, invite her to a women's Bible study or ask if she would be interested in doing one with you.

G. Communicate clearly.

Communication is of primary importance, whether you are involved locally or overseas. There can be no relationship without communication. We tend to think of communication primarily as verbal, but nonverbal communication sends equally important messages to the one we seek to reach. Both verbal and nonverbal communication are important when one is seeking to represent Jesus, especially in a foreign culture or to one who is unfamiliar with our ways of relating.

1. Nonverbal Communication

Body language, attitudes, behavior, and dress all play a part in our nonverbal communication. In a culture where the sexes do not freely mix, a woman giving a man a hug or even shaking his hand can easily be misinterpreted as a sexual advance. Similarly, many countries have expectations about how a person will dress. The wise evangelist studies these differences and adapts to them.

In the same way, remember that your attitudes toward your family or fellow missionaries will be minutely scrutinized. How you treat a fellow co-worker or family member will often speak far more clearly than your words. Jesus respected all persons. If we want those around us to see how much He cares for them, they need to first experience our care for them. In most cases, our first lesson or sermon will be based on our actions, not our words.

Finally, do you treat all people with the same respect that you accord to those from your own culture? In other words, does your behavior convey to those you are trying to reach that you think bringing the message of the Gospel to them is a privilege that you value? Do those you are trying to reach feel respected and accepted by your words and actions?

2. Verbal Communication

a. Use simple language.

Numerous books and articles have been written about the importance of the spoken word, but most authors and lecturers on the subject will agree on several points. First, it is important that the communicator use clear, simple language that is easily understood by the audience. It is theologically accurate to speak of God as "immanent" or "omnipresent," but such terms would undoubtedly confuse most illiterate, nomadic peoples who have not had the opportunity to formally study theology. Likewise, a foreign student struggling to learn English will usually find such terms difficult to comprehend. It is far better to speak of God as "wanting to have a relationship with every person" or describe Him as being "everywhere at the same time." Theological concepts are often difficult for people to grasp. It is vital, then, that we use the clearest words possible to convey the truth as accurately and simply as possible.

b. Listen for feedback.

Even with simple language, it is still crucial to use feedback to discover whether the audience has accurately perceived the truth which the evangelist has presented. More than once a grave misunderstanding has occurred because of such an error.

> *Okot p'Bitek, an unbeliever, describes missionary efforts to find points of contact with the Luo of East Africa. They asked, "who created you?" The Luo did not hear the word "create" the way the missionaries thought it, and decided that the missionaries wanted to know who molded them. That was nonsense, since they had all been given birth by their mothers. They replied, "We don't know." Pressed for a better answer, one of the elders remembered that although a person may be born normally, when he is afflicted with tuberculosis of the spine, he loses his normal figure and gets "molded." So, the old man said, "Rubanga is the one who molds people." This was name of the evil spirit believed to make the hump on the back of those afflicted with tuberculosis of the spine. The missionaries were satisfied and began preaching that Rubanga was the God who created them.[11]*

Difficulties also arise when a missionary attempts to explain a concept that is not found in the vocabulary of the people. For instance, Elisabeth Elliot speaks of the problem of teaching the Auca Indians about abstract ideas such as "love," "sin," "faith," "redemption," and "salvation." The Auca language did not contain words or phrases that could be employed to explain these basic Christian truths. During her two years in their villages, the people would usually respond in a favorable manner to her teaching, but the young missionary wisely recognized that their polite agreement did not necessarily indicate a real understanding of what she attempted to teach. From their responses, she surmised that they were only saying words that they hoped would please her. Given the feedback that she received, it would have been a fatal error to assume that their apparent agreement actually constituted a real understanding of these basic doctrines.[12]

c. Build bridges.

Most missionaries—either foreign or home—do not consider themselves engineers, but they should. They need to be vitally concerned with building bridges, especially in environments where Christianity is not acceptable culturally. What are the problems that new Christians will face from their families, friends, or community? If becoming a Christian is unacceptable, how and where will the new believers find the support that they need to maintain their commitment to Jesus?

Although it is not always possible to win the support and encouragement of every family and community, the cross-cultural evangelist must seek opportunities to demonstrate to the community that she is one to be trusted. By looking for ways to present in love what is being preached, the missionary lays the foundations for sturdy bridges. For instance, if you plan to work with inner city or ethnic youth, get to know their parents as well. Look for ways that you can encourage, help, or otherwise display the love of Christ to them.

d. Pitfalls to avoid.

1) Do not mistake a point of contact for one of agreement. General revelation comes from those things that we can see, observe, or discover using our natural abilities. The beauty and complexity of the earth usually leads people to conclude that there is a creator who is greater than they are. Even though this assumption points them in the general direction of God, it is not the same as knowing the work of God the Father as Creator and Sustainer of the universe. A person from another culture may agree with you that there is a God, but this is only a point of contact. However, it would be a point of agreement if that same person acknowledged the Triune God.

Sometimes in our great desire to see the souls of others safely harbored in God's kingdom, we look for points of contact rather than points of agreement. For instance, most people will feel some guilt if they deliberately hurt someone else. However, a guilty conscience does not automatically mean that the person will also recognize herself as a sinful person who needs the atoning death of Jesus. Guilt may be a universal human reaction, but it does not automatically follow that guilty persons recognize their need for redemption in Jesus. Points of contact should only be viewed as ways to begin or as a base on which the evangelist can build.

2) Recognize that some people would rather seek truth than find it. Most people in the world today are willing to seek spiritual knowledge, but they do not necessarily expect or want to find it. In some cultures, the *pursuit* of spiritual understanding is seen as the great goal for life. They mistakenly believe that truth is elusive and cannot be discovered in any absolute way. Such thinking will not readily accept Christ's assertion that He "is the way, the truth and the life" [John 14:6]. In such a setting, the temptation will be to engage in endless philosophical arguments. Nonetheless, our goal, to introduce them to the Living Christ free of our cultural trappings, needs to remain central.

V. CONCLUSION

The Bible tells us that as early as the Tower of Babel, *people were seeking knowledge about God*, but Christians know that *God seeks relationships with people*.[13] Christianity differs from the other religions of the world because we understand that in Jesus, God sought to bridge the gap brought by sin that separates us from Him. Because of Christ's death, we have immediate access to the throne of a loving God. Our goal as cross-cultural ministers is not to introduce people to another philosophical concept of God, but to the person of Jesus.

STOP AND APPLY

Circle the correct answer:

1. The call to missions should come first and foremost from:
   a. God.   b. Your parents.   c. Your pastor.

2. According to Robertson McQuilkin, the first step in any Christian ministry begins with:
   a. financial and prayer support.
   b. complete surrender and obedience to Christ.
   c. an evaluation of your spiritual gifts.

3. You should recognize the power and leadership of:
   a. The Holy Spirit.
   b. Your prayer partner.
   c. A leader in the culture with whom you are working.

4. In testing the soil, we need to look for a person or group who:
   a. are like us.
   b. are pagans.
   c. display a favorable reaction to our message.

5. Anyone seeking success in cross-cultural ministries must adopt:
   a. a child of that particular culture.
   b. Christ's selfless attitude.
   c. the culture's political platform.

6. John Robb underscored the need for including which of the following in the life of the evangelist:
   a. a quiet time.
   b. a consistent prayer life.
   c. strategy.

7. In planning your *strategy* it is important that you know your:
   a. language.   b. focus.   c. customs.

Fill in the blanks:

8. Clear communication is important. It can be non-_____ or _____. The steps in verbal communication are:
   1) Use _____ language.
   2) _____ for feedback.
   3) Build _____.

9. For those who cannot go to the mission field, begin to examine the world at your doorstep. Do you know any internationals who are not Christians? What groups of people live near your home who have little or no Christian witness? Are there international students (community colleges often have a large number of such students), business people, or ethnic groups near you who have recently arrived in the United States?

Now if you haven't already done so, listen to cassette tape #5B in the series featuring *Evangelism and a World Christian View* by Melody Green. Also on the tape are excerpts of messages from Marilyn Laszlo and Colleen Townsend Evans.

ENDNOTES

[1] Sherwood G. Lingenfelter and M. K. Mayers, *Ministering Cross-Culturally* (Grand Rapids: Baker Book House, 1986), pp. 15–16.

[2] *Ibid.*, p. 11.

[3] *Ibid.*, p. 17.

[4] Stephen E. Talitwala, "Cross-Cultural Communication (I)" *The Work of An Evangelist,* edited by J.D. Douglas (Minneapolis: World Wide Publications, 1984), p. 455.

[5] Ralph D. Winter, "Rejoice" (a mini-poster) published by WCL, Pasadena, CA, 1992.

[6] Elisabeth Elliot, talk given at Wheaton College, Wheaton, IL, April 23, 1991, pp. 7–8 of transcript.

[7] Robertson McQuilkin, "Who's Calling? An Exploration of the Missionary Call," Columbia Bible College & Seminary, 1984.

[8] *Ibid.*

[9] John Robb, "Evangelistic Strategies for the Evangelist," *The Calling of an Evangelist*, edited by J. D. Douglas (Minneapolis: World Wide Publications, 1987), p. 338.

[10] *Ibid.*

[11] Talitwala, "Cross-Cultural Communication (I)," p. 457.

[12] Eliot.

[13] *Ibid.*

SESSION ELEVEN
Evangelism and Disciplemaking

GOALS FOR THE CHAPTER:

After reading this chapter, you should be able to:

1. Understand the importance of disciplemaking.

2. Develop an eight-week plan for working with a new convert to establish her in her faith.

3. Learn the steps needed so that a young Christian will be equipped to share her faith and then disciple others.

4. Be aware of and avoid some of the pitfalls that frequently cause disciplemakers to stumble.

I. INTRODUCTION

Just taking a child into a school building does not mean that she will learn anything new. Someone needs to teach students, and students should want to learn. The same is true with evangelism and discipleship. Without continued learning and growth in the faith, new believers will stagnate or fall away. Unfortunately, much evangelism today is centered on encouraging a person to make a verbal decision for Christ (an event) rather than establishing or equipping the convert (a process). However, the call to make disciples is the last command that Christ gave to His church, and it must be taken very seriously.

A. What is a Disciple?

A disciple is simply a learner, a student, or an apprentice. For the new Christian, she is one who responds to Jesus' personal invitation: "learn from me" [Matt. 11:29].

B. What Is Disciplemaking?

Disciplemaking is the program and plan for equipping and establishing those who have accepted Jesus Christ. This is a lifelong course as the new Christian sets out to respond to Jesus' personal invitation to learn from Him. As the Apostle Paul put it in his letter to the church at Ephesus, the body of Christ has prophets, evangelists, pastors, and teachers whose primary calling is "to prepare God's people for works of service, so that the body of Christ may be built up until we all reach unity in the faith and in the knowledge of the Son of God and become mature, attaining to the whole measure of the fullness of Christ" [Eph. 4:11–13]. We know we will not be fully conformed to the image of Jesus until He comes again, but in the meantime we are on a pilgrimage to become more like Him and help others to do the same [1 John 3:2]. This is what disciplemaking is all about.

II. WHY IS DISCIPLEMAKING IMPORTANT?

There are many reasons why discipleship is important, but four will suffice to underscore the point. First of all, the Bible teaches that from the beginning of time God intended to call a people to Himself who would follow Him, praise Him, and bring glory to Him forever. Jesus became flesh to begin a church of the Spirit that will never perish because it is preordained to be comprised of great multitudes of men and women from "every nation, tribe, people, and language" who will praise God forever (see Rev. 7:9–12).

Secondly, the command to make disciples comes from the Lord Jesus Himself. As Jesus ascended into heaven, the words of the Great Commission echoed in the ears of His disciples. The last command of Jesus to those responsible for building His church was to *make disciples* [Matt. 28:18–20]. Evangelism is but a part of the Great Commission. This Scripture requires us not only to witness to the unsaved, but also to *teach* those that are saved to obey everything He had commanded. Two thousand years later, nothing has changed. Christians are still charged with the responsibility to make disciples.

Establishing a new Christian is a very important work. Unfortunately, many converts remain as babies or immature Christians because no one took an interest in their growth. No one would think of saying to a new baby: "When you are hungry, the bottles are in the kitchen and when you are wet, the diapers are on the changing table." If newborn babies need physical parents to feed, protect, train, and provide for their growth and well-being, it is only natural to assume that spiritual children need the same kind of care.

A third reason that Christians should be intent on making disciples emanates from the example of Jesus. Christ used people, not plans or methods, as His model. He chose twelve men and worked diligently to teach them the truths about Himself and His kingdom. Eventually, He sent them out to build the church by making disciples in the way that He had shaped them.

Furthermore, the success of the early church serves as a model. There were not many disciples when Jesus ascended into heaven—maybe 500 at the most—yet within the next thirty years, this tiny band grew to include over 200,000 people called Christians. This astounding testimony proves the effectiveness of a discipleship program based upon the model given to them by Jesus. In the book of Acts alone, there are at least thirty-two references to "follow-up" and eighteen times where encouragement is extended to new believers. If believers today multiplied at the same rate, the whole world would be kneeling at the feet of Jesus in less than one generation.

Finally, disciplemaking is important because new Christians are very vulnerable to the attacks of Satan, who will cause doubts to arise and temptations to entice. Young Christians are often easily discouraged. They have not learned to use the knowledge of the Word of God as a defense and thus are more likely to feel defeated. They do not have the spiritual resistance which comes from Scripture. Ephesians 6:13 reminds us to: "Take up the full armor of God, that you may be able to resist." But a new Christian does not possess much of an armor. She has a helmet of salvation and a very small shield of faith. Follow-up helps with the process of clothing the new believer with the rest of the armor.

STOP AND APPLY

1. Define a disciple:

2. Using your own words, define disciplemaking:

Fill in the blanks:

3. From the beginning of time, God intended to call a people to Himself who would follow Him, praise Him, and bring _____ to Him forever.

4. Jesus Himself _____ us to make disciples.

5. Jesus served as our _____ in making disciples.

6. The success of the early church serves as a_____.

III. HOW DO WE MAKE DISCIPLES?

A. Establishing the New Christian in Her Faith

"So then, just as you received Christ Jesus as Lord, continue to live in him, rooted and built up in him, strengthened in the faith as you were taught, and overflowing with thankfulness" [Col. 2:6–7]. When souls are born of the Spirit, they will either begin to grow and become more like Jesus, or they will atrophy and die. C.S. Lewis said that humans are like eggs. Either they mature and hatch or die and rot.

Most new Christians recognize their need for salvation, but this is only the beginning of what God wants for His children. Indeed, after their spiritual birth He wants them to grow in knowledge of Him and in obedience to what He has called them to do. In this way, God will be glorified and the believer will be transformed and filled with joy. New believers need a pattern or plan to follow.

The Essentials

1. Devotion

Establishing a devotional life should be the first priority for the new Christian. She needs training to learn how to have a "quiet time" and meditate on God's Word. She needs teaching on the Word of God and also how to study the Bible on her own. Furthermore, women who are trying to be "personally acquainted with Jesus" spend quality time in prayer each day. They praise him, tell Him about their fears, ask for help in overcoming sins, and seek His assistance in meeting the needs of the day.

2. Worship

A daily period of prayer and Bible reading should be comple-mented by regular worship in a local church. This normally hap-pens on Sunday mornings, but also might include Sunday evenings or midweek services as well. A new convert needs to become incorporated into a local church. She needs the sound teaching, as well as a place to observe people in ministry and eventually find a place of ministry and service herself.

3. Fellowship with Other Believers

Going to church to worship God is an essential element in growing toward maturity (particularly because the focus is on God), but growth also comes from fellowship with other believers. God does not intend for His followers to walk alone. They are now a part of the church—the Body of Christ. They are to interact by sharing one another's joys and happiness, in addition to bearing one another's burdens during seasons of distress.

4. Doctrine

The new believer needs to become doctrinally grounded and scripturally oriented. She needs to be taught the basic theology revealed in the biblical drama of the creation, fall, redemption, and future hope.

5. Witness

It is important to help the young Christian learn to be a faithful witness in bringing others to know Christ. John 15:16 tell us: "You did not choose me, but I chose you to go and bear fruit—fruit that will last." No matter how inexperienced, God can and will use anyone as a witness. Although the recent convert may not know much doctrine, she will be able to tell others what has happened and how God's grace has changed her life. Every Christian life is a testimony to God's goodness and our individual stories, when guided by the Holy Spirit, can be used to bring others to faith.

6. Giving: Money and Service

Growth also springs from giving—giving of both time and money. Everything we have comes from God, and He expects us to use our talents, abilities, possessions, and money wisely. Investing in His kingdom helps us to solidify and build on our commitment. Our allegiance and identification with God's kingdom increases in proportion to the amount that we invest of ourselves and our resources.

7. Character

All Christians are in the process of becoming conformed to the image of Christ. As we surrender control of ourselves, the Holy Spirit shows us weaknesses in our character which need to be changed. For instance, we might find ourselves dealing with selfishness, pride, laziness, lack of discipline, or a critical spirit. With the help of the Holy Spirit, we can and should weed out these sinful habits or tendencies and replace them with virtues that will bring glory to God and help to further His kingdom.

B. Implementation of Follow-Up

The process of follow-up is often divided into two time periods: the initial weeks where the person gets *started* growing in Christ, and the ongoing follow-up which helps the young believer become more deeply rooted in her faith.

The following suggestions are intended to help you get started. They do not represent the only (or necessarily) the best method to follow in all circumstances, but they should give you an idea of the goals you will want to keep in mind.

1. The Initial Period

Get together with the new Christian as soon as feasible (preferably within the first forty-eight hours) after conversion. This is the time when Satan will try to cast doubts into her mind.

a. Develop the friendship. Express a sincere personal interest in her life. If you have already established a friendship, you will just want to keep going. However, if the new convert is someone you do not know well, spend some time building your friendship. Look for areas where you share common interests and goals.

b. Clarify and confirm the commitment. Clarify and confirm her commitment to Christ. New Christians are sometimes unclear about their commitment, so begin by asking her to explain her decision to follow Christ. If she understands the basic outline of the Gospel (that she is a sinner; that she is saved through the death of Christ on the cross, and that she has now entered into a personal relationship with Christ), then go on to show her the wonderful promises of assurance of eternal life and fellowship with God found in John 3:16, 1 John 5:12–13, and John 10:27–29. When possible, let your friend read the verses for herself, and then ask her to explain God's promise in her own words. This will help you to quickly spot any areas where she might be confused about Scripture.

If she is uncertain about the source of her salvation, go back and use James Kennedy's questions from Evangelism Explosion: "If you were to die tonight, do you know for certain that you would go to heaven?" and "If you were to die tonight and stand before God and He were to say to you 'Why should I let you into My heaven?' what would you say to Him?" You will then want to present the steps to salvation again, stopping frequently to see if she has questions. Study chapter two of this manual so that you will feel comfortable dealing with her doubts or concerns.

c. Stress the importance of prayer and Bible study. Reiterate that she has entered into a *personal relationship* with Christ; He is now her friend. Within this context *briefly* explain the role of prayer and the reading of Scripture, and encourage her to begin praying and reading the Bible a few minutes each day.

Decide on a modest goal for prayer and Bible reading for the coming week. For instance, you might agree to pray for five minutes each day and read one chapter of the Bible.

Prayer should be thought of as a two-way conversation with God. The new believer will want to spend some time telling God how much she loves Him and also thanking Him for His gifts in her life. If she is uncertain about what to do, suggest that she try to praise and thank Him for five good things that have happened to her each day. These can be commonplace or significant occurrences. Then she will want to move on to confession and intercession for others or herself.

The Gospel of John is often an excellent place to begin in the Bible. Make sure that your friend has a modern translation that she can readily understand. Suggest that she keep a notebook where she can write down any questions she has about the text, and also record any ideas she has about applying the passage to her own life.

d. Plan for growth. Work out a plan for regular meetings during the next six to eight weeks. (The remaining sections of the chapter will help you get started.) Everyone is more comfortable when they know what to expect. At this stage, it is vitally important to *set an attainable goal*. You might agree that you will each spend 10–15 minutes a day on prayer and Bible reading and that you will hold each other accountable. Promise to call her daily during the first week so that she can have quick feedback with any problem or difficulty she might encounter. In succeeding weeks, you will probably want to talk with each other at least twice each week so that you can be aware of any needs or problems that might develop.

i. As her spiritual parent, you will want to **pray daily** for the new believer that she will grow in her faith and be strong when tempted. Also remember to pray for the Holy Spirit's guidance and wisdom when you are working with her and planning future sessions.

ii. Offer to **take her to church** with you if she needs a place to worship. During the next few weeks, you will want to introduce her to the importance of becoming involved in a church family.

iii. *Pray aloud* with the new believer so that she will become familiar with the format for prayer and also the concept of praying for others. If she feels comfortable, encourage her to pray aloud, assuring her that God is looking at the sincerity of our hearts and not the elegance of our words.

iv. Finally, *encourage, encourage, encourage!* It is much easier to succeed when we receive positive reinforcement. Try to find at least one reason to compliment your new friend each time you talk with her.

2. Ongoing Follow-Up—Two Weeks to Two Months

Begin with a time of informal sharing and then move on to a discussion of her quiet times during the last week. If she is struggling with consistency, try to pinpoint the problem and deal with it. For instance, if she has not set aside a regular time for her devotions, help her to do so. Answer any questions she might have. Encourage her to relate what she is learning to her daily life and continue to encourage practical application through the development of the following areas:

a. Prayer

Introduce her to the idea of using a prayer log. Help her to learn how to record petitions and answers. Encourage her to keep her prayer log in a notebook so that she will have a permanent record of how God is working in her life.

Help her to see that we cannot always know which answer God will give us when we pray for material blessings, but we do know that He will always give us those spiritual blessings that He has promised in Scripture. For instance, in James 1:5, God promises wisdom to those who ask for it; Hebrews 2:18 assures us that there is help and understanding from God when we undergo temptation; and Romans 8:28 assures us that everything believers experience can be used for good if we surrender to the will of God. The Bible is a repository for the promises of God to believers of all generations. Help the young convert to begin to pray about the ones that will specifically help her to grow spiritually. Write one or two of these down and agree to pray for them daily.

b. Bible Study

Continue to work on your study of Scripture. See the chapter on "Evangelism and Bible Study" for ideas about doing an inductive bible study. Concentrate your energies on helping your friend to discover the importance and relevance of Bible study in her life.

c. Scripture Memory

Introduce the topic of Scripture memory and explain its importance:

1. We are commanded to memorize Scripture [Deut. 6:6–9; Prov. 7:1–3].

2. It helps us to resist temptation [Ps. 19:11; Ps. 119:1–11].

3. Christ gives us an example [Matt. 4:1–11].

4. It helps us in witnessing [Heb. 4:12; 1 Pet. 3:15; Acts 4:13].

5. It helps direct our path. It fills our minds with the Word, which helps us in making decisions and in keeping our minds pure [Ps. 119:105].

Set a goal. Most people start off with a verse a week. There are several good programs available to help you with this, or you may choose the verses yourself. In any case, select verses that will either reinforce her commitment or help her to see the promises and attributes of the Christian life more clearly.

d. The Local Church

Discuss the nature and importance of baptism and identification with a local church. It is in this setting that we usually find God's provision for fellowship and teaching.

e. Testimony

Each Christian has a story to tell of God's working in her life. Your friend may not know much theology, but she should be able to relate how God has cleansed her from sin and saved her for Himself. Chapter Two of this manual contains the guidelines for developing a testimony. As soon as you are able, you will want to help the new convert to put together a two- or three-minute testimony that will clearly relate the message of the Gospel to her friends and family. God frequently uses these first weeks in a special way. New Christians often express an enthusiasm for Christianity that is contagious. Their exuberance and obvious joy in their new relationship with Jesus will cause people who are close to them to stop and take notice. This will give them a unique opportunity to witness to family and friends. Remind the new believer that many will also watch to see if this is just "a passing stage" or a real life change. The new believer will want to work on the consistency of her actions and words.

f. Lifestyle and Christian Witness

After covering the basics, work on areas that are of special concern or difficulty. For instance, the new convert may struggle with bitterness and resentment, or she may have trouble managing her time wisely. Christians are called to be holy and to live a life that consistently reflects the one led by Jesus. To that end, each of us should be striving to conform our actions increasingly to those of Jesus. Help the young believer to see that this is a lifelong privilege and blessing. There are many resources available to help you meet these needs. (See the list of selected resources at Appendix C.)

4. Accountability

It is very easy for new Christians to slip back into old habits and sins, or to never develop the spiritual disciplines that will result in healthy growth. Mutual accountability will result in a blessing for her life as well as yours. When you get together, hold each other responsible for maintaining quiet times, Scripture memory, prayer times, and also sharing prayer requests and answered prayers. Avoid overwhelming her, but stress the importance of establishing good habits. This kind of reciprocity will encourage her to begin to take responsibility for helping other Christians and will provide a natural transition to the next steps in disciplemaking.

STOP AND APPLY

1. Match the following descriptions with the essentials of discipleship that each describes:

    ___ Dealing with lack of discipline   a. Devotion

    ___ Learning to share Christ with   b. Worship
    others   c. Fellowship

    ___ Establishing a regular quiet time   d. Doctrine

    ___ Learning basic theology   e. Witness

    ___ Attending church regularly   f. Giving

    ___ Getting together with other   g. Character
    Christians

    ___ Using talents and being generous with money

2. Number the following to reflect the steps for working with a new believer:

    ___ Clarify and confirm the commitment.

    ___ Plan for growth.

    ___ Develop the friendship.

    ___ Explain the importance of prayer and Bible study.

> 3. How would you suggest that she begin a short prayer and Bible study time?
>
> 4. List five or six areas to cover in ongoing follow-up. What are some other areas that you think may be important?
>
> _____   _____
>
> _____   _____
>
> _____   _____
>
> _____   _____

IV. DISCIPLESHIP

A. *Equip the Growing Christian to Minister to Others*

The definition of equipping is "the process of preparing a growing disciple for service." To put it another way, equipping is the process of training the disciple for ministry to others. The ultimate goal is not just inward, but also that her relationship with God will result in service to others. Once a Christian is established in her spiritual life, you should teach her how to work with someone younger in the faith.

The best plan for doing the work of disciplemaking is found in the life of Jesus, and the Gospels are replete with stories of His interaction and training of the twelve. Robert E. Coleman's important book, *The Master Plan of Evangelism,*[1] provides an extremely helpful summary and explanation of the methods used by Jesus. Christ devoted most of His time to discipling twelve men with whom He worked closely for three years. Then He commissioned them to go forth and repeat the process that He had taken them through, and the church spread from Jerusalem to Judea, to Samaria, and to the uttermost parts of the world. The plan of Jesus, as presented by Coleman, is simple, clear, and useful to follow. It can be easily repeated using the following steps.

1. *Selection*

Select one or two people. Most Christians cannot devote their full time to discipleship and will fail if they try to work with twelve people. Even Jesus narrowed His focus. He made no attempt to disciple the large crowds that followed Him, and although He selected twelve Apostles, He concentrated the most attention on just three. Women with a family, job, or both have a limited amount of time and energy. Consider working with one woman or a small group of five or six, but recognize that a group will limit the amount of time that can be spent with each. *Pilgrims in Progress* by Jim and Carol Pleuddemann (Harold Shaw Press, 1991) will prove useful for those who choose to work with a group rather than an individual.

Begin by prayerfully asking God to give you someone who is a true believer and is willing to learn. It is very important to work with willing learners rather than those who have to be dragged into the discipleship lifestyle.

2. Association

Jesus spent three years working with His men. School was always in session. Time was the key element. He gave of His time by truly associating with them in a quantitative and qualitative fashion.

Jesus understood (as should we) that He was working with individuals and not machines, and took into account their unique needs. He recognized that He was investing in the future of the church and was content to start with a small group in whom He could build a firm foundation. The worldwide church of today has proven the wisdom of His methods.

3. Consecration

Jesus required obedience. Though kind, loving, and fair, He called them to costly discipleship—the way of the cross. It took them time to understand it and He was patient with them, but there was no compromise in the commitment expected from them. Personal agendas and goals had to be set aside. Christ's purpose for their lives became their highest calling.

The same holds today. Disciples must learn to walk with Jesus. Our commitment must always be to Christ and never to another human. When working with a disciple, we must always point her attention to Jesus and never to ourselves.

4. Impartation and Demonstration

His discipleship program called the disciples to give up everything, but it was no more than He gave to them. Jesus did not train His disciples through words alone. On the contrary, His instruction often took the form of demonstration. Jesus did not just command them to serve others; He washed their feet. He did not merely tell them to pray; He showed them how. Jesus imparted all the Father had given Him [John 15:5], including His joy [John 15:11], and even the keys to His

Kingdom [Matt. 16:19; Luke 12:32]. And when He called them to give everything by taking up the cross, He demonstrated at Golgotha what He asked of them. Truth is best communicated when it is presented simultaneously by example and precept.

5. Delegation

It is important to delegate responsibilities to those you disciple. Jesus allowed His followers to put into practice what He had taught and demonstrated. The Savior understood that people learn best by doing. Having been a carpenter before He took on the task of discipling twelve men, He knew from experience that an apprentice needs more than demonstrations; the learner must try the task himself. Therefore, Jesus gradually delegated responsibilities to them. He sent them for food, allowed them to baptize, and eventually sent them out two-by-two to heal the sick and preach the good news of the Kingdom of God.

Most young Christians are both eager and timid about getting involved in ministry. They usually fear that they are not "spiritual enough," but nearly all are eager to get actively involved in a tangible way. Your role as the discipler is to help them get started. Try to find an activity that suits their talents. For instance, those gifted in the area of education may choose to work with Sunday School or other educational groups; good listeners who interact well with people are ideal to visit shut-ins or the elderly. If possible, go with them the first time and show them how to do the job. After watching you, most will feel comfortable about becoming more actively involved.

6. Supervision

Always the master craftsman who knew how to direct the apprentices, Jesus not only delegated, He offered supervision. He oversaw what He delegated, and He called them together to review their effectiveness with the tasks He assigned to them [Mark 6:30; Luke 9:10]. Rejoicing that even the demons submitted to them, the disciples sometimes celebrated with their Master [Luke 10:17]. In other instances, the disciples failed to achieve the desired results and Jesus had to reshape the areas where they were weak and therefore failing. For instance, following their successful preaching trip, the perplexed disciples questioned Jesus about their inability to cast out a demon from a little boy (see Mark 9:17–29; Matt. 17:14–20; Luke 9:37–43). Pointing out the need for greater faith and prayer, Jesus sought to help them grow in their spiritual maturity and understanding.

7. Reproduction

Selection, association, consecration, impartation, demonstration, delegation, and supervision all pointed to Christ's pre-planned goal—reproduction. After His crucifixion, resurrection, and forty-day ministry preceding the ascension, Jesus turned over to the disciples the task of going out and making still more disciples.

B. The Way to Reach the World.

No one reaches full spiritual maturity until they die or Christ returns for them. Discipleship, then, is an ongoing process, even for those who have had a personal relationship with Jesus Christ for decades. The accompanying illustration dramatically underscores the power of discipleship.

Some time ago, there was a display at the Museum of Science and Industry in Chicago. It featured a checkerboard with 1 grain of wheat on the first square, 2 on the second, 4 on the third, then 8, 16, 32, 64, 128, and so on. Somewhere down the board, there were so many grains of wheat on the square that some were spilling over into neighboring squares—so here the demonstration stopped. Above the checkerboard display was a question, "At this rate of doubling every square, how much grain would you have on the checkerboard by the time you reached the 64th square?"

To find the answer to this riddle, you punched a button on the console in front of you, and the answer flashed on a little screen above the board: "Enough to cover the entire subcontinent of India 50 feet deep."[2]

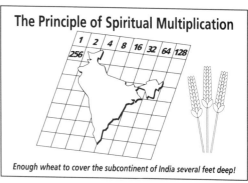

The Principle of Spiritual Multiplication

Enough wheat to cover the subcontinent of India several feet deep!

To look at this same principle in terms of evangelism and discipleship, if you won one person to faith in Christ and spent six months establishing her in the faith and equipping her to witness, at the end of six months there would just be two of you. But if both of you won other persons and trained them in the same manner for six months, at the end of a year you would have four. If this process of multiplication were to continue without stopping, in a little over 16 years you would have won the entire world to faith in Christ. This obviously assumes that there is no weak link in the chain, an assumption that we can never make when people are involved. But think of the potential of this approach! Instead of one person doing all the work of evangelism, the process of discipling systematically increases the number of laborers and results in an even greater harvest.

STOP AND APPLY

Circle the answer which best describes a step of disciplemaking:

1. When Jesus focused on a small group of men, He demonstrated the principle of:
   (a) Consecration (b) Selection   (c) Delegation

2. Seeking to train someone by example is:
   (a) Association   (b) Demonstration (c) Supervision

3. Allowing someone to put into practice the things that have been learned illustrates:
   (a) Reproduction (b) Impartation   (c) Delegation

4. Overseeing what has been delegated demonstrates:
   (a) Supervision   (b) Impartation   (c) Association

5. The goal of the eight-step plan is:
   (a) Delegation   (b) Reproduction   (c) Supervision

C. Practical Guidelines

A few points of caution need to be examined for those who, with God's help, are going to be obedient to the call to make disciples.

1. God Is the Source of Growth.

God wants every believer to grow toward maturity [Col. 1:28]. Colossians 2:6–7 speaks of the need to be *rooted* and *grounded* in the faith. The Christian, like a plant, needs a healthy root system if she is to grow and reproduce. No one should ever try and disciple someone else without remembering that the whole process is dependent on God's direction and guidance. *God is the source for spiritual growth* [1 Cor. 3:6; John 15]. Furthermore, the Christian who attempts to usurp God's role and work in her own strength will fail.

2. Count the Cost.

Count the cost before beginning. Quitting midstream will not only cause embarrassment to the discipler, but irreparable pain to the disciple who will feel abandoned.

Young disciples, like small children, need much care and attention. They get into difficulties, make messy mistakes, and take one step back for every two forward. The discipler should realize that this process will demand a commitment of time, energy, emotional strength, and spiritual involvement. The rewards, however, of seeing a young Christian grow to the point of being able to reproduce and become a vital, active part of the Kingdom ministry more than outweigh the costs.

3. Beware of the Overly-Dependent.

Every woman who sets out to make disciples should be on her guard against the parasitical person who wants to drain her time and energy (making her useless for effective Kingdom work). For example:

> *Several years ago Michelle agreed to work with Lynn, another young mother. Lynn claimed to be a Christian, but explained that no one had ever helped her to grow. Furthermore, Lynn came from an abusive home which compounded her problems. Touched by her story, Michelle enthusiastically agreed to Lynn's appeal for help. Yet signs of trouble soon appeared. No matter what Michelle counseled or suggested, Lynn always rebelled. She showed no real signs of spiritual interest. What she craved and then demanded were inordinate amounts of Michelle's time. When Michelle tried to tactfully withdraw, Lynn used guilt to manipulate her. Michelle sought the counsel of some spiritually mature women in her church and they, too, reached out only to be drawn into the destructive cycle.*

> *Lynn's sinful, self-centered behavior patterns never changed. When confronted, she would tearfully weep and ask for forgiveness, but she soon fell back into her old ways. Eventually Michelle came to dread the sound of the phone or doorbell, because she felt helplessly trapped by the other woman. Michelle expected some regressive behavior, but this was different. Eventually she confronted Lynn and told her that there would be no more involvement unless she was serious about surrendering her life to Jesus. Michelle then laid out several specifics that she expected of Lynn if they were to continue. After Lynn thought for a few minutes, she decided that she really didn't want what Michelle was offering. Although saddened, Michelle was now free to work with women who really desired spiritual growth and maturity.*

This story is far more typical than some realize. That is why it is vitally important to pray for the discernment to know when a woman really has no intention of surrendering her life in obedience to Christ.

4. Examine Your Motives.

Christian women should never encourage disciples to cling to them, but should help them to become dependent upon the Lord Jesus. Disciplers need to regularly examine their motives. Younger Christians frequently admire and compliment the more mature woman's spiritual discipline, but this kind of flattery can be deceptive. Motives and egos need to be carefully guarded. The task of the discipler is to point others to Jesus that they might learn of Him, love Him, and eventually make Him known to others.

5. Disciple Those of the Same Sex Only.

Those who liberate lives from the clutches of the evil one should expect him to strike back. Frequently he tries to draw naive, well-meaning Christians into a relationship with a person of the opposite sex. Do not be deceived on this point. Except in unusual circumstances where there are no alternatives, it is best for women to disciple women and men to disciple men. Intimate involvement of the kind described in the Master's plan is not designed for parties of the opposite sex. Jesus, after all, discipled twelve men. Women were included in the larger group of regular followers, but they were not part of the intimate circle (even though some like Martha, Mary, and Mary Magdalene were close friends). Never did Jesus discriminate against women. The opposite is true. Many sources and stories reveal His equal regard for men and women. Yet He was also extremely careful to avoid any appearance of immorality. The wise learn from Him. Many Christian leaders fall into sinful temptation and relationships every year because of carelessness in this area.

6. Expect Some to Fall Away.

Counterfeit or apostate disciples appear in every generation and locality. Even Jesus lost one of His twelve. Although disappointing, no one should be devastated if a disciple chooses to backslide into sin. Many people come to the Lord as long as the going is fashionable and easy. Once the trials of life (let alone persecutions) arise, they flee from the action. Usually this is not the fault of the discipler, who should not blame herself and wallow in guilt. This is merely one more way the enemy seeks to immobilize Christian warriors.

7. Tough Love is Required.

Related to the issue of backsliding, on the other hand, is the need for tough love. Following Christ's pathway for making disciples requires that they be held accountable, and sometimes a firm kick is required. Even the earnest seeker who genuinely wants to grow in her knowledge and love of Christ will need to be held accountable. If she slides back on her daily prayer time, Bible study, worship attendance, and obedience in areas that are not open to debate, then discipline becomes necessary. This painful task is made somewhat easier by establishing ground rules before entering into a discipling relationship. If, for instance, daily devotional time will be required for membership in a discipleship group, then make it clear that anyone who habitually fails in this area will be asked to withdraw.

8. Do Not Set Impossible Standards.

Although tough love is essential for the slothful or errant disciple, do not err on the other side and demand more than a young Christian can deliver. Never set a standard that a new believer cannot realistically sustain. Mature Christians may find it easy—even enjoyable—to spend an hour or even two in early morning devotions, but this amount of time will overwhelm the new Christian (who will probably find five minutes of prayer and a brief period of Bible and devotional reading to be sufficient). Demanding or expecting too much too soon will discourage and disillusion the new believer. It is far better to start small and let them experience success. The Holy Spirit treats each soul individually, and He never exactly duplicates the pattern found in any other life. Get the disciple started on a pattern of spiritual discipline, and the Holy Spirit will soon increase her desire for more. Remember, too, that Jesus began slowly with His disciples. He took three years before He felt ready to turn them loose to reproduce.

9. Do Not Be Jealous of Other Input.

No one should assume that she is the only person who will disciple a young believer. Most people learn from more than one person at a time. After investing huge quantities of time in the disciple, it is tempting to feel jealous when she begins to meet with someone else (or to extol the virtues and wisdom of another Christian). Rather than feeling resentment, the wise woman rejoices in God's provision for this young one. Some disciples need prolonged contact with one woman, while others move in and out of several lives. It may be that the disciple will only remain for a period of weeks or months before moving on to another woman. This is often part of God's plan and should not cause distress. Whether the discipler plays a major or minor role in someone else's journey is not important. Leading others to a closer relationship with Christ should always be the consuming passion.

10. Learn from Others.

It is vital to remember that no one knows everything. Even the person who has faithfully followed Jesus for seventy-five or eighty years can learn more about the Master and sometimes the young teach the old. No one in the Women's Bible Study group at a local church will ever forget what they learned the day the newest Christian in the group excitedly shared "the most wonderful verse" that she had "just discovered." Everyone was teary-eyed as seasoned Christians found fresh meaning in John 3:16, and attention was directed back to the great love of the Father for His children.

11. Know When You Lack the Proper Expertise.

Finally, everyone needs to humble themselves and admit there are people and situations which are more than they can handle. Some psychological or emotional problems require professional help. In such circumstances, it is imperative to bring in qualified Christian counselors.

Young Christians who go through a particular problem (such as the death of a loved one or marital problems) will often find it more helpful to be discipled by an older woman who has faced and conquered similar difficulties. Everyone must remember that the Body of Christ is made up of many parts. Each member has had different experiences and each one possesses special gifts. It is God's will that *all share* in the work of reaching the lost and making disciples. There are no "lone rangers" in the Kingdom. The effort should involve the community, not just individuals, because ultimately it is a task aimed to bring glory to Jesus Christ—and this glory will never be stolen by anyone.

V. CONCLUSION

Helping a new believer to become established in the faith is one of the most exciting tasks that a Christian can undertake. It is similar to the thrill experienced by gardeners as they watch spring bulbs appear in previously frozen ground. Green shoots signal the beginning, but no one wants the process to end there. The gardener knows that the plant still needs care if a perfect flower is going to unfold. Furthermore, each plant is different, and so is the type of care it will require. Some need sun and lots of water; others thrive in shade. The same is true of new Christians, and there are many options available for discipleship. The suggested resources in Appendix C are provided as a starting point. Christian bookstores contain a wealth of current materials and suggestions. Pastors and Christian Education Directors can also help disciplers and new believers to find materials that will meet many different needs or goals.

The wonderful thing about discipleship is that it is only complete when we enter heaven. *Spiritual growth is a lifelong process—no one has "arrived."* This is a comfort, because we realize that we do not have to have all the answers. It is also a challenge, because we are involved in a lifelong spiritual adventure that should daily draw us nearer to God. The next step is up to you. Will you take seriously the command of Christ to "go and make disciples"?

STOP AND APPLY

Fill in the blanks:

1. We must recognize that _____ always be the source of growth.

2. Count the _____ before beginning a discipleship relationship.

3. Examine your _____ to make sure disciples become dependent upon the Lord rather than you.

4. Realizing that some people come to the Lord thinking that it is fashionable and easy, expect some to _____ _____.

5. Do not be _____ of someone else's input.

6. Discuss with your mentor your personal vision for discipleship.

Now if you haven't already done so, listen to cassette tape #6A in the series featuring *A Study on Discipleship* by Kay Arthur. Also on the tape are excerpts of messages from Nita Outhous, Vonette Bright, and June Moss.

ENDNOTES

[1] Robert E. Coleman, *The Master Plan of Evangelism* (New Jersey: Fleming H. Revell Co., 1963).

[2] Walt Henrichsen, cited in *Discipleship*, ed. by Billie Hanks, Jr. (Grand Rapids, MI: Zondervan, 1981), p. 86.

SESSION TWELVE
Women Need Women

GOALS FOR THE CHAPTER:

Evangelism should never be viewed as an event. Instead, our lives (like Jesus' life) should be a consistent witness that draws others to the Father. After reading this concluding chapter, you should be able to:

1. Understand the unique role for women in evangelism.

2. Make a serious commitment to a life of discipleship.

3. Realize your circle of influence in evangelism and disciplemaking.

4. Be encouraged if you are discouraged.

5. Develop a life goal of reaching others for Christ.

I. INTRODUCTION: WOMEN NEED WOMEN

God has a unique role for women in evangelism, a special calling for women to minister to other women. As women, we need to understand the enormous value God has placed on us. We should realize the influence He has given us in the lives of other women.

Women have some needs that only other women can fully appreciate. Only a single, middle-aged woman who has desperately desired to be a wife and mother can truly empathize with another woman struggling with the same problem. Who can help the bereaved mother more than someone who has been through similar circumstances? Only women can fully understand difficulties with the desire for marriage, pregnancies, the stresses of balancing a career and home life, the trials and tribulations of mothering several preschool children, the pain of an unfaithful husband, and the list could go on and on.

Tired, lonely, discouraged, depressed, or confused women are searching for a sense of worth. You, as a woman, have an unique opportunity to share with others the solution to these deep needs. You can show them God's love, His plan of salvation, His forgiveness, and His hand on your life. You do not have to be "experienced" to do this—you do not need to be a graduate of a Bible college or seminary, or have any kind of formal training to share. No matter what your circumstances or background, you can share your story. You have your own joys and sorrows, disappointments and successes, victories and failures. You may be married or single, divorced or widowed, a mother or childless. You may be old or young. Whatever the case, you have something priceless to offer. You know Jesus Christ in a personal way, and you can share that wonderful relationship with others.

Titus 2:3–5 says: "Likewise, teach the older women to be reverent in the way they live, not to be slanderers or addicted to much wine, but to teach what is good. Then they can train the younger women to love their husbands and children, to be self-controlled and pure, to be busy at home, to be kind, and to be subject to their husbands, so that no one will malign the word of God."

You as an "older" woman, no matter what your age, can minister to a "younger" woman. Each contact provides a valuable opportunity to either bring her to a saving knowledge of Christ or to help her deepen her commitment and reliance on Him.

Everyone is in need of encouragement today. Encouragement is the affirmation that spurs someone on to want to be a better Christian, even when the going is tough. Ecclesiastes 4:9–12 says: "Two are better than one, because they have a good return for their work: If one falls down, his friend can help him up. But pity the man who falls and has no one to help him up! Also, if two lie down together, they will keep warm. But how can one keep warm alone? Though one may be overexposed, two can defend themselves. A cord of three strands is not quickly broken." Women especially need other women to encourage them. Each Christian is precious in the sight of the Lord, because we are adopted into His family as joint heirs with Christ. Share this with someone!

STOP AND APPLY

1. List several reasons why women have a unique opportunity to share with other women.

   _____ _____

   _____ _____

   _____ _____

   _____ _____

2. Read Titus 2:3–5. Is there a "younger woman" you can teach? Is there an "older" woman from whom you can learn?

II. PERSONAL COMMITMENT

A. A Call to Radical Obedience

If women are going to do their utmost to glorify God and obey His command to make true disciples (rather than mere converts), they need to be purposeful about their walk with God. New believers require help in developing this trait. This is what Jesus meant when He told us to "make disciples." If we are to be true disciples, we must continually "learn from Him." Then we must teach others to know and obey Him, so they in turn can become teachers who assist other new believers along the way.

God desires that we grow and become like Christ, but this is a process. Each day we need to let Him take control of every area of our life. Further, we must learn to be obedient to His commands. This obedience should never spring from fear but from a desire to please God. Psalm 40:8 says: "To do your will, O my God, is my desire; your law is within my heart."

The true disciple recognizes that God's law provides a safety barrier between us and evil. Obedience to God never deprives us of fun, but rather protects us from all that would injure or harm us. The law is God's gracious provision for our well being.

Hannah Whitall Smith, a Christian teacher, lecturer, and great devotional author from the last century, understood this principle of obedience and in response penned a beautiful prayer of commitment:

> Here Lord, I abandon myself to thee. I have tried in every way I could think of to manage myself, and to make myself what I know I ought to be, but have always failed. Now I give it up to thee. Do thou take entire possession of me. Work in me all the good pleasure of thy will. Mold and fashion me into such a vessel as seemeth good to thee. I leave myself in thy hands, and I believe thou wilt, according to thy promise, make me into a vessel unto thy own honor, sanctified, and meet for the master's use, and prepared unto every good work.[1]

B. Seven Elements of Discipleship

Although there are scores of books on discipleship, one of the best is a slim, seventy-seven page volume by William MacDonald entitled *True Discipleship*. Following the advice found in this tiny book has inspired countless souls to become better disciples who then helped others follow the pathway themselves. MacDonald says "true discipleship begins when a person is born again," but it must be followed by "an all-out commitment to the Lord Jesus Christ."[2] According to the author, "The Savior is not looking for men and women who will give their spare evenings to Him—or their weekends—or their years of retirement. Rather He seeks those who will give Him first place in their lives."[3] MacDonald suggests seven elements that are essential to true discipleship which he gleaned from the Bible:

1. A Supreme Love for Jesus Christ
In Luke 14:26, Jesus says we cannot be His disciples if we love anyone else—mother, father, spouse, children—more than we love Him. Anything less than this, He said, is unacceptable. The same can be said about loving things—especially money or fame—more than the Savior. The first and greatest commandment will always be to "Love the Lord your God with all your heart and with all your soul and with all your mind" [Matt. 22:37].

2. Self-Denial
Self-denial is the second element. In Matthew 16:24, Jesus said, "If anyone would come after me, he must *deny himself.*" This is not a matter of self-denial (such as giving up coffee, candy, or some bad or sinful habit). Rather, it involves submission of all one's "rights" and "will" to Him. In short, it is saying to God, "I give up all claims to myself. You will be my master." Luke 14:33 quotes Jesus as saying that only the person who gives up everything can be His disciple.

If this sounds radical, MacDonald's third point is even more so. The true disciple must not only love Jesus supremely and deny herself, she must take a further, deliberate step described in Matthew 16:24.

3. Taking Up The Cross
The cross is not the pain suffered when a loved one dies or the doctor prescribes major surgery. No indeed. These things happen to nonbelievers as well as believers. Taking up the cross is the shame, criticism, and pain received from family, friends, and even some Christians for living a life of radical obedience to Jesus Christ. Of course the cross can be avoided. Everyone is free to choose to be con-

formed to the ways of the world rather than the pathway set forth by Christ.

4. A Life of Following Jesus

A fourth element of discipleship requires Christians to spend their lives following Christ. Again as found in Matthew 16:24, Jesus says, "If anyone would come after me, he [she] must deny himself [herself] and take up his [her] cross *and follow me*." By "following Jesus," MacDonald means emulating His example. We need to learn to live as He did in the power of the Holy Spirit, giving unselfish service to others, and demonstrating complete obedience to everything commanded by the Father. Then we will become like Jesus.

5. Love for the Body of Christ

Element five is "a fervent love for all who belong to Christ." Jesus said that others will know we are His disciples by the way we love one another [John 13:35]. This is the kind of love that considers others better than ourselves [Philippians 2] and seeks the welfare of others before our own. In brief, it is being lovingly responsible for others, rather than selfishly seeking to secure our own privileges and rights—a revolutionary world view in these times.

6. Uncompromising Commitment to His Word

The sixth factor of true discipleship demands continuance in His Word. Jesus said, "if you hold to my teaching, you are really my disciples" [John 8:31]. Many people start their new life in Christ with great enthusiasm, only to turn away and give up once the novelty wears off or life becomes difficult. Fair-weather Christians (or those who join Christ's army for glamour or ease of life) soon fall by the way. They are not true disciples.

7. Willingness to Forsake All

Note that it is Jesus who sets forth these elements—not some overzealous and misguided modern teacher. In Luke 14:33, Jesus said in a way that must have astonished His followers, "any of you who does not give up everything he has cannot be my disciple." Jesus did not say you must be willing to forsake all. He said you must do it. He did not say that He required this of full-time Christian workers (such as missionaries, pastors, or evangelists). Rather, He said this is the standard He demands of *all* disciples.

This way of true discipleship is presented quite clearly and succinctly by Robert E. Coleman in *The Mind of the Master*:

> We are sent into the world, not to satisfy our own whims of ambition, but to do the will of Him who commands us. For us the cross does not mean that we will die for the world. That has been done by Jesus. But in accepting the benefit of His vicarious death, we are made aware that we are no longer our own, and compelled by the mandate of His love, we must give ourselves to the purpose for which He died [that is to see people reconciled to God through faith in Jesus Christ]....[4]

The demands of discipleship require that we live in a state of spiritual mobilization, bringing our thoughts into the same captivity as the obedience of Christ. Reflecting this commitment means a strict discipline and simple lifestyle, unencumbered with the things this world seeks, that we might give our maximum energy to God's mission. In the same spirit, we should hold our material resources with an open hand, recognizing that they belong to Christ, and are His to use for the furtherance of the Gospel.

Daring faith is required if we are to walk such a pathway. Most people will call this fanaticism rather than discipleship, but those following the steps of the Master know it means freedom and joy. As Robert Coleman noted, "Jesus is looking for such persons to follow Him—disciples who will throw caution to the wind and live like fools for His sake."[5]

STOP AND APPLY

1. If we are to be true disciples, we must continually
   _____ _____ _____.

2. Then we must teach others to _____ and _____
   Him so they can become teachers as well.

3. List the seven elements of discipleship and briefly describe what each one means.

   1) _____

   2) _____

   3) _____

   4) _____

   5) _____

6) _____

7) _____

4. Write a prayer to God, expressing your desire to be committed radically to Him.

_____

_____

_____

_____

III. CIRCLES OF INFLUENCE IN EVANGELISM AND DISCIPLEMAKING

You are a woman of influence. The way you live influences others. Whether we realize it or not, this is part of God's plan. God values not only our relationship with Him, but also our relationships with others. Every life either "gathers" (that is, attracts) or "scatters" (that is, distracts) others for the Kingdom of God.

A. Influence as a Single Woman

Singleness is a *gift* given to some people. In Matthew, the disciples ask Jesus about divorce. He instructs them that it is only permitted when one partner commits adultery. The amazed disciples respond: " 'If this is the situation between a husband and wife, it is better not to marry.' Jesus replied, 'Not everyone can accept this teaching, but *only those to whom it has been given*' " [Matt. 19:10–11]. In other words, for many the single life is a gift to be enjoyed because it is a special calling from God. Likewise, Paul writes to the Corinthians: "I wish that all men were as I am. But each man has his own gift from God; one has this gift, another has that" [1 Cor. 7:7]. If you are single, do you view your state as a blessing or a burden?

Singleness often brings time and opportunities that married people do not have. Singles have more freedom and mobility to "pick up and go" than a person with children has. There may be more flexibility to go to the mission field for either short- or long-term mission assignments. In addition, singles often have more time for education and training for ministry.

Without the distractions of a husband and children, the single woman can develop many varied friendships and ministries. John Fischer (author of the pamphlet, *A Single Person's Identity*) reflected on this topic:

> I have a strange feeling that the single person who is always wishing he were married will probably get married, discover all that is involved, and wish he were single again! He will ask himself, "Why didn't I use that time for the Lord when I didn't have so many other obligations? Why didn't I give myself totally to him when I was single?"[6]

Singleness is not better or worse than marriage—just a different life path. Whichever way God has chosen for you, each Christian should live a life that brings glory to God. If you are single, praise God for the gift He has given and see how you can take full advantage of your calling to advance the Kingdom of God.

There are others, however, who are single because of circumstances. Divorce or the death of a spouse has placed them into a single state. While it is not something they chose, they need to believe God is not only at work in them, but through them. God can take the pain they have experienced and through the comfort He has given them, enable them to comfort others and share God's faithfulness in difficult situations.

B. Influence as a Wife

Each Christian wife has an unique opportunity for evangelism in her own home. The wife of a nonbelieving spouse has the all-important task of seeking to introduce her husband to faith in Jesus as Savior and Lord. Equally exciting, the Christian wife of a Christian husband has the unique opportunity to work *in tandem with her spouse* in leading others to Jesus. She realizes this goal through actually witnessing to her faith and also by encouraging her Christian husband in his ministry of evangelism.

A wife can be a refreshing spring for her husband. Sarah Edwards, the wife of the great eighteenth-century preacher Jonathan Edwards, has been described as "the resting place of Jonathan's soul."[7] Besides her own witness to her family and community, Sarah gave needed support and encouragement to her husband.

Likewise, Maria Taylor, the wife of Hudson Taylor (the great missionary to China), dramatically influenced his life and ministry:

> Maria tempered without quenching his zeal, was largely responsible for the common sense and balance characteristic of Taylor at the height of his power. She made him take holidays. He became more assured, grew up. Her passionate nature fulfilled his

warm-blooded yearning to love and be loved. She gave him full response, fostering and feeding affection so that together they had such a reservoir of love that it splashed over to refresh all, Chinese or European, who came near them.[8]

C. Influence As A Mother

It is our children who will carry the Gospel to succeeding generations. Therefore we must carefully nurture it in their lives until the message of salvation burns brightly through them to the world. Hannah Jowett profoundly influenced her son, John Henry Jowett, whose preaching touched lives on all continents. Arthur Porritt, John Jowett's biographer, writes that:

> Jowett went through life chanting the praises of his mother. To the end of her life she was the object of his solicitous care. He never wearied of acknowledging the immensity of his indebtedness to her. "At my mother's knee," he said once, "I gained my sweetest inspirations." To a friend who once asked him whence came his gift for felicitous illustration he replied, "From my mother! It was she who taught me to see—she taught me to see things, and the things within things."[9]

In a similar way, Hudson Taylor's mother prayed earnestly for him:

> Leaving her friends she went alone to plead with God for his salvation. Hour after hour passed while that mother was still upon her knees, until her heart was flooded with a joyful assurance that her prayers were heard and answered.[10]

Mothering can often seem very mundane, unexciting, and of little consequence when you are up to your ears in diapers, bottles, or turbulent teenagers. At these moments, it helps to imagine what your child can become when he or she is surrendered fully to the Lord. Remember that the cake in the mixing bowl bears little resemblance to the iced delicacy on the china plate. It takes time and patience to get to the finished product.

Mothers need to keep a sense of perspective about household duties and responsibilities that can easily dim the little joys of life. No matter how pressing the demands of the day, it is imperative that Christian moms spend quality time with God and their families. The reward is not always instantaneous, but it will come.

If children feel neglected by Mom, they will not see the message of God's love shining through her life. It is difficult for a child to believe that he or she is important and loved by God when they do not experience similar reactions from their earthly parents. Although it is difficult to imagine when you are surrounded by preschoolers, children grow up quickly and each day of their young  years is precious. Investing time in your child's life will pay eternal dividends. Irene Foster's poem, *Time is of the Essence*, whimsically sorts out priorities.

Time is of the Essence

Now is the time to get things done…
wade in the water,
sit in the sun,
squish my toes
in the mud by the door,
explore the world in a boy just four.

Now is the time to study books,
flowers,
snails,
how a cloud looks
to ponder "up",
where God sleeps nights,
why mosquitoes take such big bites.

Later there'll be time
to sew and clean,
paint the hall
that soft new green,
to make new drapes,
refinish the floors
later on… when he's not just four.[11]

If you find yourself stressed out and in need of spiritual restoration, set aside time to be alone with God. Get your husband or a friend to watch the children for several hours. Pray for guidance and direction. Ask the Holy Spirit to reveal things in you that need to change. Pray for each of your children—for their strengths and weaknesses. Finally, beseech God to give you the ability to become a better model of His love to your family.

Keep praying for your children, no matter what their age. If they do not have a relationship with Christ, pray that they would recognize Him as Lord and Savior. For your Christian children, pray that Christ will shine through their lives and that He will use them to bring others to faith.

Besides your children, recognize that your circle of influence extends to other mothers. A struggling mother will more readily turn to a fellow mother for help and guidance. Keep your eyes open. Opportunities to minister surround each person.

D. As a Senior Citizen

The potential for senior citizens to influence others is enormous. Older, mature Christian women have more experience to draw upon, more wisdom, and often more time to minister than do other women of younger ages.

All soul winners recognize that prayer is the greatest work in evangelism, and many have been won to Christ as the result of an older person who prays consistently for the work of salvation.

Hilda, an eighty-nine-year-old member of a church, was so crippled with arthritis that she could not write, play the piano, or walk easily. But she spent countless hours praying for souls to be won to the Lord. People would ask her to pray for someone, and she would be faithful until they accepted Christ. Only eternity will reveal the number of Hilda's spiritual children.

Sybil Warren, a pastor's wife from North Carolina, began praying daily for Ann, a young visitor to the church. Ann went on to college and seminary before becoming the wife of a professor of evangelism. Unknown to Ann, Sybil prayed for her for twenty years. Imagine how encouraging it was to Ann when she received a note from Sybil and learned of the older woman's faithfulness as an effective prayer warrior.

Senior adults often find wonderful evangelistic opportunities when they become foster grandparents to children whose own grandparents live far away. Or consider what a difference might be made in the life of a young child who has no one else who really loves and cares for her.

Mature Christian women are urgently needed as role models for women who want to learn about personal discipleship, churchmanship, and giving. If you find yourself in this era of life, rejoice that you have flexibility with your schedule. Get involved with the teaching ministry of your church, or perhaps take a lead in evangelistic endeavors such as Vacation Bible School, Backyard Bible Clubs, or Evangelism Explosion. Ministry to young families provides an outlet not only for you to share what God has taught you about mothering, but it offers a chance for service as well. Offer to baby-sit for a housebound young mother who desperately needs a break.

Some seniors feel called to work with those in their peer group. Taking meals, tapes, or simply offering companionship to shut-ins brings the love of Christ in a tangible way. Providing chauffeuring services to the grocery store, doctor, or other appointments can open the door for spiritual conversations.

All ministries can be used as bridges to share the gospel to those in need. No matter what our age, we are never to forget our charge of reaching others for Christ and being faithful to the Great Commission.

STOP AND APPLY

Choose one or more answers for each question:

___ **1.** Singleness is:
   a) better for everyone.
   b) a gift from God to some people.
   c) neither of these

___ **2.** A single woman can offer more:
   a) money
   b) flexibility in ministry
   c) undivided devotion to the Lord

___ **3.** A married woman can aid in evangelism by:
   a) witnessing to an unsaved husband
   b) encouraging a saved husband in his ministry
   c) leaving her family and going to seminary

___ **4.** Mothers should:
   a) pray daily for children
   b) fill all their time with Christian activities to set an example of ministry
   c) set an example of time with the Lord each day
   d) realize their incredible influence on their children

___ **5.** Christian senior citizens:
   a) are valuable prayer partners in evangelism
   b) often have more time to minister
   c) have much wisdom to offer younger women

IV. ENCOURAGEMENT

A. When Feeling Guilty and Overwhelmed by Needs

There are "seasons" in every person's life. It is understandable if you are discouraged in a season of dirty diapers, preschoolers, sick parents, bereavement, or other difficult circumstances. But try to remember that God does not expect us to be superhuman. He knows our limitations. Frequently Satan tries to bog us down in guilt for all that we are not doing. Needs surround us, and the evil one's voice accuses us unceasingly because it seems we are failing at every turn. It is then that we must go back to the cross and seek God's direction. Every need is not a call, and no one can conquer every need that presents itself.

Our model is Jesus. His example and Spirit will encourage us. He was *swamped* with needs and feelings of concern and compassion for the lost. Even so, He did not despair or fall apart. The first chapter of Mark illustrates this point vividly. Jesus was in Capernaum, surrounded by people who came to Him for physical or spiritual healing. The text says: "The whole town gathered at the door" [Mark 1:33]. Jesus has had an exhausting day, but Mark goes on to relate that "very early in the morning while it was still dark," Jesus went off to "a solitary place" to pray. Jesus recognized His own need for spiritual refreshment and direction in His ministry.

Later that morning Peter reports to Jesus, "Everyone is looking for you" [Mark 1:36]. But instead of going back to Capernaum (where the crowds were waiting to welcome Him), Jesus followed the direction received during His morning prayer time and moved on to nearby villages who also needed to hear His message. There will always be more places and people with spiritual needs than can be met by any one person. Our primary job is not to run frantically from one to another, but to seek God's guidance prayerfully and then work in His strength to fulfill His specified plans for certain tasks. If you find yourself overwhelmed by the number of needs or you are consumed with guilt, set aside time alone with the Lord and seek His specific direction for your ministry.

If at all possible, perhaps even try to set aside a couple of hours, a half day, or even a whole day for *a season of prayer* where you can focus your mind on Him and allow Him to lead and refresh you. It is important to remember that Jesus did not try to meet every need. On the contrary, He concentrated on a few people and sent them out to do the same. This geometric progression has spread the Gospel all over the world.

B. When Suffering from Spiritual Burnout and Depression

Electrical burnout occurs when too much heat in the current overloads the circuit. Christians can suffer from "overload" as well. Spiritual burnout can occur even if we are doing good things in the right way with pure motives. Only God can be everywhere and everything to all people.

Susie, a young single woman, was involved in every ministry of her small church. She taught Sunday School, played the piano, was a member of the evangelism team, did consistent church visitation, volunteered in the nursery, chaperoned youth functions, and worked in the kitchen. She got to the point where she did not want to go out and tell anyone about anything, much less share her faith. She was tired and weary from doing good things. She wanted to quit everything and move far away. Susie was suffering from spiritual burnout.

The pace of modern life can be destructive. On top of all the hustle and bustle, there is an intense spiritual battle as well. "Our struggle is not against flesh and blood, but against the rulers, against the authorities, against the powers of this dark world and against the spiritual forces of evil in the heavenly realms" [Eph. 6:12]. "If the enemy cannot get to us via lust, money or power, he'll attack by twisting our virtues into vices. He will lead us into spiritual burnout."[12]

There are countless instances in the Bible where strong spiritual leaders fell victim to burnout and depression. Moses suffered from the pressures of ministering to a multitude of ungrateful complainers (Ex. 12:37–38; 15:24; 16:3) who worshipped idols (Ex. 32–33). As a result, Moses became angry and depressed (Num. 11:4–6), lost sight of God's power (Num. 11:13), and forgot God's promises (11:14). But God understood his problem (Ex. 33:2–3) and guided Moses to divide responsibility among seventy men to whom He gave the Holy Spirit (Num. 11:17). God wants you to recognize His strength and His ability to meet your needs. Christians who labor in their own strength will always fail.

Jeremiah also went through severe burnout and depression. After he faithfully proclaimed God's prophetic message, the people of Judah turned against him. Lonely and rejected because of his obedience, he felt alienated from his family (Jer. 12:6). Because of his calling he could not marry and have children (16:2, 8) and the people refused to believe his message (20:7–8). How did Jeremiah handle his depression? He continually turned to the Lord and talked to Him about his problems (15:10, 15). Jeremiah obeyed God, thus keeping his line of communication open (12:1–7), and he concentrated on God's character (Lam.

3:22–23). God promised and gave him protection (Jer. 15:20–21), and then Jeremiah rested in personal victory, finding joy and comfort in his relationship to God (15:16).

Or consider Elijah, God's mouthpiece to Israel. His ministry led to a great spiritual awakening in the land, but he was personally hated by Jezebel, the evil Queen of Israel. She persecuted Elijah because of his influence. At one point, Jezebel was so enraged by Elijah's actions that she sent him the message: "May the gods deal with me, be it ever so severely, if by this time tomorrow I do not make your life like that of one of them." In other words, "If I don't kill you within twenty-four hours, I'll be ready to kill myself."

Elijah, who had fearlessly obeyed God's commands for three years, suddenly buckled under the threats of this powerful woman and ran to the desert where he abjectly cried to God:

> *Elijah was afraid and ran for his life. When he came to Beersheba in Judah, he left his servant there, while he himself went a day's journey into the desert. He came to a broom tree, sat down under it and prayed that he might die. 'I have had enough, Lord,' he said. 'Take my life; I am no better than my ancestors.' Then he lay down under the tree and fell asleep [1 Kings 19:3–5].*

But the merciful and omnipotent Lord became Elijah's comforter. He confronts, comforts, and encourages Elijah, who picks himself up and continues in obedience to God. There are several lessons to be learned from Elijah.

1. ***Focus on facts, not feelings*** (v. 3). Elijah felt like a failure and assumed that he was (since he ran away). Some days you may not "feel" like a Christian, but being a Christian is based on fact, not feeling.

2. ***Do not compare yourself with others*** (v. 4). It is common to compare your weaknesses with others' strengths. You may get down on yourself for not being the Christian you ought to be, not spending enough time reading the Bible, or for not witnessing to as many people as you think you should. Acknowledge your strengths and weaknesses, determine to set some goals to work on (one weakness at a time), and don't wallow in self-pity.

3. ***Do not take false blame*** (v. 10). Elijah could not change the nation so he blamed himself. You can influence others, but you are not responsible for the decisions other people make. You can share the gospel, but you are not responsible for another person's decision to accept or reject Christ.

4. ***Do not exaggerate the negative*** (v. 10). Elijah said, "I'm the only one left and now they are trying to kill me too." The "they" that Elijah mentions really refers to just one person, Jezebel. If she really wanted to kill him, she would not have sent him a messenger but a murderer.

God's remedy in Elijah's case has profound implications for each person in a similar situation:

1. ***Take care of your physical needs.*** Elijah "lay down under the tree and fell asleep. All at once an angel touched him and said, 'Get up and eat.' He looked around, and there by his head was a cake of bread, baked over hot coals, and a jar of water. He ate and drank and then lay down again" [1 Kings 19:5–6]. God did not condemn him, but provided for his physical requirements.

   Maybe your pace of life has left you physically exhausted and you have not been taking care of your nutritional or exercise needs. Billie Hanks, an evangelist with International Evangelism Association, has said, "The most spiritual thing you can do when you are tired is sleep."

2. ***Talk to God and express your feelings to Him.*** In verse 10, Elijah poured out his feelings to the Lord: "I have been very zealous for the Lord God Almighty. The Israelites have rejected your covenant, broken down your altars, and put your prophets to death with the sword. I am the only one left, and now they are trying to kill me too."

   All of us have moments when we need to pour out our fears honestly to God. No matter how trivial or seemingly unimportant, God hears and cares.

3. While you are alone, ***try to gain God's perspective on your life and allow God to give you a fresh awareness of His presence in your life.***

The Lord said, "Go out and stand on the mountain in the presence of the Lord, for the Lord is about to pass by." Then a great and powerful wind tore the mountains apart and shattered the rocks before the Lord, but the Lord was not in the wind. After the wind there was an earthquake, but the Lord was not in the earthquake. After the earthquake came a fire, but the Lord was not in the fire. And after the fire came a gentle whisper. When Elijah heard it, he pulled his cloak over his face and went out and stood at the mouth of the cave. Then a voice said to him, 'What are you doing here, Elijah?' " [1 Kings 19:11–13]

4. *Clarify your goals and ask God to give you new direction for your life.* It has been said, "If you shoot at nothing, you will hit it every time." Paul says, "I press on toward the goal to win the prize for which God has called me heavenward in Christ Jesus" [Phil. 3:14].

God gave Elijah a new assignment in verse 15. Maybe God wants to change your assignment. Perhaps He does not want you to be involved in so many areas of service. Could it be that you have a problem with saying "no" to people? Some Christians think God will be pleased if they over-extend themselves—even if this causes them to neglect their family or their physical, emotional, and spiritual health.

If this has been your problem, confess it to God and ask Him to help you break old patterns that lead you astray. Then seek God's true direction and purpose for your life.

5. *Do not isolate yourself. Find someone to nurture or mentor you.* You may be so busy trying to witness and disciple that you fail to realize that you need a trusted mentor as well. You need another Christian woman to pray for you, challenge you, support you, and hold you accountable. All Christians need fellowship and encouragement from others. Look for ways to slip out of your regular routine every week or two for a quiet breakfast or lunch with a Christian friend or mentor. If this is not possible, at least talk on the phone. Plan times of refreshment and encouragement into your schedule.

There are many sources of depression: problem situations, fatigue, life changes. Such causes usually produce temporary periods of depression and will pass. For prolonged depression, it is always wise to seek medical counsel.

C. When Storms Come And Life Seems Out of Balance

God has always calmed storms and brought peace. When the circumstances of life are swirling around us like a hurricane, we need to learn to abide in the calm of the storm. We do this by

continually centering ourselves in His Word and staying on our knees close to the cross of Christ.

Whether we realize it or not, people are watching us. How we handle difficult circumstances is often a living testimony of the grace of our Lord Jesus. The recently bereaved, ones who have experienced great personal disappointment, the newly unemployed, or the mother of a handicapped newborn will testify with their actions to the reality of Jesus in their lives. If He is real, others will see Him shining through their pain and sustaining them in their difficulties. Such a witness often influences more people than a mighty sermon or book.

But sometimes it is the little waves, not the major storms, that keep us out of balance: the piles of laundry, the never-ending task of cleaning, the way "Murphy's Law" works—your daughter spills her apple juice AFTER the floor was mopped, the unexpected business trip, the prolonged visit of a very talkative neighbor. Again, our lives become a spiritual mirror for those around us. Will people see Christ or an angry woman more clearly?

Keep in mind through all circumstances that God is sovereign. God is all-powerful, all-knowing, and He loves you. Also look at how Jesus used ordinary events as opportunities for evangelism and discipleship.

Jesus used the unexpected intrusion of 5,000 people on his rest time to teach the disciples compassion. He used the interruption by Zacchaeus (the little man in the tree) as an occasion to change a man's life in order to demonstrate to a community the meaning of repentance. The Apostle Paul used prison time for worship, for evangelism, for teaching, and for writing to young congregations that he had previously established. Biblical men and women of God never saw any circumstance as pointless.[13]

STOP AND APPLY

1. Put a check by the lessons learned from Elijah:
   - ❒ Don't exaggerate the negative
   - ❒ Don't admit your problem
   - ❒ Run away from the problem
   - ❒ Don't take false blame
   - ❒ Focus on facts, not feelings
   - ❒ Don't compare yourself to others

2. List four practical things you can do to deal with your depression:

   a. _____

   b. _____

   c. _____

   d. _____

3. Identify some of the storms and waves in your life:

   _____

   _____

   _____

   _____

4. What are some specific things you can to do to overcome them?

   _____

   _____

   _____

V. CONCLUSION

Now is the time to begin reaching the world for Christ. We must not wait until we are fully trained or until we feel a miraculous "personal call." God has commanded all Christians to join in this task! God has called you!

An incident from the life of swimmer Florence Chadwick underscores a profound truth:

> *The California coast was shrouded in fog that fourth of July morning in 1952. Twenty-one miles to the west on Catalina Island a 34-year-old woman waded into the water and began swimming toward the mainland, determined to be the first woman to do so. Her name was Florence Chadwick, and she had already been the*

first woman to swim the English Channel in both directions. The water was numbing cold that July morning and the fog so thick that Florence could barely see the boats in her own party. But still she swam, mile after mile.

After more than 15 hours, her body numbed with cold, she asked to be taken out. "I can't go on." Florence Chadwick had never before quit. Her mother and her trainer urged her not to give up, assuring her that the coast was just a short distance away. But in the California fog, Florence could not see land. She swam for 15 more minutes before finally giving up.

Later when her body began to thaw, she blurted to an inquiring reporter, "Look, I'm not making excuses, but if I could have seen land, I would have made it." When she quit, she was only a half-mile from the coast. The fog defeated her because it obscured her goal.

It was the only time Florence Chadwick ever quit. Two months later, she swam the same channel, again in fog. But this time, things were different. This time Florence didn't allow the fog to blind her reason, her eyes, and her heart. This time her faith kept her swimming toward a goal she knew was there but couldn't see. She made it, not only as the first woman to swim the Catalina Channel, but also the fastest swimmer, beating the men's record by two hours.

Do not let a fog dim your vision of reaching people for Christ. Ask God to give you His vision for your life. Then make it your goal to honor and glorify Him by submitting all of your life to His plan.

> *"Since we are surrounded by such a great cloud of witnesses, let us throw off everything that hinders and the sin that so easily entangles, and let us run with perseverance the race marked out for us. Let us fix our eyes on Jesus, the author and perfecter of our faith, who for the joys set before him endured the cross, scorning its shame, and sat down at the right hand of the throne of God. Consider Him who endured such opposition from sinful men, so that you will not grow weary and lose heart" [Heb. 12:1–3].*

Susanna Wesley, the mother of John and Charles Wesley, took time each day to be alone with God in order to study her Bible and pray. One of her daily prayers was: "Dear God, guide me. Help me do Thy will. Make my life count."[14] As a young woman, she wholeheartedly dedicated her life to evangelism: "I hope the fire I start will not only burn all of London, but all of the United Kingdom as well. I hope it will burn all over the world."[15]

May we have that same kind of vision to reach our world for Christ!

Now that you have completed the manual, you can gain an appreciation for the developing role of women in evangelism by listening to the last cassette tape in the series, featuring a historical essay presented by Edith Blumhofer.

ENDNOTES

[1] Hannah W. Smith, *The Christian's Secret to Happy Life* (Westwood, NJ: Fleming H. Revell, n.d.), p. 39.

[2] William MacDonald, *True Discipleship* (Kansas City, MO: Walterick Publishers, 1975), pp. 64–65.

[3] *Ibid.*, p. 5.

[4] Robert E. Coleman, *The Mind of the Master* (New Jersey: Fleming H. Revell Co., 1977), pp. 100–101.

[5] Ibid., p.101.

[6] John Fischer, *A Single Person's Identity* (Palo Alto, CA: Discovery Publishing, 1973), p. 4.

[7] Elisabeth Dodds, *Marriage to a Difficult Man: The Uncommon Union of Jonathan and Sarah Edwards* (Philadelphia: Westminster Press, 1971), p. 203.

[8] John Pollack, *Hudson Taylor and Maria* (New York: McGraw-Hill Book Co, 1962), p. 102.

[9] Arthur Porritt, *John Henry Jowett* (Hodder & Stoughton, 1900), p. 4.

[10] Howard Taylor, *Hudson Taylor's Spiritual Secret* (China Inland Mission, 1958), p 13.

[11] Jean Fleming, *A Mother's Heart* (Colorado Springs: NavPress, 1982), p. 56.

[12] Charles Bradley, "Spiritual Burnout—When There's Nothing Left to Give" (*Decision Magazine*, February 1991), pp. 14–16.

[13] Gail MacDonald, *High Call High Privilege* (Wheaton: Tyndale House, 1981), p. 58.

[14] Charles Ludwig, *Susanna Wesley* (Milford, MI: Mott Media), p. 30.

[15] *Ibid.*, p. 88.

$\mathcal{A}$PPENDICES

A. The Bridge Illustration

B. Resources

C. References

D. *STOP AND APPLY* Answer Sheets

PPENDIX A

THE BRIDGE ILLUSTRATION

Let's walk through a practice presentation as I share with "Sally":

Get a sheet of paper and write on it: "PEOPLE" and "GOD" (Fig. 1). Explain that people have always tried to know and reach God.

Share the fact that there is a big problem that keeps us from having the quality rela-

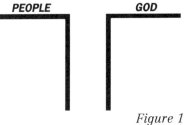

Figure 1

tionship with God that we really need and that He wants us to have. The Bible tells us about that problem in Romans 3:23—"For *all* have sinned and fall short of the glory of God." (If you have a Bible with you, let the person read it for herself.)

"Now, Sally, that verse you have just read says *all* have sinned. That means you and me and everyone in the world. We need to understand that sin is not only *doing* those 'big' things that we know are wrong, but it is also the 'little' things we do such as gossiping about our neighbor, telling white lies, thinking bad thoughts, having the wrong attitudes, etc."

Write the reference "Rom. 3:23" under "PEOPLE," and then "All have Sinned" under it. Next draw in the chasm between "PEOPLE" and "GOD" and write "SIN" in that space. (Fig. 2).

"Now, Sally, read Romans 6:23."

Figure 2

"For the wages of sin is death; but the gift of God is eternal life in Christ Jesus our Lord."

"Sally, you know what wages are, don't you?"

"Of course. It is the paycheck you receive for your work every week or month or so. It is something you deserve."

"That's right, Sally. The Bible says that sin earns death. When we face God at the end of our life, death is what we will have earned. When a person sins and is separated from God, she is dead toward

God and has no relationship with Him. That means all of us deserve spiritual death."

At this point write "Rom. 6:23" in your illustration and the words, "Sin Earns Death" under it (Fig. 3).

"Now let's read Hebrews 9:27."

"Just as man is destined to die once, and after that to face judgment..."

"This verse speaks of physical death. Every person will die at some time. We just don't know when that will be. We hope it won't be for a while, but nobody can know when that will happen. Sally, some day you and I are both going to die.

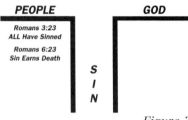

Figure 3

After that we will face God's judgment. According to what we have read so far, the result would be eternal death."

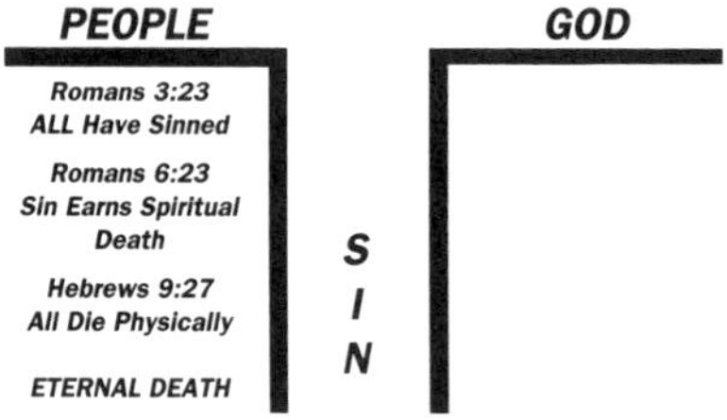

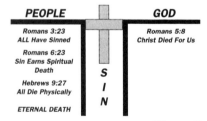

Figure 4

Now write "Heb. 9:27" under the other verses with the notation "All die physically" under it. Then draw a line under these three verses to show that they add up to eternal death (Fig. 4).

"But Romans 5:8 gives us some good news":

"But God demonstrates his own love for us in this: While we were still sinners, Christ died for us."

On the right side of your illustration under "GOD," write "Rom. 5:8" and under it the words "Christ died for us." Then draw a cross, bridging the gap between "GOD" and "PEOPLE" (Fig. 5).

"This is why Jesus went to the cross: to pay the penalty of our sin."

Figure 5

"Now, Sally, look at what Ephesians 2:8–9 says":

"For it is by grace you have been saved, through faith—and this not from yourselves, it is the gift of God—not by works, so that no one can boast."

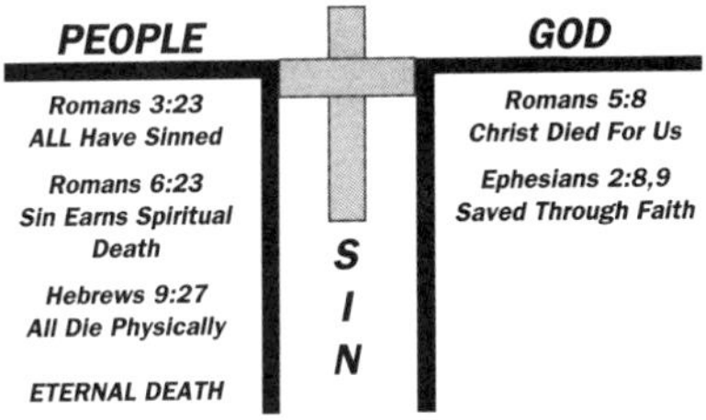

"Sally, it is by God's *grace* that we are able to become Christians and receive eternal life. It is a gift that we cannot earn or deserve. God gives us this gift because He loves us. We can receive this gift through *faith*."

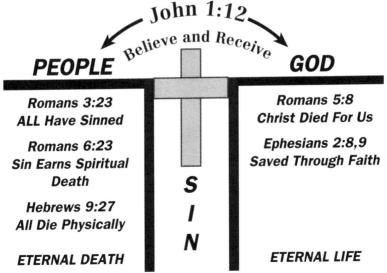

Figure 6

Write "Eph. 2:8–9" on the right side and under it the words "Saved through faith" (Fig. 6).

"Sally, now read John 1:12":

"Yet to all who received him, to those who believed in his name, he gave the right to become children of God."

"Sally, there are two steps in this verse that explain how to become a child of God. The first is to *believe* in Jesus Christ. You must accept that He is who He claimed to be. Do you believe that Jesus is the infinite God/Man? He was both fully God and fully man who lived a perfect life. If you do, then there is a second step, which is to *receive* Him as your own Savior and Lord."

"Intellectual belief is not enough. In the Bible, there is a verse in James 2:19 that says, 'You believe that there is one God. Good! Even the demons believe that—and shudder.' One must receive Christ by a personal choice and act of the will."

Figure 7

At this point, draw a bridge across the top of the cross on your diagram, and write "Believe and Receive" and "John 1:12" over the top of the bridge; also write "Eternal Life" on the right side (Fig. 7).

To illustrate the difference between believing and receiving, take a pen or pencil and ask, "Sally do you believe that I have a pen in my hand?"

"Yes, I do."

"Well, do you believe it enough that if I offer it to you, you will take it?"

(You offer it and she takes it.) "Sally, what did you just do?"

"I took it."

"Why did you take it?"

"*Because you offered it to me.*"

"In other words, you believed me when I said I would give it to you, so you were willing to reach out to receive it."

"That's right."

"Sally, the pen was potentially yours the moment I decided to offer it, but it wasn't yours experientially, until you acted in faith and received it.

"What Christ did on the cross was potentially for everyone in the world. The gift has already been paid for, and the loving hand of God is now extended. He is simply waiting for you and every other person to believe in Him enough to receive His gift that He offered in the Person of Christ."[1]

"Sally, where are you on this diagram? Have you reached the point of believing?"

When that question is asked, the average person will put her finger between the "BELIEVE" and "RECEIVE." Most people believe in the historical Jesus existed and the facts about His life, but have never received Him into their life. This diagram helps pinpoint exactly where the person is in her spiritual pilgrimage.

Assuming Sally put her finger on the "and" between believe and receive, you could continue our conversation: "Sally, you have already taken the first step; you already believe in Christ. Would you like to take next step and actually *receive* Him into your life?"[2]

If she says "Yes," you can clarify what that means and lead her in a sinner's prayer. (More will be said about making a decision for Christ in the next section, so keep reading!) If she says "No," then ask if she has any questions you can answer. Give her the diagram and encourage her to think about it later.

STOP AND APPLY

Write down the six verses used in the Bridge Illustration:

1.   4.

2.   5.

3.   6.

Commit to memorize one verse a week for six weeks.

ENDNOTES

[1] Billie Hanks, *Everyday Evangelism* (Fort Worth, TX: International Evangelism Association, 1983), pp. 74–75.

[2] Billie Hanks (adapted), pp. 69–75.

APPENDIX B

RESOURCES

Music:

Check your local Christian bookstore for the latest offerings of available music.

Drama Groups

A.D. Players
2710 W. Alabama
Houston, TX 77098
(713) 526-2721

Toymaker's Dream
Impact Productions
807 South Xanthus Place
Tulsa, OK 74104
(918) 582-4464

Lamb's Players
500 Plaza Blvd.
P.O. Box 26
National City, CA 92050
(619) 474-4802

Youth With a Mission
Academy of Performing Arts
P.O. Box 1324
Cambridge, Ontario N1R7G6
(519) 622-2008

The Refreshment Company
801 Dayton Avenue
St. Paul, MN 55104
(612) 227-3157

Drama Publications:

Acting out Faith: Christian Theater Today (1986) by Gordon C. Bennett
CPB Press, Box 179
St. Louis, MO 63166

Super Sketches for Youth Ministry (1991) by Debra Poling & Sharon Sherbondy
Zondervan Publishing House
Grand Rapids, MI 49506

15 Surefire Scripts. Ed. by Kerry Cederberg Meads and Robert Smyth
World Wide Publications
1303 Hennepin Ave.
Minneapolis, MN 55430

Theater Craft: Creativity and the Art of Drama (1990) by Nigel Forde
Harold Shaw Publishers
Wheaton, IL 60187

Lamb's Players Presents: How to Develop a Drama Group
World Wide Publications
1303 Hennepin Ave.
Minneapolis, MN 55430

Time to Act by Paul Burbridge and Murray Watts
Hodder and Stoughton Publishers

Lightning Sketches by Paul Burbridge and Murray Watts
Hodder and Stoughton Publishers

Using the Bible in Drama by Steve and Janet Stickley and Jim Belben
Bible Society Publishers

List of Drama Publishing Companies:

Agape Drama Press, Ltd.
Box #1313
Englewood, CO 80110

Dramatists Play Service
440 Park Ave., South
New York, NY 10016

Augsburg Publishing House
426 S. Fifth St.
Minneapolis, MN 55415

Dramatic Publishing Co.
P.O. Box 109
Woodstock, IL 60098

Creative Arts Productions
Box #7008
Santa Cruz, CA 95061

Impressions Drama Resources
4166 Brentwood Lane
Waukegan, IL 60087

Baker's Plays
100 Chauncy St.
Boston, MA 02111-1783

Lillenas Publishing Co.
Box #419527
Kansas City, MO 64141

I.E. Clark Publisher
St. John's Road
Schulenberg, TX 78956

Samuel French, Inc.
45 W. 25th Street
New York, NY 10010

Broadman Press
Baptist Convention Press
127 Ninth Ave., North
Nashville, TN 37234

Seeds Resources
Willow Creek Comm. Church
67 East Algonquin Road
S. Barrington, IL 60010-6143

Contemporary Drama Service
Box #7710-B5
Colorado Springs, CO 80933

The Jeremiah People
(Sketch Books)
Box #1996
Thousand Oaks, CA 91360

Help in Drama Skills:

Voice and the Actor by Cicely Berry
An Actor Prepares by Constantine Stanislavski
One Hundred Plus Ideas for Drama by Anna Scher and
    Charles Verall
Improvisation Games by Viola Spolin

Art:

For a catalog of the Sacred Arts:
        Billy Graham Center Museum
        500 E. College Ave.
        Wheaton, IL 60187

Film and Videos:

Campus Crusade for Christ
Media Distribution
Arrowhead Springs
San Bernardino, CA 92414

Baptist Film Centers
1235 Hurstbourne Lane
P.O. Box 24086
Louisville, KY 44022

Gospel Films, Inc.
P.O. Box 455
Muskegon, MI 49443

Word Publishing Resources
Waco, TX 76796

Josh McDowell Ministry
P.O. Box 5585
Richardson, TX 75080

World Wide Pictures
1201 Hennepin Ave., South
Minneapolis, MN 55403

Mark IV Pictures
5907 Meredith Dr.
Des Moines, IA 50322

Christian Film & Video Center
Lubbock, TX 79401

Moody Films
12000 E. Washington Blvd.
Whittier, CA 90608

Christian Supply Center
Portland OR 97266

Outreach Films
P.O. Box 4029
Westlake Village, CA 91359

For a magazine reviewing new Christian films and videos (as well as suggestions for film and video use), subscribe to:

Christian Film and Video
P.O. Box 3000, Dept. Y
Denville, NJ 07834

PPENDIX C

References

I. Sample List of Objectives of a Social Ministry.

The following is a list of Social Ministry Objectives of College Church, Wheaton, Illinois. It relates to the social ministry discussion found in Session Nine.

> *We believe our people need to involve themselves in a holistic ministry whereby we are confronted with 'human needs' more basic than our own.*
>
> *We affirm the work of the South Carol Stream Community Center and desire to establish an intimate working relationship with them in attempting to work for the betterment of the citizens of South Carol Stream.*
>
> *We commit ourselves to evangelism with the hope of bringing individuals to a saving knowledge of Christ through our efforts.*
>
> *We desire to see an increase in giving on the part of College Church; we shall give of our people, our time and our finances to see the work go forward.*
>
> *We envision taking initiative for various ministries which we deem appropriate in conjunction with the South Carol Stream Community Center.*

II. Services and Objectives of Life Choice Ministry.

Life Choice Ministry is a representative example of a community organization with specific services and objectives in social ministry.

A. Services Available.

> *A free pregnancy test is usually the reason for the first visit to our offices. Many girls are unaware they already carry a real baby by the time they suspect pregnancy.*
>
> *We tell her about her physical condition and the development of her baby. We also share information about abortion and what it would really mean to her body and her life.*
>
> *We present ALL her options and alternatives because we believe she is entitled to make an informed decision. There is never any pressure or condemnation.*

If she decides to carry her baby to birth, she will receive a "friendship helper" to walk alongside as she completes her pregnancy. . . a trained volunteer who is also a mother, experienced in life, who will share love and encouragement.

During this time, in deciding whether to rear her baby or place it up for adoption, LIFE CHOICE again presents all sides of either course so she can make a fully informed decision based on what is best for herself and her baby.

If she chooses to keep her baby, she is encouraged to finish her schooling. If she chooses adoption, she can read the application information from Christian families and choose the best one for her baby.

The art of responsible decision making is a LIFE CHOICE goal for each girl. For the one who chooses abortion, LIFE CHOICE wants to be the friend to whom she can turn when she is having physical pain, nightmares, fears, temptation to suicide. . . whatever her situation. Many have returned, and many have referred their friends.

The message is the same. Jesus loves you and finds you precious and special. LIFE CHOICE is here to help you.

B. Specific Objectives.

1. To focus on the pregnant woman, meeting her needs by offering physical and spiritual support.

2. To share Christ's unconditional love and plant the seed of salvation, sharing the Gospel of Jesus Christ.

3. To protect the life of the unborn.

4. To specify the alternatives to abortion.

5. To educate individuals on the facts of abortion and the development of the unborn child.

6. To provide a comprehensive plan for the care and development of the woman with a problem pregnancy in order to prepare her in needed or desired skills to become self-supporting.

7. To serve women who have experienced abortions and are seeking help.

8. To educate women regarding God's design for sexual morality, and to encourage chastity.

9. To offer services to those who desire help and are directly concerned with the pregnancy.

10. To establish and operate a pregnancy crisis center which will offer hope and encouragement to women.

11. To offer services without regard to race, color, legal residence, prior marital status, economic status, or religious affiliation.

III. Resources and Addresses for Further Information on Social Ministry

Bill Glass Evangelistic Association, P.O. Box 1105, Cedar Hill, TX 75104

Christian Life Commission, SBC, 901 Commerce Street, Number 550, Nashville, TN 37203-3620

Evangelicals for Social Action, P.O. Box 76560, Washington, DC 20013 (this group offers resources to become active in issues such as peace, nuclear disarmament, abortion, poverty, the family, racial and sex discrimination, human rights, and protection of the environment)

Good News Jail and Prison Ministries, 1036 South Highland Street, Arlington, VA 22204

Institute for Prison Ministries, Billy Graham Center, Wheaton College, Wheaton, IL 60187

Joni and Friends, P.O. Box 3225, Woodland Hills, CA 91365 (offers resources in becoming more aware of the needs of the handicapped)

National Association of Evangelicals, Social Action Commission, 1405 G Street, N.W., Washington, DC 20005

National Ministries/Social Ministries, American Baptist Churches, Valley Forge, PA 19481

Prison Fellowship in America, P.O. Box 17500, Washington, DC 20041

Salvation Army, National Headquarters, 799 Bloomfield Avenue, Verona, NJ 07044 (assists the poor and does evangelistic work all over the world)

World Relief, P.O. Box WRC, Wheaton, IL 60187 (offers resources in refugee resettlement and disaster relief)

Youth With a Mission, P.O. Box 4600, Tyler, TX 75712 (channels Christians into missionary work and offers resources in "mercy ministries," such as hunger and disaster relief)

IV. Resources on Evangelism & Disciplemaking

Adsit, Christopher. *Personal Disciplemaking: A Step-by-step Guide for Leading a Christian From New Birth to Maturity.* Here's Life, 1988.

Aldrich, Joseph. *Life-Style Evangelism*. Multnomah, 1980.

_____. *Gentle Persuasion: Creative Ways to Introduce Your Friends to Christ.* Multnomah, 1988.

Berry, Jo. *Beloved Unbeliever.* Zondervan, 1981.

Brestin, Dee. *Finders Keepers: Introducing Your Friends to Christ and Helping Them Grow.* Harold Shaw Publishers, 1983.

Bright, Bill. *Witnessing Without Fear.* Here's Life, 1987.

Chapman, John C. *Know and Tell the Gospel.* NavPress, 1985.

Christenson, Evelyn. *Battling the Prince of Darkness: Rescuing Captives from Satan's Kingdom.* Victor Books, 1990.

Coleman, Robert. *The Master Plan of Discipleship.* Revell, 1987.

_____. *The Master Plan of Evangelism.* Revell, 1963.

_____. *The Spark that Ignites.* World Wide Publications, 1989.

Coleman, Robert and Tim Beougher, Tom Philips, William Shell, editors. *Disciplemaking.* Billy Graham Center Institute of Evangelism, 1994.

Coppedge, Allan. *The Biblical Principles of Discipleship.* Zondervan, 1989.

Eims, LeRoy. *The Lost Art of Disciple Making.* Victor Books, 1981.

_____. *One to One Evangelism.* Victor Books, 1990.

Ford, Leighton. *Good News is for Sharing.* David C. Cook, 1977.

Fryling, Alice. *Disciple-Maker's Handbook.* InterVarsity, 1989.

Hanks, Billie, Jr. and William Shell, editors. *Discipleship: Great Insights from the Most Experienced Disciple Makers.* Zondervan, 1993.

Hanks, Billie, Jr. *Everyday Evangelism.* Zondervan, 1983.

Heck, Joel. *The Art of Sharing Your Faith.* Revell, 1991.

Henrichsen, Walter A. *How to Disciple Your Children.* Victor Books, 1981.

Hull, Bill. *The Disciple-Making Pastor.* Revell, 1988.

Jacks, Bob and Betty. *Your Home a Lighthouse.* NavPress, 1989.

Kincaid, Ron. *A Celebration of Disciple-Making: How Church-centered Evangelism Can Excite Your Congregation to Growth. Victor* Books, 1990.

Knechtle, Cliffe. *Give Me An Answer.* InterVarsity, 1978.

Little, Paul. *How to Give Away Your Faith.* InterVarsity, 1966.

Mainhood, Beth. *Reaching Your World: Disciplemaking for Women.* NavPress, 1987.

Metzger, Will. *Tell the Truth: The Whole Gospel to the Whole Person by Whole People.* InterVarsity, 1981.

Ortlund, Anne. *Discipling One Another.* Word, 1979.

Peterson, Jim. *Evangelism for Our Generation: The Practical Way to Make Evangelism Your Lifestyle.* NavPress, 1988.

Pickard, Nellie. *What Would You Have Said? Witnessing with Confidence and Sensitivity.* Baker, 1990.

Pippert, Rebecca Manley. *Out of the Salt Shaker.* InterVarsity, 1979.

Plueddemann, Jim and Carol. *Pilgrims in Progress: Growing Through Groups.* Harold Shaw Publishers, 1990.

Posterski, Donald. *Reinventing Evangelism.* InterVarsity, 1989.

Riggs, Charlie. *Learning to Walk with God.* Worldwide, 1988.

Rinker, Rosalind. *You Can Witness with Confidence.* Zondervan, 1962.

Robinson, Bill. *Getting Beyond the Small Talk.* Worldwide, 1989.

Shaver, Charles. *The Bible Speaks to Me About My Witness.* Beacon Hill, 1991.

Strobel, Lee. *Inside the Mind of Unchurched Harry & Mary.* Zondervan, 1993.

Swithinbank, Kim. *The Natural Touch: Reaching Others for Christ.* Marshall Morgan and Scott, 1988.

VanAtta, Lucibel. *Women Encouraging Women.* Multnomah, 1987.

Warr, Irma. *The Godly Woman.* Creative Resources, 1976.

Whitman, Virginia. *The Power of Positive Sharing.* Tyndale, 1974.

APPENDIX D
Stop & Apply Answers

Session 1: "The Message of Evangelism"

Page 5

1. You can write your own that is something like this: "The compassionate sharing of the Good News of Jesus Christ with lost people, in the power of the Holy Spirit, for the purpose of bringing them to Christ as Lord and Savior, that they in turn might share Him with others."
2. Jesus; Lord; Savior

Page 13

1. Holy Spirit
2. companionship; harmony
3. all; death
4. sin; nature; holy
5. God's; death
6. Christ; God
7. love; Christ; punishment
8. acknowledge; recognize; turn
9. all; all

Page 17

It gives God glory.
We are commanded to evangelize.
Everyone should have the opportunity to hear.
People burdened by sin cannot have lasting peace.

Session 2: "A Verbal Witness in Evangelism"

Page 25

1. b
2. c
3. An open nerve is a need a person is experiencing. Two examples are marriage problems, and parenting problems.
4. Answers will vary.
5. Choose three of the ones listed in the session.

Page 30
This will be different for each person.

Page 32
1. True
2. False
3. True
4. True
5. False
6. True
7. True
8. False

Page 37
1. a. sense
   b. receive
2. Ask if you have explained everything clearly enough. Be courteous and express appreciation for letting you share.
3. One example is: "Dear Jesus, I know that I am a sinner and need Your forgiveness. I believe that You died for my sins. I want to turn from my sins and ask You to take over the control of my life. I commit myself to You as Lord."

Page 39
1. preclude; postpone; answer; research

Session 3: "Evangelism and Prayer"

Page 49
1. c
2. b
3. c
4. a
5. c
6. b

7. <u>D</u> Prayers for protection for the Christian who is evangelizing.
   <u>O</u> Prayers to soften hearts and prepare hearers.
   <u>O</u> Prayers to block Satan in the lives of unbelievers.
   <u>D</u> Prayers to clothe Christians with spiritual armor.
   <u>O</u> Prayers to send forth workers into the field.

Page 58
1. specific times
2. Adoration; Confession; Thanksgiving; Supplication
3. power; conviction
4. varies for individuals

Session 4: "Evangelism with Children"

Page 71
1. True
2. True
3. False
4. False
5. True

Page 74
1. parents; homes
2. example; consistent

Page 81
1. individual; Savior
2. seeds
3. see session for ideas
4. varies with individuals

Page 84
1. respond
2. theology
3. yes; no
4. spiritual need

Page 87
1.
   - **5** Tell them God expects them to respond positively.
   - **3** Explain that sin leads to punishment.
   - **1** Tell of the fact of God's love.
   - **6** Give the opportunity to respond.
   - **2** Present the issue of sin.
   - **4** Share the main points of the Gospel.

Session 5: "Evangelism with Spouses and Other Family Members"

Page 101
1. commitment; obedience
2. yourself
3. Prayer
4. a
5. c
6. b
7. b

Page 106
1. superior; ignore
2. prayer
3. how; when
4. love
5. communication
6. patient

Session 6: "Relationship Evangelism"

Page 113
1. False
2. True
3. True
4. True
5. True

Page 115
Answers vary with individuals.

Page 120
Answers vary with individuals.

Page 128
1. <u>5</u> Use hospitality to help build your relationship.
   <u>3</u> Establish additional points of contact.
   <u>4</u> Deepen the relationship with her.
   <u>6</u> Share spiritual things and eventually present the Gospel.
   <u>1</u> Identify the people with whom you come in contact on a regular basis.
   <u>2</u> Narrow your list to a realistic number of people.
2. clear; open doors; materials; outreach

Session 7: "Evangelism and Bible Study"

Page 135
1. "A Bible study where believers and nonbelievers meet to discuss in an open and nonthreatening way the claims of Christ."
2. a. True   c. True   e. True
   b. False   d. True   f. False

Page 143
1. b.
2. co-leader; place; time; length; baby-sitting

Page 146
Check all except "Dominates discussions," "Has all the answers," and "Lectures well."

Page 152
1. 1) What does the passage say? (observation)
   2) What does the passage mean? (interpretation)
   3) What does the passage mean to me? (application)

Session 8: "Evangelism and the Creative Arts"

Page 157

1. a) message b) attention; focus
   c) blessing d) talents; abilities
2. answers vary with individuals

Page 163

1. b 4. d 6. rehearsal
2. c 5. people 7. spiritual
3. b

Page 172

1. Relaxes an audience, Teaches the Bible, Makes money, Inspires worship, Sows spiritual seed, Helps the preacher
2. artistic; spiritual 5. False 8. False
3. visual 6. False 9. True
4. True 7. True

Page 176

1. preach; portray 4. Home
2. Christ 5. Gospel
3. audience; discussion

Session 9: "Evangelism through Social Ministry"

Page 184

1. individuals; conditions
2. change
3. evangelism (the Gospel)
4. Because lasting social change will only take place as people are transformed through the message of evangelism.
5. Jesus' healing of the paralytic who was lowered through the roof.

Page 187

1. a 3. d
2. b 4. c

Page 191

1. False 3. False
2. True 4. True
Arrange in order (by column)
Column 1 — 3, 5, 1, 8 Column 2 — 2, 4, 6, 7

Session 10: "Cross–Cultural Evangelism"

Page 211

1. Culture is the distinctive characteristics of a people's way of life.
2. 1) E-0 the winning of nominal Christians in a similar culture to personal faith and commitment.
   2) E-1 evangelism within homogeneous groups.
   3) E-2 evangelism of geographically close and culturally or linguistically related groups.
   4) E-3 evangelism of culturally distant groups in which the evangelist is separated from the people to be evangelized by monumental cultural distances.
3. E-3 evangelism
4. 150%
5. host culture
6. Great Commission

Page 224

1. a	4. c	7. b
2. b	5. b	8. verbal; verbal;
3. a	6. c	simple; listen;
		bridges

Session 11: "Evangelism and Disciplemaking"

Page 229

1. A disciple is a learner.
2. Disciplemaking is the program and plan for equipping and establishing those who have accepted Jesus Christ.
3. glory   5. example
4. commanded   6. model

Page 236

1. g; e; a; d; c; b; f
2. <u>2</u> Clarify and confirm the commitment
   <u>4</u> Plan for growth
   <u>1</u> Develop the friendship
   <u>3</u> Explain the importance of prayer and Bible study
3. answers will vary
4. prayer; study the Scripture; Scripture memory; importance of the local church; developing her testimony; lifestyle

Page 241
1. b
2. a
3. c
4. a
5. b

Page 246
1. God
2. cost
3. motives
4. fall away
5. jealous

Session 12: "Women Need Women"

Page 250
1. Shared experiences such as being a single woman, an unfulfilled marriage, pregnancy, parenting, balancing a career with home life, an unfaithful husband, an aging parent and many others.

Page 254
1. learn from Him.
2. know; obey
3. see pages 252–253

Page 260
1. b
2. b
3. a, b
4. a, c, d
5. a, b, c

Page 267
1. Don't exaggerate the negative.
   Focus on facts, not feelings.
   Don't take false blame.
   Don't compare yourself to others.
2. a. Take care of your physical needs.
   b. Talk to God and express your feelings to Him.
   c. Gain God's perspective on your life and allow God to give you a fresh awareness of His presence in your life.
   d. Clarify your goals and ask God to give you new direction for your life.
3. answers will vary
4. answers will vary

Page 275
1. Rom. 3:23
2. Rom. 6:23
3. Heb. 9:27
4. Rom. 5:8
5. Eph. 2:8–9
6. John 1:12